KV-384-109

Religion, Education and Employment

Aspects of Equal Opportunity in Northern Ireland

Edited by R J Cormack and R D Osborne

Appletree Press

First published and printed in 1983 by
The Appletree Press Ltd
7 James Street South
Belfast BT2 8DL

For our Parents and Families

British Library Cataloguing in Publication Data
Religion, education and employment.
1. Discrimination—Northern Ireland
I. Cormack, R. J. II. Osborne, R. D.
306'.09416 HM146

ISBN 0-904651-87-8

Acknowledgements

Many friends and colleagues have helped, in a number of ways, in the formation of this book. However, we would like to thank, in particular, Peter Daly, Bob Eccleshall, Liz McShane and Professors A. H. Halsey and Roy Wallis for reading and commenting on various chapters. R. G. Cooper, Chairman on the Fair Employment Agency, kindly gave us and fellow contributors permission to draw upon research conducted for the Agency. The preparation of the book was greatly aided by Merle Osborne's work in drawing the maps and diagrams, Fred Vincent's help in assembling the bibliography, Sandra Maxwell's accurate and speedy typing, Jenitha Orr's skilful formulation of the index, and particularly Douglas Marshall's seemingly endless patience as Appletree's editor in dealing with our delays and revisions.

The researches reported in the chapters of this book were funded by a variety of sources. Hepburn received an SSRC award for the research reported in chapter 3; Miller derived his data in chapter 4 from the Irish Mobility Project supported also by the SSRC. Miller and Osborne's work, reported in chapter 5, was funded by the Nuffield Foundation and based on data generously made available by the Department of Manpower Services (now the Department of Economic Development). Trewsdale, in chapter 6, was assisted by Queen's University Computer Centre. Murray and Osborne's work, in chapter 7, benefited from comments from Professor J. Fulton. Cormack and Osborne's study, in chapter 8, was greatly aided by data preparation work done by Mark Hart and Eddie Rooney. Osborne, Cormack, Reid and Williamson, in Chapter 9, received an SSRC grant for this research and were ably assisted by Betty Cole-Baker and Roz Goldie. Finally we would like to thank the Economic and Social Review and the Modern Law Review for permission to publish versions of the papers by Aunger and McCrudden respectively.

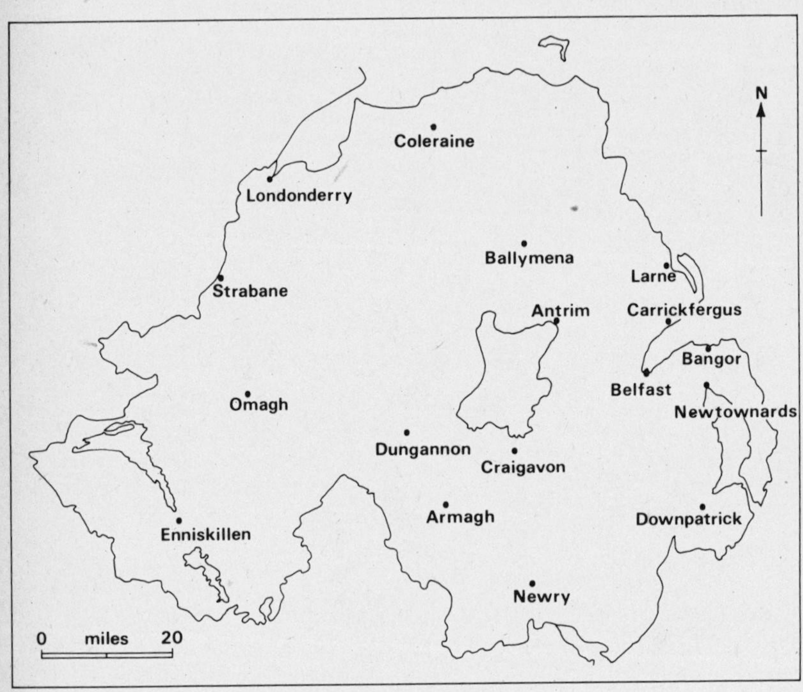

Northern Ireland

Contents

Contributors

Edmund A. Aunger	Assistant Professor Economics and Political Science Faculté Saint-Jean, University of Alberta, Edmonton, Alberta, Canada
Frederick W. Boal	Reader in Geography Department of Geography, The Queen's University of Belfast, Belfast BT7 1NN, Northern Ireland
Robert J. Cormack	Lecturer in Sociology Department of Social Studies, The Queen's University of Belfast, Belfast BT7 1NN, Northern Ireland
John Darby	Lecturer in Social Administration Social Administration, School of Social Sciences, New University of Ulster, Coleraine, BT52 1SA, Northern Ireland
Anthony C. Hepburn	Senior Lecturer in History Department of History, New University of Ulster, Coleraine, BT52 1SA, Northern Ireland
John A. Jackson	Professor of Sociology Department of Sociology, Trinity College, Dublin, Ireland.
J. Christopher McCrudden	Fellow and Tutor in Law Lincoln College, University of Oxford, Oxford, OX1 3DR, England
Robert L. Miller	Lecturer in Sociology Department of Social Studies, The Queen's University of Belfast, Belfast, BT7 1NN, Northern Ireland
Dominic Murray	College Lecturer in Education Education Department, University College, Cork, Ireland.
Russell C. Murray	Formerly Lecturer in Sociology University of Edinburgh. Home address: 12, Castle Street, Crail, Fife.

Robert D. Osborne Senior Lecturer in Social Policy
School of Sociology and Social Policy, Ulster Polytechnic, Newtownabbey, Co. Antrim, BT37 0QB, Northern Ireland

Norma G. Reid Research Fellow in Mathematics
Department of Mathematics, New University of Ulster, Coleraine, BT52 1SA, Northern Ireland.

Janet M. Trewsdale Lecturer in Economics
Department of Economics, The Queen's University of Belfast, Belfast BT7 1NN, Northern Ireland

Arthur P. Williamson Lecturer in Social Administration,
Social Administration, School of Social Sciences, New University of Ulster, Coleraine, BT52 1SA, Northern Ireland.

Foreword

J. A. Jackson

One cannot approach the subject of Northern Ireland without an acute awareness of the dangers of misinformation and bias. The period since 1969, which brought the affairs of the 'six counties' into international prominence, has been scattered with frustrated solutions based on attempts to understand the complexities involved. Many of the failures in comprehension were due to insufficiencies of imagination and learning of the lessons of history. Even the most well-intentioned were deemed to be unfitted to make the attempt by virtue of their deficiencies of shared experience and identity with one or other of the contending groups. Where passions run high there may even be some doubt about the value, let alone the possibility, of dispassionate inquiry. In a Province where two separate histories have been presented in the schools, where two separate communities have established different and contentious criteria for the identity of the Province itself, it is hardly surprising that there should have been no certain agreement about the facts of the case—facts, which, if they could but be established, would give a starting point to a rational assessment of problems and the development of solutions.

Facts, however, have been very hard to come by. Even where available they did not necessarily reveal the nature of the problem. Certainly the extent of cross-cutting relations between the two communities is concealed by categories which assume that divided and parallel communities do not exist. Thus Aunger's incisive re-analysis of 1971 Census data on occupations, re-printed in this volume, shows how valuable it is to disaggregate the broad categories if one is to reveal the distinctions of power and position which operate internally within the different occupational areas.

A series of studies, reported in this volume, demonstrate the extent to which Protestant majority and Catholic minority exist in a complex interdependence, in apparent 'apartheid' of separate and equal, in which the realities of discrimination and dominance are 'misrecognized' in a situation of apparent social equality. So powerful indeed are the ideological forces operating to bring about this misrecognition that measures of 'life-chances' in relation to access to education or the labour market, and measures of social mobility do not, as Miller and Osborne indicate, readily reveal the polarity of experience represented by the alternative sets of structures through which these social processes are experienced.

Many of those who were in Northern Ireland in the early 1970s believed that most of the apparent problems would respond to the effects of hard information and communal education. Such traditions of liberalism were perhaps too naive as were no doubt the associated policy intentions of the Northern Ireland Community Relations Commission or later even the Fair Employment Act. But the attempt to set about to establish the facts of the case still represents a necessary starting point and is where the granity exterior of Northern Ireland can be used to hone the tools of research rather than frustrate the intentions of the venture. Far too many imported theories have been sunk against those cliffs. Political arithmetic remains as a potent reality to be addressed in the Province.

The papers in this volume represent the results of that research by a group of young scholars whose attention has been focussed by the empirical reality and the need to examine and explain the problems by establishing the facts of the case. They represent a tradition of social and statistical inquiry with deep roots in social science endeavour, going back to Farr and Galton, Booth, and Rowntree and more recently Hogben and Glass. It is fitting that the last of these, an honorary graduate of Queen's University, should be associated in a tradition of scholarship so clearly and succinctly expressive of liberal social thought and policies. As the editors indicate, the theme of liberalism—indeed its theoretical purpose—has been a concern with equality of opportunity and human rights. The liberal issues, slavery, poverty, education, progress, social change, life-chances, race relations, have all had to do with the amelioration of the grosser inequities of capitalist society. The instinct has been pragmatic—to find ways of ameliorating problems rather than to worry overmuch about their origins or the broad theoretical debates that lie around them. An instinct which, as the editors point out, was, at least until recently, a distinctive feature of Anglo-American sociology, and may have its origins in the different paths to liberal democracy taken in Britain, North America and Europe.

It is a climate of opinion that has tended to take something of a back seat in the heady days of major theoretical debate and reorientation in the social sciences during the late 1960s and 1970s. Even the calculus of economics has been affected by the inroads of theoretical debate regarding its principles and their application. The epistemological assumptions that lie behind the inquiry itself have been questioned by some of the debates on the nature of the capitalist state, on ideology and on the extent to which the institutions of education and science are themselves compromised by the very acts of 'misrecognition' that they seek to uncover.

John Whyte in an important assessment of the theoretical debates about the situation in Northern Ireland (1978) concludes that no one theoretical posture, Marxist or non-Marxist, appears to provide an adequate way forward. He writes that 'anyone who studies the Ulster conflict must be struck by the intensity of feeling. It seems to go beyond what is required by a rational defence of the divergent interests which undoubtedly exist' (Whyte, 1978:278).

Sweet reason may not be sufficient to solve the problems of a people so divided and so distrustful within as well as between the communities of Protestant and Catholic. Nevertheless without it there can be no way forward at all. The elaboration of the issues in the papers included in this volume marks a necessary step in assessing the experience of the decade of the 1970s in this sadly fractured society and measuring the extent to which government and public policy can respond to good intention with initiatives that at the least recognise and at best reflect the facts of the case.

In their conclusion the editors stress the ways in which the key issues of religion, education and employment open up the central themes of Northern Ireland life. What their volume establishes beyond doubt is that the relations between the two communities, divided in the name of religion, are neither new or simple. Hepburn's study of a fifty-year period, 1901–1951, shows convincingly that there is little evidence to suggest that Protestant advantage and Catholic disadvantage are likely to disappear or be much mitigated by policies directed at the structure as a whole. Other work in the volume shows how disadvantages that arise from one condition such as religion have to be linked to other factors such as being a woman—an area so far given little attention in public debate in the Province and consequently under-researched.

The overall emphasis in all of the studies reported in this collection is on disadvantage, since it has been shown that overt discrimination is relatively rare and indeed only the tip of the iceberg as has been shown also in race relations in the UK and elsewhere.

The editors in their conclusion reach toward a policy of quota allocation as a tangible response to the real situation of disadvantage and inequality of opportunity that persists in Northern Ireland. This policy involving what has been described, perhaps unfortunately, as 'positive discrimination', has been tried in the USA and elsewhere to help resolve conflicts. Its success depends on two things. The first of these this book goes a long way to help provide: that is a factual basis for the disadvantage recognized and accepted by all to be accurate and true. The second and more difficult, even to the limited extent suggested by the editors, depends on the political will to bring it about.

Sadly, I do not believe that the parties to the political debate in Northern Ireland yet see the social issues of disadvantage as the central issues of political debate and contest. Unless the human condition of the people of Northern Ireland can become the central issue of debate rather than issues of sovereignty it seems unlikely that measures addressed to the protection of individual rights as indicated recently by Garret FitzGerald or measures intended to remove institutionalized but misrecognized disadvantage can have much hope—especially in a recessionary climate.

But, that said, the starting point lies in establishing the basis for the constructive social engineering which ultimately will be required if a reasonable possibility of government is to be explored and developed. The research reported in this book shows the need for government to take seriously its responsibilities with regard to the monitoring of social change and policy effectiveness. The inadequacy of official statistics and the need to elaborate an informed debate about the social issues must be central to any government object that is committed to revealing rather than concealing the real condition of the governed.

It is precisely because these facts are intractable and difficult to disentangle that the kind of research reported in this book is so important. The Rothschild inquiry into the work of the Social Science Research Council has done much to reinforce the view that the social sciences have a role in providing a continuing critical analysis of the social fabric. It is undesirable for government to be the sole arbiter and umpire of its policy intentions. Nevertheless it can do much directly and indirectly to make it possible for this research to be done—to provide the substance of a political arithmetic which can be applied to the complex equations of Northern Ireland.

1. Introduction: Political Arithmetic and Social Policy

R. J. Cormack and R. D. Osborne

The chapters of this book offer the beginnings of a *political arithmetic* of Northern Ireland. The *arithmetic* has to do with, for example, the numbers of Protestants and Catholics in and out of jobs, the numbers in different types of jobs in terms of function and status, the numbers of young people gaining secondary level qualifications and higher degrees, the types of jobs found by these young people from the two communities. The *political* implications are most usually drawn in terms of equality of opportunity and the social policies fashioned to advance this principle.

While we focus specificially on the two divided communities of Northern Ireland, the issue of *inequality* in opportunities is of increasing significance throughout the developed world. The lead given by the United States in formulating policies of 'positive discrimination' and 'affirmative action' has found many followers in Europe. In particular, as the Women's Movement has advanced, and as so-called 'gastarbeiters' have become much less welcome 'guest' workers, agencies have been formed, either directly by governments or indirectly with government support, to pursue equality of opportunity in terms of sex and race.

The strength of the chapters which follow lies in the *empirical* evidence they provide on topics which are the focus of often contentious and frequently ill-informed debate. However, before leaving the stage to such empirical evidence a few words of *theoretical* introduction seem appropriate.

Notwithstanding A. H. Halsey's (1980) best efforts the term 'political arithmetic' has fallen into disrepute if not disuse. Despite this lack of currency in fashionable circles, it has a long and venerable history. Broadly speaking political arithmetic can be defined as argument, disciplined by facts and figures, addressed to issues of government.

William Petty in *Political Arithmetik* in 1686, and other works, had much to say about economic and social policies of the government of his day, especially in relation to Ireland (Petty, 1899). In the nineteenth century Henry Mayhew inspired Dickens among others with his *London Labour and the London Poor* (1968). Charles Booth continued and added to the tradition in his voluminous *Life and Labour of the People in London* and was a major influence on the development of this type of work in North America (Pfautz, 1967). In 1938, Lancelot Hogben, an influential member of what has been called a 'visible college' of socialist scientists (Werskey, 1978), published *Political Arithmetic.* One of the contributors to Hogben's volume became the doyen of the tradition in the post-war period. David Glass in *Social Mobility in Britain* (1954), while the starting point for so many histories of British sociology, can be seen in the present context to have been contributing to an ongoing tradition. The contributions of Douglas (1967), Goldthorpe (1980) and Halsey et al (1980) are but a few examples of the more notable contributions in the recent past. Political arithmetic has been central to, if it has not defined, the British tradition in sociology (Abrams, 1968). However all too often political arithmetic is presented as mere 'number crunching' or, to use a term coined by Mills (1959), 'abstracted empiricism'. Even Halsey (1980) would appear to think political arithmetic lacks a clear *theoretical* foundation. This we would dispute. The tradition of political arithmetic has been directly engaged in providing a critical analysis and assessment of liberal social thought and social policies. Liberalism, as with other theories of society, presents a set of propositions which require scrutiny and testing in the light of available evidence. The tradition of political arithmetic has been in the forefront of this critical task.

Equality of opportunity has been a central principle of liberal social thought and policy throughout its many transformations (e.g. Bramsted and Melhuish, 1978; Collini, 1979). Political arithmeticians have sought, in particular, to identify and measure inequalities in opportunity and the degree to which social policies have either directly or indirectly enhanced or restricted the growth of opportunities. The focus has been primarily on disadvantages associated with social class, but more recently attention has been directed to disadvantages associated with sex and race. In the circumstances of Northern Ireland if *religion* is a source of disadvantage then it is of direct social, economic and political importance. The chapters in this book are primarily directed to assessing the extent to which religion acts as a disadvantage in the pursuit of various activities, particularly the pursuit of a job on the labour market.

In 1975 Aunger published an article analysing 1971 census data in terms of religion and occupational class. (The 1971 census provided the first opportunity since 1911 to investigate relationships between occupation and religion.) This article, adapted and reprinted here as chapter two, encouraged much subsequent work in political arithmetic in Northern Ireland. Aunger found a sizeable Catholic middle class, albeit substantially smaller than the Protestant middle class. Noticeably, the members of this Catholic middle class were to be found primarily servicing their own community as doctors, lawyers, teachers, publicans. By contrast, members of the Protestant middle class serviced their own community but, in addition, provided Province-wide services in, for example, banking, insurance and public administration. In terms of manual work, Catholics were found to be substantially over-represented in semi-skilled and unskilled work, and in unemployment. Hepburn, in chapter three, provides historical information on the development of these patterns of disadvantage. It would seem that already by 1901 quite significant differences existed between the two communities to the disadvantage of Catholics. Throughout the book, chapters deal with various aspects of these patterns and, somewhat more indirectly, with their policy implications.

Miller, in chapter four, contributes an analysis of inter- and intragenerational mobility of Protestant and Catholic males controlling for education and age. Differences in mobility are attributed primarily to a widening split resulting in the dominance of Protestants in upper middle or 'service class' categories, and Catholics in working-class categories. In chapter five, Miller and Osborne provide an analysis of unemployment based on data collected in a survey conducted by the Department of Manpower Services. These 1976 data confirm a continuing pattern of Catholic over-representation in unemployment and the analyses suggest some possible factors contributing to this recurring pattern. In some areas of Northern Ireland women have found it easier to find jobs than men, e.g. in Londonderry the shirt-making factories have traditionally provided female employment in areas where opportunities for men are relatively fewer. Trewsdale, in chapter six, provides an analysis of this and other features of women and work in the Province concluding that women's disadvantaged position in the labour market can be attributed more to sex than to any other factor.

An argument often advanced to explain Protestant/Catholic differences in employment is differential performance in school-based examinations. Murray and Osborne, in chapter seven, tackle this issue with data on examination performance for 1971 and 1975. While levels of attainment in Catholic schools in the past were lower than those for Protestant schools, the differentials have narrowed considerably. The relationships between qualifications and the occupational hierarchy provide the basis for the discussion of these differentials. In the subsequent chapter young school leavers are the focus. Cormack and Osborne's chapter on male school leavers in Belfast, and Murray and Darby's study in Londonderry and Strabane suggests that levels of examination performance of boys from the two communities are remarkably similar. However, such qualifications appeared to have little currency in the labour market; rarely were boys asked whether or not they had examination qualifications. Much more significant in securing employment was the network of family and friends in work. Since this mechanism for finding a job depends on having family members and friends who have jobs it is found to be a central factor in the reproduction of existing patterns of advantage and disadvantage.

In terms of access to higher education the signs of major changes are evident. Osborne et al, in chapter nine, provide extensive detail on higher education entrants in 1973 and 1979. By 1979 Catholics were represented in higher education in about their proportion in the relevant age cohort. Some concern, remains, however, in terms of subjects studied. Catholic underrepresentation in science-based subjects continues to be noticeable feature.

Finally, McCrudden, in chapter ten, leaves the statistical side of political arithmetic behind and takes-up the policy implications. The major instrument of policy in this area is the Fair Employment Agency set-up in 1976 to promote equality of opportunity in employment between the two communities. McCrudden assesses the experience of the FEA in the six years of its existence and places its achievements and deficiencies in a comparative perspective. In the conclusion to the book, Osborne and Cormack address the major themes and issues raised by a political arithmetic of Northern Ireland and discuss some policy implications.

Theoreticians and 'Number Crunchers'

Readers who are satisfied they are now sufficiently informed about our approach are advised to proceed to chapter two. However, those who feel more questions have been raised than answered may well want to read on. More we think needs to be said about our conception of political arithmetic, about its relationship to liberalism, sociology and social administration[1], about its contribution to social policy, and the relevance of these issues to the divisions in Northern Ireland.

We argued above that political arithmetic is not 'mindless empiricism', 'mere number crunching', 'aimless fact gathering', rather it addresses central issues and principles of liberalism and liberal social policy. Historically, political arithmetic has been at the centre of the British tradition in sociology and, as such, has been the focus of frequently voiced accusations (which have now been elevated to the level of received wisdom) that British sociology is atheoretical and empirical. One of the early versions of this argument was advanced by John Rex (1961:28) in a highly influential book which appeared just as sociology was on the point of expansion in the 1960s:

> In the main the problems investigated by sociologists are those which have arisen in the course of philanthropic work or in the struggle for some social reform. In England, for example, there are many who would regard Charles Booth's studies of the incidence of poverty among different groups in London as the main starting point of empirical social investigation in their society. The assumption behind this appears to be that when argument occurs about social reform, the task of the sociologist is to collect the objective facts, as Booth, and later, Rowntree did, when they cleared away a lot of the prevailing myths about the causes of poverty.

Rex denigrates these researches because they are not, in his interpretation of them, guided by theory. Rex tells us that the 'scientific approach to sociology' he advocates is one 'which emphasises the role of theoretical models in the orientation of the sociologist to his research problems' (Rex, 1961). Similar views have been expressed since, often in more carefully qualified ways, but nevertheless making the same essential point (Abrams, 1968; Anderson, 1969; Kent, 1981; Payne et al, 1981).

It is certainly true that many of the central figures in 19th and early 20th century sociology did not engage in extended theoretical discussions. German and French sociology of the period was much more taken-up with theoretical issues (Maus, 1962). However, when the intellectual and ideological environment in which British, French and German sociologists were working is taken into account this difference in focus is more readily understood. In Britain the creation and accommodation of capitalist institutions was achieved without turmoil on the scale engendered on the Continent (Moore, 1967). Liberalism, the ideology most in harmony with the ideas and interests of the bourgeoisie, had established an almost hegemonic place in the life and thought of the society by the time the founding fathers of sociology were writing in the latter half of the 19th century (Gamble, 1981; Eccleshall, 1979; Lichtman, 1969). The new order came about much less easily in France and Germany and, once established, faced much more severe opposition (Moore, 1967). British sociologists lived and worked in an environment in which liberal principles had assumed a normative force (Hawthorn, 1976). Their work was conducted within the parameters of liberalism. Their researches were directed to issues, disputes and problems raised by liberal principles and policies. The pressures and conflicting influence on British sociologists were much less direct and distracting than those faced by sociologists on the Continent (Giddens, 1971, 1972; Lukes, 1975).

This is not to suggest, however, that sociology in Britain developed within the framework of an harmonious liberal consensus. Nothing could be rather from the truth. The divisions within liberalism were as wide and as passionately fought over as any between left and right, between conservatism and socialism.

The 'new' versus the 'old' liberalism

In tracing out the liberal roots of sociology one could go back to Hobbes and Locke, or to the founding father of liberal political economy, Adam Smith, as early American sociologists often did (Martindale, 1960; Schwendinger and Schwendinger, 1974). However, for our purposes the period at the end of the 19th century is a useful point to break into the story. From 1880 onwards the 'old' or 'classical' liberalism was under attack, while the 'new' liberalism was slowly emerging. Laissez-faire liberalism was being supplanted by a liberalism which increasingly recognised that the state had a significant role to play. Sociologists were to be found in both camps. Herbert Spencer was the most prominent and strident advocate of laissez-faire liberalism, while L. T. Hobhouse, the first professor of sociology at the University of London, was, in his journalism for the *Manchester Guardian* and in his academic work, a powerful advocate of the need for the state to intervene to guarantee social justice. It is remarkable the contemporary relevance of much of this debate as Thatcher and Reagan administrations pursue Friedmanite policies inspired by a faith in laissez-faire and an antipathy to solving problems through state intervention (Friedman, 1980).

Spencer was an advocate of social and economic laissez-faire, a militant defender of individualism, and a foe of collectivism, especially in the form of an interventionist state. Spencer combined the competitive aspects of the free market found in Adam Smith and the classical political economists, with the population theory of Thomas Malthus.[2] Simply, Malthus argued that population has a constant tendency to increase beyond the means of subsistence. As a result there were frequent 'struggles for existence' in which the 'fittest survived'. Similarly, in a free society with a free market, there is equally a struggle for existence in which the fittest survive and flourish. As an ideological justification of Victorian Britain and its Empire such a theory had great force and attraction.

Perhaps the point is best made in considering the implications of the following passage from Spencer (1854:241):

> The poverty of the incapable, the distresses that come upon the imprudent, the starvation of the idle, and those shoulderings aside of the weak by the strong, which leave so many 'in swallows and in miseries', are the decrees of a large, far-seeing benevolence. It seems hard that an unskilfullness which with all his efforts he cannot overcome should entail hunger upon the artisan. It seems hard that a laborer incapacitated by sickness from competing with his stronger fellows should have to bear the resulting privations. It seems hard that widows and orphans should be left to struggle for life or death. Nevertheless, when regarded not separately, but in connection with the interests of universal humanity, these harsh fatalities are seen to be full of the highest beneficence—the same beneficence which brings to early graves the children of diseased parents and singles out the low-spirited, the intemperate, and the debilitated as the victims of an epidemic.

Life is a struggle for existence and any attempt, particularly by the state or charitable bodies, to interfere with this process of 'natural selection' do so at the risk of weakening the principle of the survival of the fittest and the positive evolutionary consequences of this supposedly 'natural' process.[3] Spencer (1884:107) wrote:

> The function of liberalism in the past was that of putting a limit to the power of kings. The function of true liberalism in the future will be that of putting a limit to the powers of parliaments.

By the 1880s laissez-faire liberalism was increasingly under attack. The pressures were numerous and various: Dickens's novels,

Engels' study of Manchester slums, Mayhew's studies of the London poor, the formation of Trades Unions, the founding of the Marxist Social Democratic Federation in 1881 and the Fabian Society in 1884, and the London riots in 1886–7 protesting about the lack of jobs. It would be wrong to single out any one author or event as being instrumental in changing the climate of opinion. However, for our purposes, Charles Booth's *The Life and Labour of the People of London* must hold a special place. Booth, as a result of this monumental work, is often given credit as the founding father of empirical sociology (Pfautz, 1967). Certainly, his influence on British and North American sociology is not in dispute (Kent, 1981; Schwendinger and Schwendinger, 1974). Booth, and later Rowntree, conducted surveys of the social conditions in London and York respectively. Hobhouse (1964:85) draws out the theoretical and practical conclusions to be made from these studies:

> The careful researches of Mr Booth in London and Mr Rowntree in York, and of others in country districts, have revealed that a considerable percentage of the working classes are actually unable to earn a sum of money representing the full cost of the barest physical necessities for an average family; and, though the bulk of the working classes are undoubtedly in a better position than this, these researches go to show that even the relatively well-to-do gravitate towards this line of primary poverty in seasons of stress . . . It is clear that the system of industrial competition fails to meet the ethical demand embodied in the conception of the 'living wage'. That system holds out no hope of an improvement which shall bring the means of such a healthy and independent existence as should be the birthright of every citizen of a free state within the grasp of the mass of the people of the United Kingdom.

The researches of Booth and Rowntree directly engaged central issues of 'old' liberal principles and policies. These researches demonstrated that the social conditions of much of the urban working class could *not* be improved through their own efforts. 'Self-help' in the circumstances was not an answer to the conditions found in the working class. The free competitive market cannot even, or so it seemed, provide a 'living wage' for the 'respectable', 'deserving' working poor, far less provide for the sick and other poor. These conditions, together with the vast inequalities they displayed in the society at large, implied that the state would have to intervene to create much greater opportunities for the poor to help themselves, and to provide for the sick and alleviate the worst excesses of poverty that charitable foundations were unable to abate. Gamble (1981:182) expresses this goal well:

> The moral case for social democracy which was pressed by progressive liberals like Hobhouse and Tawney was that only if industrial societies were organised on the basis of an equality that went beyond abstract rights and signified equality of opportunity and an equality of basic condition, would they create a social order accepted as legitimate by all their citizens.

As Gamble rightly argues, the 'new' liberalism places a greater emphasis on equality of opportunity. Genuine respect for the individual required that society provided, at the very least, a basic minimum standard of living together with social institutions, particularly education and employment, allowing the full potential of each and every individual to develop.[4] The political arithmeticians had demonstrated empirically the overwhelming handicaps poverty and low wages placed on the working class. Churchill expressed the new policy well:

> We want to draw a line below which we will not allow persons to live and labour, yet above which they may compete with all the strength of their manhood. We want to have free competition upwards; we decline to allow free competition to run downwards. (Churchill, quoted in George and Wilding, 1976)

A 'new' liberalism and a new set of social policies were required to advance and protect the 'rights' of *all.*

'Butskellism'

British politics for the last hundred years has been greatly shaped by arguments and polemics underpinned by the 'old' and the 'new' liberalism. George and Wilding (1976:21) in an otherwise commendable book suggest:

> . . . liberalism today stands for such a wide spectrum of political ideology that it has lost all meaning. The term liberalism confuses rather than clarifies discussion today.

We would disagree with this assessment. Since that was written British politics has undergone a transformation which has resulted in much greater ideological clarity than perhaps has existed for a century. We are confronted by much clearer choices than ever before. The Conservative Party now offers a revitalised version of the 'old' liberalism. The Labour Party is in the process of seeking out a more authentically socialist voice than has been the case for most of its history. The Social Democratic Party in alliance with the Liberal Party has striven to maintain the 'middle' ground *vacated* by the other two Parties; a middle ground variously described as 'Butskellism'—a term named for R. A. Butler, a major force in reshaping the Conservative Party after the War, and Hugh Gaitskell, leader of the Labour Party from 1955 to 1963, a term which suggests the remarkable cross-party consensus that existed until recently in post-war British politics (Eccleshall, 1980).

Butskellism has its roots in the 1880s in the reaction of progressive liberals to laissez-faire liberalism and in the programme of the Fabians. The confusion pointed to above by George and Wilding stems from the similarities in *some* of the policies advanced by the new liberals and the Fabian socialists. In particular both groups shared a belief in the ability of government to intervene to alleviate poverty and the worst excesses of social condition resulting from the operation of the free market system. They disagreed about equality and how it was to be defined, but this will be taken up later. The Fabians, the 'new' liberals, and, slowly, some political economists came to recognise a role for the state (Wolfe, 1981).

By the 1930s it looked as if the capitalist system was on the verge of collapse with no obvious *liberal* solution available. Hunt (1981:155) describes the period well:

> What had happened to reduce the output of goods and services so drastically? Natural resources were still as plentiful as ever. The nation still had as many factories, tools, and machines. The people had the same skills and wanted to put them to work. And yet millions of workers and their families begged, borrowed, stole, and lined up for a pittance from charity, while thousands of factories stood idle or operated below capacity. The explanation lay within the institutions of the capitalist market system. Factories could have been opened and people put to work, but they were not because it was not profitable for businessmen to do this. And in a capitalist economy production decisions are based primarily on the criterion of profits, not on people's needs.

Not only were firms going bankrupt; so too, it seemed, were the old liberal verities. The 19th century versions of liberalism were obsolete and demonstrably so. It was an age of great confusion. Marxists offered a persuasive solution which appeared to have its practical counterpart in the post-Revolution expansion of the Soviet economy. The Fascists in Europe offered their own solutions which as Galbraith (1977:213) ironically points out prefigured the post-war liberal solution adopted in Western economies:

> The Nazis were not given to books. Their reaction was to circumstance, and this served them better than the sound economists served Britain and the United States. From 1933 Hitler borrowed money and spent—and he did it liberally as Keynes would have advised.

But it was practical experience gained in the conduct of World War II more than the persuasion of theory that brought about a change. Wars on the scale of World War II could not be fought without the state organising production and distribution. On both sides of the Atlantic the state intervened so effectively that the 'new' liberal arguments about a new role for the state no longer fell on outraged ears.

The new liberalism, after more than sixty years of incubation, came to underpin the post-war consensus of British politics. Both political parties recognised the need for the state to intervene in economic matters, and in social and welfare provision. The state, instead of acting as ringmaster, as it had done in the days of laissez-faire, now had to get into the ring and help out in all kinds of ways. The state moved from a passive to an active role.

Political Arithmetic and Equality of Opportunity

The principle of equality of opportunity has been central to many of the progressive social policies pursued in the post-war period. Social justice, it is argued, demands that each and every individual be given the opportunity to develop his or her abilities and talents to the full. From Adam Smith onwards liberal economists have argued that innovation greatly depends on the market rewarding those who are skilful, inventive and industrious. A healthy and vigorous society is one in which social status is individually achieved rather than ascribed, for example, at birth.

Political arithmetic has been primarily engaged in investigating the handicaps and hurdles which diminish the opportunities available to specific groups in the population. As we have seen, the 19th century poverty studies, particularly Booth's, demonstrated the difficulty of working people rising above their condition. Increasingly, however, the attention focused on education as a means to upward social mobility. At the 1896 TUC, a motion was presented urging 'that our education system should be completely remodelled on such a basis as to secure the democratic principle of equality of opportunity' (Silver, 1973). Tawney's famous statement in *Equality* in 1931, that 'the hereditary curse upon English education is its organisation upon lines of social class', sought to focus attention on the major source of inequality: the class structure. Towards the end of the 1930s Lancelot Hogben collected together a series of empirical studies on education and social mobility under the title *Political Arithmetic* (1938). One of the findings will perhaps suffice to give the flavour of this seminal book:

> . . . while nearly all the children of the larger business and the professional classes who possess ability have the opportunity of higher education, the correspondng figure for clerical and commercial employees is approximately 50 per cent, for skilled wage-earners 30 per cent, and for unskilled wage-earners 20 per cent. (Gray and Moshinsky, 1938:416)

Social justice in liberal terms cannot and does not pertain when children of equal ability, but from different class backgrounds, have visibly different chances of entering institutions of higher education.

The post-war sociology of education can almost be read as a catalogue of continuous monitoring of opportunities available, particularly in class terms, but latterly in terms of sex and race. Floud, Halsey and Martin (1956) found significant class differentials in access to grammar schools. Douglas in 1964 found '. . . a substantial loss of ability (to the nation—eds) in the manual working-class children which could be prevented'. Halsey et al (1980:204) reported in 1980 that:

> . . . class differentials widen at each rung up the educational ladder. The boy from the working class was much more likely than his service-class contemporary to drop out of school as soon as the minimum leaving age was reached, was less likely to continue his school career into the sixth form, and less likely to enter a university or some other form of education after school . . . A service-class boy in our sample was four times as likely as his working-class peer to be found at school at the age of 16, eight times as likely at the age of 17, ten times as likely at the age of 18, and eleven times as likely to enter a university.

In policy terms a series of government reports—Early Leaving (1954), Crowther (1959), Newsom (1963) and Robbins (1963)—demonstrated the 'wastage of ability' and recognised the need for changes to be made to increase the equality of opportunity (Mortimore and Blackstone, 1982).

In the late 1960s the 'new' sociology of education made its

appearance, deflecting attention away from the central issues of political arithmetic. This 'new' sociology of education sought to focus attention on the actual processes of schooling, i.e. what goes on in the classroom (Young, 1971; Banks, 1982). Fashion plays an important role in sociology; sociologists keep reinventing the wheel and declaring what went before as square. In their focus on classroom activities little mention was made of much earlier material (Waller, 1933). However, although never quite living up to its promises the 'new' sociology of education has contributed much useful material on the curriculum and on the micro-sociology of the school (Bernbaum, 1977). Nevertheless, it has now been overtaken by a neo-Marxist perspective which has much in common with political arithmetic. The seminal book here has been Bowles and Gintis' *Schooling in Capitalist America.* Gintis was one of the co-authors with Christopher Jencks of *Inequality* (1978), a major study of equality of educational opportunity in the United States. However, Bowles and Gintis, in their own book, part company with Jencks' egalitarianism.

The credentialism in modern society has resulted in educational institutions being much more directly involved in the process of social stratification (Bowles and Gintis, 1976:103):

> The educational system legitimates economic inequality by providing an open, objective, and ostensibly meritocratic mechanism for assigning individuals to unequal economic positions. The educational systems fosters and reinforces the belief that economic success depends essentially on the possession of technical and cognitive skills—skills which it is organized to provide in an efficient, equitable, and unbiased manner on the basis of meritocratic principle.

Bowles and Gintis take issue here with the liberal meritocratic principle which equality of opportunity policies are geared to fulfil. *If* full equality of opportunity were attained then we would have a highly stratified society where placement on the hierarchy would depend solely on merit. Liberals most usually argue that differential material rewards are necessary to *motivate* individuals to compete for well-paid high prestige positions.

In sociology the functional theory of stratification is a good example of such an argument. Davis and Moore argue that social stratification is a functional mechanism '. . . by which societies insure that the most important positions are conscientiously filled by the most qualified persons.' (Davis, 1949). Society must distribute its members in such a manner that social positions are filled by qualified individuals who are motivated to perform the duties attached to these positions. It does this by allocating the highest rewards to the functionally most important positions. Such rewards provide the motivation for individuals to compete and train for the top positions; a training which often involves a lengthy period on low income. Thereafter, high rewards further serve to motivate such individuals to fulfil the requirements of such top positions once they have been attained. Hence, the functional theory of stratification is essentially the classical liberal model rendered sociological (Wrong, 1959).

This meritocratic model was heavily satirised in Michael Young's *The Rise of the Meritocracy* (1958). Young suggested that *if* the model worked, that is if all the documented disadvantages and inequalities could be wiped out, society would become a 'meritocracy': a society which distributed rewards on the basis of the formula: I.Q. + EFFORT = MERIT. But he asked whether intelligence should be given such a major role in the allocation of the social rewards. Is it fair that those with sub-average I.Q.s should be denied access to the greatest rewards the society has to offer? Are there qualities other than measured intelligence which are socially valuable?

The measurement of I.Q. and the purposes to which I.Q. tests are put became a contentious and hotly debated issue in its own right at the end of the 1960s. Much of the discussion arose from the perceived failure of certain 'compensatory education' programmes in the United States. Jensen argued that Blacks were genetically inferior in intelligence and this, rather than poverty, explained why as a group they underachieved in schools (Jensen, 1969). In Britain the argument was taken-up and extended by Eysenck to include the Irish along with Blacks (Rose and Rose, 1976; Halsey, 1977). On the one side of the debate were to be found arguments somewhat similar to those advanced by the 19th century eugenicists that intelligence is inherited and the stratification patterns come to reflect inherited advantage or disadvantage (Mackenzie, 1981). On the other side were Marxists such as Bowles and Gintis and others who argued that the meritocratic principle was used as an ideological legitimation for the existing patterns of stratification, i.e. that inequalities were justified on the basis of the unequal distribution of intelligence. Bowles and Gintis (1976:123) argued:

> Differences in I.Q., even were they genetically inherited, could not explain the historical pattern of economic and educational inequalities.

> The intractability of inequality of income and of economic opportunity cannot be attributed to genetically inherited difference in I.Q. The disappointing results of the 'War on Poverty' cannot be blamed on the genes of the poor. The failure of egalitarian school reforms reflects the fact that inequality under capitalism is rooted not in individual deficiencies, but in the structure of production and property relations.

Equality of Opportunity and Positive Discrimination

'Compensatory education' in the United States, and to the extent that it developed in Britain following the Plowden Report (1967), involved 'positive discrimination'. As Silver (1973:XXIII) put it:

> In an unequal society, it was argued, equality of opportunity could only have meaning if those who began with unequal chances had unequal support from the the educational system. The underprivileged, insisted the Plowden Report, needed *more* money spent on their education, *better* primary schools, a *larger* number of teachers and helpers than did other children.

While the Plowden Report (1967) established 'positive discrimination' as a new option in British educational and social policy it also created a certain ambivalence over what was meant by the term. Was positive discimination to be applied to *areas,* to *schools,* or to *individuals?* Experimental educational priority areas in several British cities were subsequently shown to contain only a minority of the educationally deprived in those cities, and only a minority of those who were disadvantaged (Barnes and Lucas, 1975). However, further area-based positive discrimination policies emerged, concentrating in particular on deprived inner-city areas. As Edwards and Batley (1978) suggest, the Urban Programme, the first of these policies, was at least partially a result of the state of race relations in Britain. Increasing evidence of disadvantages experienced by ethnic minorities disproportionately located in the inner cities, coupled with the notorious 1968 Enoch Powell speech in Birmingham, resulted in the perceived need to respond directly to racial disadvantage. Under this programme additional resources were to be given to specified areas to benefit disadvantaged black *and* white alike but in effect benefiting the black population disproportionately. The specific issue of racial discrimination was to be tackled through a mechanism for investigating individual complaints under the strengthened Race Relations Act of 1968. Area-based positive discrimination could be justified in terms of the conventional philosophy of the Welfare State, and hence *not* be seen as a new racially-conscious policy development (Jones, 1977). The race relations legislation could be justified as a narrow form of intervention to deal with the specific issue of discrimination.

In Northern Ireland, area-based positive discrimination policies have developed, albeit on only a limited scale, in response to the identification of areas of multiple deprivation (Boal et al, 1974; Project Team, 1976). A recent call for positive discrimination for 'priority schools' (McIntyre Report, 1980) has to date, however, met with a negative response from government.

Area-based positive discrimination programmes have been increasingly criticised on a number of fronts: they can stereotype areas as 'problem' districts, they commit the 'ecological fallacy' by predicting individual circumstances and performances from areal statistical measures and averages, and they ignore the deeper structural factors generating localised expressions of deprivation. Nevertheless, such policies have enabled successive British governments to develop racially inexplicit programmes towards Britain's ethnic minorities. Political elites from both major parties have been inordinately fearful of the 'white backlash' (Studler, 1980) and have regarded area-based policies as a major means of 'doing good by doing little' (Kirp, 1979).

The contrast with the racially explicit policies in the United States, particularly as they have developed towards 'goals' or 'quotas' to secure equality of opportunity, could not be greater. Racially explicit policies can be justified by the complex interaction between social disadvantage and racial discrimination, but their particular development in the United States has owed much to a sense of guilt amongst whites for the collective experience of blacks, allied to direct political pressure especially in the 1960s, and the capacity for the United States Constitution to be reinterpreted in the light of contemporary demands and expectations. These policies have been under continuous debate and reassessment as Sindler (1978:27) has noted:

> . . . the exquisitely complicated problems . . . (of equality of opportunity) . . . are enduring problems not amenable to full resolution at any one time but in process of partial and changing resolution at all times.

Particularly influential in questioning these policies has been Glazer (1975, 1978), an American sociologist with impeccable liberal credentials. He argues that they represent a move away from the traditional concern with 'individual' rights in the United States towards collective or 'group' rights, i.e. all blacks are preferentially assisted by these policies while all whites are regarded as jointly responsible for the past treatment of blacks. Hence, for example, the famous case of Alan Bakke, who was refused entry to medical school in favour of less well qualified blacks. Glazer further argues that the commitment to equality of opportunity is being distorted into equality of outcomes or results to be achieved in terms of statistical representation rather than merit; moreover, such developments are not supported by a majority of either blacks or whites. Glazer continues that the need to classify and categorize people into groups further offends against individual rights and will tend to sustain ethnic and racial cleavages, whereas the long-term trend in United States society is towards assimilation and integration. Glazer is in favour of strong anti-discrimination legislation but not 'quotas'. Many writers responded to Glazer in order to counter his assumptions and arguments contradicting his statistical material and arguing that 'group' rights are, especially on a fixed-term basis, compatible with United States social goals (Livingston, 1979).

Fuel has been added by the argument of a black sociologist (Wilson, 1978) who suggests that middle class blacks have gained primarily from these policies while there is increasing evidence of an emerging black underclass for whom the policies are irrelevant. But, with scant regard to this debate, the Reagan administration has been concerned to 'liberate entrepreneurs and businessmen from bureaucratic interference' and, as a result, has dismantled some of these policies (Robbins, 1982).

In Britain some moves towards 'quotas' policies seem to be developing around pressures for greater sex equality as a result of the perceived failure of equal pay and anti-discrimination legislation. Patently area-based policies are irrelevant in this context and the strengthening of policy is being seen in terms of 'quotas'. Paradoxically it was the introduction of sex-discrimination legislation in 1975 which extended British policy beyond a narrow conception of discrimination to include 'indirect discrimination' (policies and practices which might not be discriminatory in intent but were so in effect) which led to a similar strengthening of race relations legislation in 1976. Most recently however 'positive discrimination' has returned to the public agenda with the Scarman Report's investigation of the 1981 urban disturbances in Britain (Scarman, 1981). Lord Scarman (1981, para. 6:32), in assessing the wider social context of the riots, advocated that:

> . . . if the balance of racial disadvantage is to be redressed, as it must be, positive action is required . . . justice requires that special programmes should be adopted in areas of acute deprivation.

It became clear however that Scarman was lending support to the continuation and further development of area-based social policies more specifically targeted on black residential areas; policies more spatially discriminatory. 'Quotas' or anything like them were to be avoided. Even here, however, the Conservative government has been reluctant to commit additional resources.

Positive discrimination programmes in Britain have tended to be piecemeal and have not been developed in a coherent and sustained fashion (Mortimore and Blackstone, 1982). Nevertheless, it does seem likely that the discussion of positive discrimination will become much more significant in Britain. The advantages and disadvantages of various strategies available to implement positive discrimination will, of necessity, have to be more comprehensively understood in terms of their potential application to specific disadvantaged groups to promote equality of opportunity.

In Northern Ireland, in typical 'step-by-step' manner, the Equal Opportunities Commission for Northern Ireland was established in 1976, a year later than in Britain. Also in 1976 the Fair Employment Agency was set-up under the Fair Employment Act. The task ahead, as seen by the Working Party which recommended the setting-up of the FEA, is instructive at this point:

> The Central Principle: As we have made clear . . . it was not our function to pass judgement upon what may or may not have happened in employment practices in the past. No one, however, who has observed the events of recent years can fail to appreciate the intense feeling of grievance generated by a conviction—be it mistaken or otherwise—that objective judgement of individual worth has been distorted by prejudice, and that the rewards for effort, qualification and general merit have been denied or diluted on account of bias.
>
> Accordingly, we decided at an early stage of our deliberations that our fundamental aim must be to promote full equality in all aspects of employment opportunity. We regard this as a positive concept. It rests upon the vision of an open, free and just society, and it is fully compatible with determined steps—through programmes of 'affirmative action' . . . to remove the constraints and impediments which at present inhibit the realisation of that ideal. (MHSS, 1973:9)

This Working Party came out very strongly against quotas arguing that there were '. . . serious objections of both a moral and practical nature to both quotas and benign discrimination'; it was further argued that 'quotas' involved '. . . the abrogation of the very principles which they seek to assert' (MHSS, 1973:11). In the face of such explicit condemnation it is hardly surprising that 'quotas' have rarely surfaced since as a possible policy option to strengthen existing legislation (these issues are discussed more fully in chapter ten and in the conclusions).

Class and Equality of Opportunity

It is fair to say that the Fair Employment Agency, and the policies out of which it arose, do not infuse and excite the minds of most politicians in Northern Ireland. Predictably Unionist politicians have seen the fair employment legislation as a threat to the community they represent, while Catholic politicians have rarely seen the Fair Employment Agency as a instrument to advance the circumstances of their community. Just as political divisions rarely follow the class-based divisions universally assumed to be 'normal' in delevoped societies (O'Dowd et al, 1980); so has a 'new' liberal voice rarely been heard in Northern Ireland in support of the interventionist policies of post-war 'Butskellism'. As Boal and Douglas (1982:344) recently observed:

> It may also be noted that many of the gains in working-class conditions in Northern Ireland, certainly since the Second World War, occurred without the need (sic) for combined working-class action in Northern Ireland itself. The gains were achieved through working-class action on the United Kingdom mainland, the welfare consequences of which were transferred subsequently to Northern Ireland.

Class in Northern Ireland has seldom been the basis for social or political action. But, in saying that, it becomes incumbent on us to unscramble what is meant by 'class'. Quite simply, political arithmetic is concerned with *distribution*, particularly the manner in which first the market, and now increasingly the educational system, distributes opportunities. Who gets what jobs? As we have seen, children from working-class backgrounds, women, and blacks have been identified as groups with diminished opportunities.

The distributive model envisages a *stratified* society—a hierarchical arrangement most usually of occupations (Davis and Moore, 1945). This geological analogy offers a model very different from the one presented when 'class' is used in a more precise fashion. 'Class', when strictly defined, tends to suggest the grouping together of strata into a few large categories. Classes so conceived are most usually thought to have some cohesive unity, e.g. shared political consciousness. In Marxist usage, class refers to the organisation of *production* in that classes are defined in terms of their relationship to the means of production. This focus on production leads to important questions about types of production, the dominant mode of production, who owns/controls the principal units, what the relationships are between the owners/managers and local, national and international capital. These questions are not the sole preserve of Marxists. Classical and neo-classical economists have been working away at these and related issues for years. However, what is significant is that they are now being confronted by a Marxist political economy of Northern Ireland (Bew et al, 1979; Rowthorn, 1981).

Our focus, however, has been exclusively on the distribution of opportunities. The issue here can usefully be expressed in terms of the degree of 'social closure' identifiable groups can attain and enforce. Parkin (1979:44), following Weber, defines social closure as:

> . . . the process by which social collectivities seek to maximise rewards by restricting access to resources and opportunities to a limited circle of eligibles . . . This monopolization is directed against competitors who share some positive or negative characteristic; its purpose is always the closure of social and economic opportunities to outsiders. The nature of these exclusionary practices, and the completeness of social closure, determine the general character of the distributive system.

Clearly closure can be conceived in terms of class, sex, race or religion and hence, we suggest, provides a useful way to advance beyond the basic data and framework provided here (Kreckel, 1980).

Conclusion

In the nearly ninety years since the TUC motion calling for equality of opportunity, various ways of 'remodelling' the educational system on this principle have been explored. In education and in employment a tradition has grown up of monitoring the equality of opportunities. At first social class was identified as a major source of disadvantage, while latterly attention has been drawn to sex and race as further sources. In Northern Ireland religion has been added to this list and the chapters in this book investigate various aspects of this phenomenon.

George Homans (1961:9), an American sociologist, once said: 'Give me a man's actual findings, and I care not what theory he may have built them into.' There is much truth in this dictum. An excellent example is the Marxist critique Bowles and Gintis develop using mainstream (liberal) research on the equality of opportunity in the United States. However, Homan's view is too close to encouraging the 'mindless empiricism' pilloried by a number of critics of British and American sociology. Sociological research has been conducted in a more context-bound environment than this dictum allows. Our argument has been that this context in Britain and the United States has been provided by liberalism through its many phases and developments.

Liberalism, in these various transformations, has provided a framework or paradigm within which both empirical research and policy formulation have been conducted. Such empirical research has, most usually, produced findings which raise serious questions regarding the efficacy of liberal policies and hence ultimately concerning liberal principles. The accumulation of such 'anomalies' should *formally*, in Kuhnian (1962) terms, lead to a search for alternative principles and policies. In *practice*, however, this is subject to the much slower processes of change which operate in the realm of politics.

Many sociologists and others, in the late 1960s and 1970s, could not wait for politicians, ideologues and policy-makers to catch-up. The early Marxists were revolutionaries first and theoreticians second; in the post-war period Marxists have been academics first with often quite tenuous links to working class political movements. The early sociologists were directly engaged and addressed the politics of their day. In the last decade sociologists have often brought ridicule upon themselves for the outlandishness of their ideas. However, it is amazing how a severe recession brings mundane politics back into focus.

The breakdown of the Butskellite consensus in British politics has acted as a further spur and opportunity. As the Conservatives have found renewed inspiration in the classical liberal policies of laissez-faire, and as the Social Democrats cling to the not-so-new liberalism of Keynes and Beveridge, the Labour Party has struck out in search of an 'alternative strategy'. Whether or not this will lead them to electoral success is something of a moot point. However, in the present context it is notable that Benn (1979) also selectively draws on the liberal tradition.

All this may seem far removed from the politics of Northern Ireland where class-based politics have yet to emerge and where progressive liberalism has rarely found much local support. The sovereignty issue, London or Dublin, remains the principal focus of Northern Ireland politics. Yet the day-to-day policies emanating from Stormont Castle, especially in this period of 'Direct Rule', carry over the current thinking in Westminster. The 'double-minority' problem (Jackson, 1971), i.e. Catholics in a minority in Northern Ireland, Protestants in a minority in all Ireland, suggests that *any* political solution will have to be sensitive to the problem of minorities and will undoubtedly lead to a search for policies geared to protecting minority interests. On this question the liberal tradition, with its roots in protecting human rights, will remain a resource to be selectively ransacked. Moreover, whatever policies are pursued, much arithmetic will remain to be done on the politics of opportunity.

Notes

1. Sociology and social administration, particularly in the last fifteen years or so, have become quite distinct if not discrete disciplines. However, they share the same roots and in the view of some authors have been tarred with the same brush (see John Rex's view, above). A more balanced view of the history of British sociology can be found in Eldridge (1980) and a useful sociologically-informed view of social administration in Mishra (1981). The common roots of the two disciplines are what concern us in this chapter and it is our view that the two disciplines should be kept in a state of mutual interaction (Townsend, 1975).
2. Charles Darwin also found inspiration in Malthus. He acknowledged 'the struggle for existence' as a significant contribution to his search for the central mechanism in the evolution of natural organic life (Jones, 1980). *Social* Darwinism was the application of Darwin's evolutionary biology to society and social evolution. It was, in fact, the *reimportation* of the model of 'the struggle for existence' and 'the survival of the fittest' back into the social sciences; but now with the mantle and aura of a fundamental principle uniting natural and social sciences. In the first instance, social Darwinism provided an account of a social order, a social hierarchy, which now assumed the status of being a 'natural' phenomenon, a 'natural' evolutionary process whereby the 'fittest' had survived and flourished.
3. In the classical liberal political economy of Smith and his followers, the free market is seen to be the central institution in society organising, as if by an 'invisible hand', the production and distribution of goods. Smith's *The Wealth of Nations* (1776) inaugurated a new form of economic arrangements; slowly, meddling mercantilist states were transformed as markets developed. In Smith's

formulation this was a progressive development, as Marx recognised, liberating individuals from the ascribed statuses of an earlier age and allowing them now to freely compete and achieve on the market (Winch, 1978). This 18th century radical reform programme had, by the 19th century, in the hands of Herbert Spencer, become a justification for the status quo. The fittest had survived. The social order reflected the underlying 'natural' process of selection. Relevant to these developments is the manner in which classical liberalism intersected with pre-modern values. This provides the basis of an alternative view emphasising not so much liberal values but rather the continuity of the conservative tradition (Eccleshall, 1979).

4. This was very similar to a theme developed by Durkheim in reaction, in particular, to Spencer's work—the need for a 'moral' individualism (Lukes, 1978).
5. Legal and political aspects had been secured by the beginning of the twentieth century and in Marshall's discussion of the evolution of 'citizenship rights' this has formed a highly influential conceptual framework in social administration. (Marshall, 1963; Parker, 1975).

2. Religion and Class: An Analysis of 1971 Census Data

E. A. Aunger

There is no consensus on the relationship between occupational class and religious persuasion in Northern Ireland, but the dominant view appears to be that the two are largely unrelated, i.e., that economic class distinctions cut across religious divisions. Frank Gallagher (1957: 208), in a detailed, if somewhat partisan, study of relations between Protestants and Catholics in Northern Ireland concluded that 'both sections are stratified in similar ways. Generally speaking, there are proportionally the same numbers in the professions, in the trades, in clerical groups, and so on'. More recent, and more objective, studies have appeared to give qualified support to this general conclusion. On the basis of an examination of the occupational structure of major religious denominations in Belfast, Budge and O'Leary (1973: 245) concluded that 'marked occupational differences did not occur among adherents of the various denominations'. Richard Rose, in a comprehensive survey of social relations in Northern Ireland, determined that economic differences between the two religious groups were very slight. Rose (1971: 280) found only 'a limited tendency' for Protestants to have a higher occupational class than Catholics and noted that the median Protestant and the median Catholic were both manual workers. In direct contrast to these surveys, however, an examination of the community of Portadown undertaken by Barritt and Carter (1962: 54) found 'a marked difference in the economic status' of the two major religious groups: 'the Protestants tending to provide the business and professional classes, the larger farmers, and the skilled labour; and the Catholics the small farmers and the unskilled labourers'.

If, as appears to be frequently assumed, the two religious persuasions are largely similar in terms of their occupational stratification, a particularly salient characteristic in the social development of Northern Ireland is the relative absence of effective class organisations containing both Protestants and Catholics.

Compared with other parts of the United Kingdom, the trade unions have been considerably weaker in social influence and their political arm, the Northern Ireland Labour Party, has not had a significant impact upon Northern Ireland politics. The failure of class organisations to cross the religious divide effectively has been widely attributed, not to any class differences between the two religious groups, but rather to the perpetuation of religious bigotry by both Protestant and Catholic middle classes. This 'conspiracy' theory asserts that the capitalist class has used the device of sectarianism to divide the working classes and thereby prevent them from threatening the economic control of the elite. The Irish historian Owen Dudley Edwards (1970: 132, 154), for example, puts the blame for the social tensions on political leaders and capitalists who have exploited religious differences within the working class in order to weaken labour organisation and to increase job competition. Liam de Paor (1970: 94, 106) suggests that the Unionist government applied a strategy of *divide et impera* in order to keep itself in power: it exacerbated religious hostility thereby keeping the working class disunited. Bernadette Devlin (1969) and Eamonn McCann (1974) have similarly attributed a large measure of the working class disunity to the promotion of religious tension by the bourgeoisie. The view is perhaps best summarised by Robert Moore (1972: 32) in a study of 'race' relations:

> Northern Ireland is a society in which social stratification derived from the social relations of an industrial society is found within the major religious groups. Attempts have been made to organise on a class basis across these groups but these have always been defeated by playing upon the hostilities and fears derived from the colonial past and expressed in modern sectarianism. These fears and hostilities have been deliberately used by groups in power to prevent the emergence of class organisations, and thus to preserve their own power.

Religion and Occupational Class

The purpose of this chapter is to examine the extent to which occupational and religious differences may or may not be related, i.e., to examine whether, in fact, both religious groups are stratified in similar ways. If there exist significant differences in the occupational class of Protestants and Catholics this may explain, in itself, the reason why class organisation has failed to cross the religious divide: it would indicate that certain class divisions reinforced the religious divisions. For while many observers have claimed that only minimal class differences exist between Protestants and Catholics, there has been insufficient empirical evidence to either corroborate or refute this claim. This chapter will attempt to provide such empirical evidence. (The second claim, that politicians and capitalists have encouraged religious tension, while a worthy subject for investigation in its own right, will not be examined here.)

The logical place to begin such an examination is with the results of the Northern Ireland census. Unfortunately, however, although the census questionnaire requests that each respondent specify his religion, full information on the relationship between religion and occupation has not been made available since the 1911 census of Ireland, i.e., before partition. A partial exception to this was the 1961 census which provided information on the relationship between religion and family size, by socio-economic group, for a restricted sample of women. The Northern Ireland General Register Office published *Religion Tables*, based on the 1971 census, in 1975; for the first time these provided reliable information on the social characteristics of the major religious denominations, and the Census Office made some of the preliminary data for these tables available for use in this study. These data provide a classification of the employed population, by religion and sex, into 222 occupational groups.[1]

In order to reduce these groups to a scale convenient for analysis, each was classified according to the Hall-Jones scale of occupational prestige.[2] The Hall-Jones scale was chosen, first, because it permits an empirically derived ranking of occupations according to their social status. Second, because it contains eight occupational classes, it gives sufficient detail for analysis. When this classification was completed, it was found that a relatively small proportion of the Northern Ireland population was contained in each of the non-manual classes. Several of these were combined, therefore, in order to simplify their presentation.

In most cases, the occupational descriptions were sufficiently precise that each occupational group could be readily allocated a position on the Hall-Jones scale. However, two groups were felt to be so broad that they overlapped several levels and they were thus omitted from the classification.[3] Further, individuals who were recorded as out of employment were added to the lowest occupational class, the class containing unskilled workers. Apart from the obvious low status of the unemployed, those who are unemployed in Northern Ireland have generally come from the ranks of the unskilled workers (see Boal et al, 1974).

The results of this classification show that Protestants are disproportionately represented in the non-manual and the skilled manual occupations, while Catholics are disproportionately represented only in the semi-skilled, unskilled and unemployed classes (table 2:1). Although the difference between the proportions of Catholics and Protestants at each occupational level does not, at first, appear to be as great as that found by Barritt and Carter in the Portadown study, some of the general trends are confirmed. It is particularly noteworthy that while the median Protestant is a *skilled* manual worker, the median Catholic is a *semi-skilled* manual worker. (The occupational differences between Protestant and Catholic will be shown to be even more pronounced when men, alone, are considered.)

Table 2:1

RELIGION AND OCCUPATIONAL CLASS 1971, ECONOMICALLY ACTIVE MEN AND WOMEN

Occupational class	*Hall-Jones classification*	*Catholic (per cent)*	*Protestant (per cent)*	*Total* (per cent)*
1. Professional, managerial	I, II, III	12	15	14
2. Lower grade non-manual	IV, V(a)	19	26	24
3. Skilled manual	V(b)	17	19	18
4. Semi-skilled manual	VI	27	25	26
5. Unskilled, unemployed	VII	25	15	18
Total		100	100	100
N = 564,682				

* These percentages are calculated only for those individuals who stated a religion. Approximately 9 per cent of the respondents at the 1971 census did not give their religious persuasion.

While there is a very distinctive tendency for Catholics to fall into a lower occupational class than Protestants, it would be misleading to over-emphasise this tendency. These results indicate that both religious groups have large proportions in each of the five classes. Although the proportion of Catholics in non-manual occupations (31 per cent) is significantly smaller than the proportion of Protestants (41 per cent), it is sufficiently large to indicate the existence of a substantial Catholic middle class. In part, the fact that such a Catholic middle class exists at all may be attributed to the high level of segregation in Northern Irish society: this segregation creates the conditions which support the existence of a professional and business class whose role is specifically to satisfy the needs of their own religious group. For example, the division of the educational system into Protestant and Catholic schools, creates the need for large numbers of Protestant and Catholic teachers. Similarly, the high level of religiosity in Northern Ireland provides the environment for large numbers of clergymen and related religious workers. Without this need of each religious community for such specific professional services, it is doubtful that the Catholic middle class would be as large as it is. Among Catholics, primary and secondary school teachers and clergymen account for over a third (34 per cent) of those in professional and managerial occupations. By contrast, among Protestants, primary and secondary school teachers and clergymen account for less than a fifth (19 per cent) of those in this class.

Further, the prominence of religion in Northern Irish society encourages a loyalty to members of one's own group which is evident in the world of small business. Where possible, Catholics will shop in Catholic shops, while Protestants will patronise only Protestant shops. In some circumstances, this may simply be the consequence of a high level of residential segregation: shopping facilities and community services tend to be located in areas which are relatively homogeneous in terms of religion and, as a consequence, tend, themselves, to employ a homogeneous staff.[4] However, even in regions which have a religious mix there appears to be a definite tendency to support the members of one's own religious group. Many observers, for example, have remarked on the large number of shops which exist in the smaller Northern Irish communities. Where Protestants and Catholics live in substantial numbers, there is inevitably a duplication of the shops of each type in order to accommodate the religious cleavage. Rosemary Harris (1972: 6), in her study of a small rural community in Co. Fermanagh, has observed:

> The advantages offered by one shop over its rival had to be very considerable before a Protestant owner could attract Catholic customers, or vice versa. One shop, no matter how good, could never monopolise the trade, and no matter how poor it could normally expect a number of faithful clients.

J. M. Mogey (1955) has similarly commented on the large number of shops and businesses in Northern Ireland, relative to its population size, noting that this is a consequence of a duplication which exists throughout the society: schools, voluntary societies, cultural festivals, sports meetings, all must have duplicate arrangements in order to satisfy the religious division.

Thus, while Catholics are proportionately under-represented relative to Protestants in the non-manual occupations, it is apparent that the very existence of a high level of religious segregation in the society has created the conditions which have led to the development of a limited Catholic middle class. Each religious community centres around its own church, school, and shops. While school and church employees make up a significant proportion of the higher grade non-manual workers, shop proprietors and employees compose the majority of those in lower grade non-manual occupations.

Non-Manual Occupations

A number of important, but generalised, distinctions may be drawn between those Catholics and Protestants who are employed in non-manual work. First, if we consider the professional and managerial class, it is apparent that the occupations filled by Catholics are largely those which respond to the felt need of each religious group to have certain services provided by their co-religionists. The need for Catholic teachers, inspired by the segregated educational system, is the most notable example of this phenomenon. By constrast, professional and managerial occupations providing services required by the whole community, rather than a specific religious section, are very disproportionately Protestant. The educational system provides an instructive, but by no means the most dramatic, illustration. At the primary and secondary level, where schools serve their own particular religious community, Catholics represent 39 per cent of the teachers in employment. At the university level, however, where the educational service is non-segregated, providing a service to the whole society, Catholics represent only 17 per cent of the teachers in employment (Scott, 1973). In comparing these figures it should be kept in mind that Catholics constitute 31 per cent of the economically active population of Northern Ireland. We should expect that this employment pattern also exists in the lower grade non-manual occupations; however, this cannot be as readily tested: there are insufficient data concerning these occupations to draw a distinction between those which serve a particular religious community, and those which serve the society at large.

Second, and closely related to our first observation, Catholics tend to be disproportionately represented in the social services, while Protestants are disproportionately represented in finance and industry. This is particularly true in the professional and managerial class. Well over half (56 per cent) of the Catholics in this class are employed either in teaching, at the primary and secondary school level, or nursing. These same occupations account for only 29 per cent of the Protestants in this class. A comparison of those employed as either agents or managers in finance and industry, however, shows that these occupations account for about a quarter (24 per cent) of all Protestants in the professional or managerial class, but less than a tenth (9 per cent) of all Catholics in the same class. A similar pattern is found among the lower grade non-manual occupations, where Catholics can frequently be found to be concentrated in the sphere of routine services. This is combined with a traditional tendency for Catholics to operate certain of the smaller businesses and shops, while Protestants dominate the larger and more substantial business concerns. This is partially illustrated by an examination of 'industrial' groups, rather than 'occupational' groups; disproportionate numbers of Catholics work in smaller businesses such as betting and gambling (72 per cent), public houses (70 per cent), hotels and other residential establishments (48 per cent), and restaurants (42 per cent).

Third, those non-manual occupations which have the largest proportions of Catholics, relative to the total number employed in the occupation, tend to be lower status occupations, compared to those which have the highest proportions of Protestants (table 2:2). Thus, even within the non-manual levels, there are significant status distinctions between what might be termed 'Catholic' occupations and 'Protestant' occupations. If we examine those occupations which are most heavily Protestant, it is evident that nearly all of them are in the top levels of the non-manual classes. The only one with a relatively lower social status, police officers and men, is clearly counterbalanced by its strategic significance. This evidence confirms what has been, in any case, common knowledge, *viz.* that Protestants control the top positions of economic and political power. Catholic are concentrated in lower status occupations, generally with minimal political influence or strategic significance.

This status difference takes on added importance if we consider non-manual occupations related because they share a common 'working context'. In the medical services, for example, Catholics represent only 21 per cent of the qualified medical practitioners, but

Table 2:2

RELIGION AND NON-MANUAL OCCUPATIONS 1971, EMPLOYED MEN AND WOMEN

Occupational Group	*Hall-Jones classification*	*total employed*	*per cent women*[1]	*per cent Catholic*[1]
'Catholic' occupations:				
Publicans, innkeepers	IV	2,026	21	73
Waiters, waitresses	V(a)	2,145	84	50
Hairdressers, manicurists	V(a)	2,828	76	49
Domestic housekeepers	V(a)	1,582	100	48
Nurses	III	12,249	90	43
Primary, secondary teachers	II–III	15,726	63	39
'Protestant' occupations:				
Company secretaries	I	347	15	7
Police officers and men	V(a)	4,046	3	10
Chemists, biologists[2]	I	711	11	11
Engineers[3]	I	3,282	—	11
Managers[4]	II	10,312	6	12
Senior government officials[5]	I	1,383	10	13

[1] The percentage of women employed in each occupation is calculated on the basis of the total number employed, while the percentage of Catholics in each occupation is calculated on the basis of the total who stated their religion.
[2] Includes those classified as chemists, physical and biological scientists.
[3] Includes those classified as civil, structural, municipal, mechanical, electrical, electronic, etc., engineers.
[4] Includes managers in engineering, building, mining, personnel, sales.
[5] Includes Ministers of the Crown, MPs, senior government officials, senior officers in Local Authorities.

In comparing these occupational groups it should be kept in mind that Catholics constitute 31 per cent of the economically active, and 29 per cent of those in employment.

43 per cent of the nurses. Thus, considering the social relations within this sphere only, it is apparent that Protestants control the superior positions of authority, while Catholics are disproportionately members of the inferior positions. In the educational services, Catholics constitute only 15 per cent of those in administration, but 39 per cent of those in teaching. Thus, when the working context is considered, the relationship between occupational stratification and religious denominations appears to be considerably stronger than might otherwise be anticipated. While a clerk may be a Catholic, it more likely that the office manager will be a Protestant; while a skilled craftsman may be a Catholic, it is more likely that the supervisor will be a Protestant; and while a

nurse may be a Catholic, it is more likely that the doctor will be a Protestant.

'Feminine' and 'Masculine' Non-Manual Occupations

A further observation which should be made about the non-manual occupations concerns the sexual distinctions existing between the two religious groups. The non-manual occupations with the highest proportions of Catholics tend to be 'feminine' occupations while those with the highest proportions of Protestants tend to be 'masculine' occupations (table 2:3). If we examine the professional and managerial class, the two occupations with the highest proportions of Catholics are nurses (90 per cent women) and teachers (62 per cent women). On the other hand, the most 'Protestant' occupations have a negligible proportion of women:

Table 2:3

NON-MANUAL AND MANUAL OCCUPATIONS 1971, BY SEX

	Non-manual per cent	*Manual per cent*	*Total per cent*
Catholic men	21	79	100
Protestant men	33	67	100
Catholic women	48	52	100
Protestant women	55	45	100
N = 564,682			

engineers are virtually 100 per cent male, while managers are 94 per cent male. By way of comparison, it should be noted that women constitute 35 per cent of those in employment in Northern Ireland. Taking the class as a whole, *men* are in the great majority (69 per cent) among Protestants, while *women* are in the majority (51 per cent), albeit slight, among Catholics.

This observation, based upon the top non-manual class only, appears to be borne out, in general, for the non-manual occupations taken as a whole. Women have traditionally made up a large number of those employed in the non-manual occupations, particularly in the lower grades which include clerical and secretarial staff, shop assistants, waitresses and so on. However, since in absolute terms women are a smaller proportion of the work force, they do not make up the majority of those employed in non-manual occupations, except within the Catholic community. For while the majority of Protestant non-manual workers, by a small margin, are men, the majority of Catholic non-manual workers are women. In absolute terms, the number of Catholic women employed in non-manual is 25 per cent greater than the number of Catholic men in these same occupations.

This evidence, combined with what is known about unemployment in Northern Ireland, suggests that Catholic men may be in a more disadvantageous position than Catholic women, in terms of employment opportunities.[5] At the 1971 census, unemployment among women amounted to less than 5 per cent. However, among Protestant men it was 7 per cent, and among Catholic men, 17 per cent. Although Catholic men are less than 21 per cent of the economically active population, of both religions, and both sexes, they represent 44 per cent of the unemployed. This pattern of high unemployment and low economic status for Catholic men creates a particular problem in Northern Ireland given the extent of role stereotyping which exists within the society. Perhaps even more than in many other western societies, the stereotype of the dominant, assertive male is firmly entrenched. According to the psychiatrist Morris Fraser (1973: 23), this is the consequence of the 'settler' traditions which Northern Ireland has inherited and holds in common with other frontier communities. Further,

> ... this is to some extent an expression of population selection, the immigrant conforming to his stereotype—tough, male-dominant, hard-working, go-getting, self-starting. It also reflects the stong religious conservatism in both Protestant and Catholic camps, with its roots deep in Old Testament Judaism—a religion in which the male daily gives thanks to God that he was not born a woman.

In the Republic of Ireland, the role of the woman in the society is made clear by the policy of the Civil Service (up to recently), and of some private employers, of dismissing female employees when they marry.

Manual Occupations

The importance of the male in Northern Irish society, and the significant discrepancy between male and female occupational class, suggests that a more accurate indicator of the occupational differences between Catholics and Protestants might be a measure which used only males, or 'heads of households'. Since it might be expected that the status of the family would most often derive from that of the male head, we have recalculated the religious distribution over the five occupational classes, for males only. It is not possible to compute the results for 'heads of households' from these 1971 census data; however, a possible approximation, for purposes of comparison, can be taken from the 1961 census. The *Fertility Report* of the 1961 census provided a classification which showed the family size of married women over age 45, by religion and socio-economic group of husband. From this information, it is possible to calculate the relationship between occupation and religion, albeit for a restricted sample of the population, i.e., mature married males.

The results of these computations give us two pictures of the relationship between religion and occupation which are considerably different in terms of their sources: (1) one is from the 1971 census, the other the 1961 census; (2) one deals with all economically active males, the other only with those who are married to wives over the age of 45; and (3) one is coded using the Hall-Jones classification of socio-economic groups. Given these differences in derivation, it is perhaps surprising that the results are so similar (tables 2:4, 2:5).

Table 2:4

RELIGION AND OCCUPATIONAL CLASS 1971, ECONOMICALLY ACTIVE MEN

*Occupational class**	*Hall-Jones classification*	*Catholic per cent*	*Protestant per cent*	*Total per cent*
1. Professional, managerial	I, II, III	9	16	14
2. Lower grade non-manual	IV, V(a)	12	17	16
3. Skilled manual	V(b)	23	27	26
4. Semi-skilled, manual	VI	25	24	24
5. Unskilled, unemployed	VII	31	16	20
Total		100	100	100

N = 365, 948

* In classifying these socio-economic groups, three were omitted because they did not clearly fall within any one occupational class. These were (1) Farmers, (2) Members of the armed forces and (3) Own account workers.

Table 2:5

RELIGION AND OCCUPATIONAL CLASS 1961, MATURE MARRIED MEN

Occupational class	*Socio-economic group*	*Catholic per cent*	*Protestant per cent*	*Total per cent*
1. Professional, managerial	I, II, III, IV	9	17	15
2. Lower grade non-manual	V, VI, VIII	14	22	20
3. Skilled manual	IX	21	27	26
4. Semi-skilled manual	VII, X, XV	25	18	20
5. Unskilled manual	XI	31	16	19
Total		100	100	100

N = 85,936

These results reveal a higher level of class distinction between Protestants and Catholics than was observed when the occupations of both men and women were examined. As noted earlier, the majority of both Catholics and Protestants are manual rather than non-manual workers; however, if modal averages are considered, it is clear that the Protestant is most likely to be a *skilled* manual worker while the Catholic will be an *unskilled* manual worker.

In spite of this tendency for Catholics to be unskilled and Protestants to be skilled, it should be noted that Protestants, because of their larger numbers overall, still constitute an absolute majority of those who are unskilled. Nevertheless, a closer examination of those employed in manual work, and especially those who are unskilled workers, reveals another form of status differentiation: differentiation based upon industry, rather than occupation. When similar occupations are compared, it becomes evident that Protestants tend to be over-represented in the higher status industries, and Catholics in the lower status industries.

The nature of this industrial segregation may be partially illustrated by examining the distribution of those classified by the Census Office as 'labourers' (table 2:6). If the labourers are matched with their appropriate industrial group, the previously observed

Table 2:6

RELIGION AND INDUSTRY 1971, LABOURERS

Classification of Labourers	*total employed*	*per cent Catholic*	*Appropriate industrial group*	*total employed*[1]	*per cent Catholic*
Engineering[2]	2,440	16	Engineering	46,945	15
Textiles	2,191	30	Textiles	41,701	25
Railways	183	33	Railways	1,296	23
Chemicals	98	43	Chemicals	1,735	27
Docks	1,439	54	Port, water transport	3,945	35
Building, contracting	12,118	55	Construction	58,058	41
Glass, ceramics	173	59	Pottery, glass	499	41

[1] Includes labourers.
[2] Includes those labourers employed in (engineering) foundries.

pattern of *occupational* differentiation is emphasised: the proportion of labourers who are Catholics is greater than the proportion, in the industrial group as a whole, who are Catholics. However, a comparison of the different industrial groups shows an additional pattern of *industrial* differentiation such that labourers in the higher status engineering and textiles industries are predominantly Protestant, while those working in lower status industrial groups, such as the docks and building-contracting, are predominantly Catholic. Even this breakdown by industrial group fails to demonstrate the full extent of this segregation however. For example, although the census data do not provide further detail, it is known that the dock workers themselves are further subdivided: deep-sea traffic is handled primarily by Catholics, members of the Irish Transport and General Workers' Union, while cross-channel traffic is handled largely by Protestants, members of the Amalgamated Transport and General Workers' Union (Barritt and Carter, 1962). Traditionally, the deep-sea work has provided casual and irregular employment; the cross-channel work, employing Protestants, offers more regular, stable employment.

The general pattern of industrial differentiation may be studied further by examining briefly the major employers of Protestant and Catholic manual workers (table 2:7). Engineering has both the highest proportion of Protestants relative to Catholics and the highest absolute number of Protestants employed, in any industry. The proportion of Protestants in engineering as a whole amounts to 85 per cent, although in certain fairly prominent sections of the industry, notably shipbuilding, the proportions are even higher. In absolute numbers, the number of Protestant men employed in engineering and allied trades is equal to more than a fifth (22 per cent) of the total number of Protestant men employed in manual work. Apart from being the industry which is the most identifiably Protestant, the engineering and shipbuilding industry is also the most prestigious and influential of the major industries employing manual workers.

Some of this influence is a consequence of the greater economic prominence which the industry once had. The shipyard in Belfast, at its peak during the war years, employed more than 30,000 men and, since it was concentrated in one region, had considerable economic and political impact on the Province. The fact that, at the beginning of 'the troubles' in 1969, many in Northern Ireland looked to the shipyards for token leadership, indicates that in spite of its subsequent economic decline, much of its historic influence still remains (McInerney, 1970). Isles and Cuthbert (1957: 71) attribute much of the shipyard's importance to its historic role in the development of the Northern Ireland economy but note that 'its

Table 2:7

RELIGION AND INDUSTRY 1971, MAJOR INDUSTRIES EMPLOYING MANUAL WORKERS

Industry	*(I) hourly earnings*[1]	*(II) total employed*	*(III) per cent male*	*(IV) per cent unem-ployed*[2]	*(V) ratio of salaries to wages 1970*	*(VI) per cent Catholic*
A. Manufacturing						
Engineering[3]	68p	46,945	80	4.9	0.44	15
Textiles	65p	41,701	58	5.7	0.32	25
Food, drink, tobacco	64p	25,797	65	4.9	0.21	23
Clothing, footwear	58p	25,289	15	3.7	0.19	44
B. Other						
Transport, communication	68p	25,894	86	7.6	—	29
Agriculture, forestry	—	44,962	95	19.6	—	34
Miscellaneous services[4]	62p	49,065	50	6.6	—	35
Construction	55p	58,058	97	18.7	—	41

[1] These figures are the earnings of manual workers during the month of October, 1971. Since 1970, such earnings have been compiled only for the month of October of each year.

[2] The percentage employed is based only upon insured employees for the month of June, 1971.

[3] This includes mechanical, instrument, electrical, and marine engineering and allied industries such as shipbuilding and vehicle construction.

[4] This includes primarily motor repairers, garages, filling stations, public houses, betting shops, cinemas, restaurants, and hotels.

Data sources:
(I), (V), Ministry of Finance (1973).
(II), (III), (VI), Census Office, Northern Ireland, unpublished.
(IV), Northern Ireland Office (1973).

influence is all the greater because the workers are almost exclusively men, a large proportion of them skilled workers, and the industry is highly localised in Belfast'. Its higher proportion of skilled labour and generally higher pay scales make it a relatively more prestigious employment, even for the relatively unskilled.

The industries employing the largest proportions of Catholics, however, offer a considerable contrast to the engineering industry. In terms of the manufacturing industries, the clothing and footwear industry has the largest proportions and the largest absolute numbers of Catholics employed. Unlike engineering, it employs predominantly women rather than men, and has both the lowest wage levels and the lowest proportion of skilled labour of the major manufacturing industries. If industries outside manufacturing are also considered, however, it is Construction which employs the largest number of Catholic manual workers. Construction accounts for more than a third (34 per cent) of all Catholic men employed in manual work. The construction industry also has the highest proportion of labourers of any major industry and this likely contributes to its lower social status. It attracts workmen, especially the unskilled who, when employed elsewhere, seek casual employment in building and contracting. Isles and Cuthbert (1957: 65) described it as the 'sump into which workmen, particularly the unskilled, tend to drift as casual workers'. Not surprisingly it also has the highest level of unemployment of any of the major industries, with the possible exception of the declining agriculture industry.

In very general terms, the comparison suggests a broad division which has Protestant manual workers tending to be employed in higher status industries and Catholic manual workers tending to be employed in lower status industries. However, since only the largest Northern Ireland, are 47 per cent Catholic. On the other hand, workers must be exercised in making these generalisations. Considerable variations exist within these industries and it would be difficult to attribute these solely to status differentiation. Nevertheless, if some of the smaller industries are examined, a similar pattern appears to exist. Workers in the leather goods industry, the lowest paid in Northern Ireland, 47 per cent Catholic. On the other hand, workers in gas, electricity and water, one of the highest paying industries for manual workers in the 1970s, are only 16 per cent Catholic.

In examining the non-manual occupations, it was noted that a look at the working context of certain occupations revealed a pattern of stratification which was otherwise concealed. This was particularly true of related occupations, such as doctors and nurses which, while differing in status, fell within the same occupational class. It is likely that a similar pattern of differentiation exists within each of the manual classes; however, without more detailed investigation, it is frequently difficult to identify these status distinctions. One such relationship which is known may be cited by way of illustration. It appears to be frequently accepted in the building trade that carpenters enjoy a superior status to bricklayers, although both are skilled occupations. This may be due to a presumed difference in skill or to the fact that bricklayers, by the nature of their work, are more likely to be exposed to the natural elements. It is worth noting, therefore, that while carpenters and joiners are predominantly Protestant, bricklayers and plasterers are, by a slight margin, predominantly Catholic (table 2:8). Nevertheless, for most related occupations, without further information we can only speculate whether differences in the religious proportions are a consequence of status distinctions or are rather due to other factors.

Table 2:8

RELIGION AND SELECTED OCCUPATIONS 1971, CONSTRUCTION AND ENGINEERING

Occupation	*Occupational class*	*total employed*	*per cent Catholic*
A. Construction			
Managers, building and contracting	I	1,025	18
Carpenters and joiners	III	10,424	35
Bricklayers, tile setters	III	4,305	51
Plasterers, cement finishers	III	1,817	51
Labourers, building and contracting	V	12,118	55
B. Engineering			
Managers, engineering	I	737	8
Fitters, n.e.c.	III	8,045	15
Electricians	III	6,613	20
Motor mechanics	III	6,102	27
Labourers, engineering	V	2,440	16

Conclusions

In summing up the results of this analysis, it should be noted that at least three principal forms of stratification exist between Protestant and Catholic occupations. First, in its most simple form, there is a marked tendency for Protestants to dominate the upper occupational classes while Catholics are found predominantly in the lower classes. Thus, the majority of Catholic men are either in semi-skilled or unskilled work or unemployed, while Protestants are most likely to be in skilled or non-manual work. This is the traditional form of horizontal stratification.

Second, there appears to be what might be described as a form of 'vertical' stratification. As well as being stratified horizontally by occupation, there is a tendency for the majoı religious groups to be partially segregated by industry: Protestants are concentrated in the higher status industries, while Catholics are disproportionately represented in the lower status industries. This is, to a limited extent, compatible with the simple form of horizontal stratification since some industries may be preponderantly non-manual, skilled manual, or semi-skilled manual.

Third, there exists a more complex form of horizontal stratification. While both Protestants and Catholics exist in varying proportions within each of the major occupational classes, these classes are further subdivided into segments of differing status. When occupations within the same class, and the same working context, are considered, it would appear that Protestants dominate the superior positions while Catholics are over-represented in the lower status positions.

An important aspect which might be pursued further is the extent to which these occupational differences are translated into the shared stereotypes of Protestants and Catholics in Northern Ireland. Multi-dimensional analysis would be useful in enabling us to distinguish between the different public images which the two groups possess, and the extent to which these are derived from their differing occupational characteristics. Some time ago, Rosemary Harris (1955: 163) observed an example of this type of relationship, in her study of a small rural community:

> The difference in the class structure of the two religious groups affects their relations with each other because in the ascription of stereotyped characteristics to the members of the other group, something which almost inevitably takes place under the local conditions, the characteristics of the poorer classes are ascribed by the Protestants to the Catholics as a whole and those of the better off group by the Catholics to the Protestants.

On the basis of our own analysis, a number of dimensions which might be further explored in an attempt to define these ascriptive characteristics can be outlined.

1. *Skilled/Unskilled.* On the basis of modal averages, the 'typical' Protestant male is a skilled worker, and the 'typical' Catholic, unskilled.
2. *Employed/Unemployed.* Although less than a third of the economically active population of Northern Ireland, Catholics constitute a majority of the unemployed.

3. *Masculine/Feminine.* Occupations which can be identified as strongly Protestant tend to be male, while a significant number of those identifiable as disproportionately Catholic tend to be predominantly female.
4. *Superordination/Subordination.* Many of the occupations which have higher levels of authority and influence tend to be dominated by Protestants, while many of the lower status services are disproportionately Catholic.

Whichever of these dimensions is considered, it is apparent that there exist significant differences in the occupational characteristics contributing to an individual's generalised social class positon, if these other characteristics follow a similar pattern, it would indicate a noteworthy congruence between the class cleavage and the religious cleavage in Northern Ireland. Such a congruence would partially explain the ineffectiveness of class organisations in crossing the religious divide.

Notes

1. For a more detailed description of these occupational groups, see: Office of Population Censuses and Surveys (1970).
2. A guide to this scale is contained in Oppenheim (1966, pp. 275–284). For more details on the construction of the scale see Hall and Jones (1950) or Moser and Hall (1954).
3. These two groups were (1) Farmers, farm managers, market gardeners, and (2) Members of the armed forces.
4. The phenomenon of segregated residential communities leading to segregated shopping activity is well illustrated by F. W. Boal's study of the Shankill–Falls area of Belfast. See, for example, Boal (1969) and Boal (1972).
5. Harold Jackson (1972) points to Londonderry, the largest city in Northern Ireland with a Catholic majority, as a prime example of the male unemployment problem. Londonderry's major industry, textiles and textile products such as clothing, is a light industry which offers employment largely to women.

3. Employment and Religion in Belfast, 1901–1951

A. C. Hepburn

In the late eighteenth century Belfast was a small, mainly Presbyterian, commercial centre. The Catholic proportion of its population amounted to less than ten per cent. During the industrial era which followed, the city's religious demography underwent a marked series of upheavals, which may be divided into three clear periods. Down to the 1830s, as the city expanded rapidly from its small base, the Catholic proportion rose to more than a third. Between 1861 and 1911, as even more migrants flooded into the city, that proportion fell to less than a quarter. Since 1911 the balance between Protestant and Catholic has remained remarkably stable, with any slight Catholic increase since 1951 being explained by differential suburbanisation beyond the city boundary. The economic development of the city may be periodised in a broadly similar way. Growth in the first half of the nineteenth century focussed on the development of a textile labour force for cotton, replaced in the 1820s by linen. From mid-century down to 1914 the city experienced a great new growth of industries offering skilled employment to men—shipbuilding, textile machinery manufacture and other engineering work—as the continued mechanisation of linen led it to depend increasingly on low-paid female labour. The new industries, from their early days, were very predominantly Protestant in the composition of their labour forces. The same period also experienced a generation of rioting, 1857–86, which was intensive even by Belfast standards (Baker, 1973; Budge and O'Leary, 1973; Hepburn, 1978, 1980; Hepburn and Collins, 1981). Since World War I the economic picture has been more complicated, although a decline in the staple industries and a measure of stagnation have been among the more prominent characteristics. The purpose of this chapter is to examine the impact of this third phase of industrialism on the relationship between religion and employment. Because of the nature of the 1951 data set, the study will be confined to the male section of the workforce.

The great staples of textiles, engineering and shipbuilding, which accounted for over 40 per cent of male and female employment on the eve of World War I, proved more vulnerable than most industries to the contraction of international trade which characterised the inter-war period. Linen entered a steep decline from the late 1920s onwards. By the end of the decade shipbuilding was beginning to contract at an even sharper rate. Engineering followed the same trend at first, although since it embraced a broader group of industries the sector was able to recover more quickly, with the growth of electrical goods and, from 1937, an aircraft factory. Unemployment for the city in its worst years, 1931 and 1938, has been estimated at 25 per cent of the workforce (Black, 1967:163). Shipbuilding had scarcely begun to recover before the renewed outbreak of war, and linen's revival came later still. Depression was mitigated to some extent by a general trend towards expansion in the distributive industries, professional services and government employment, while the demands of World War II gave a large, if temporary, boost to shipbuilding and engineering, and to a lesser extent linen.

The immediate post-war years favoured most manufacturing industries, as consumer demand began to revive. The long-term base was not a sound one however, and the linen industry had begun to enter a near-terminal decline by 1952, although one writer tells us that at this time 'the economy of the city was buoyant and most of the workers obtained other jobs quickly' (Black, 1967:164–5). The early sixties witnessed a similar decline of shipbuilding in all parts of the United Kingdom. Developments in engineering continued to generate some new employment, but more new jobs were provided

Table 3:1

CHANGES IN INDUSTRIAL DISTRIBUTION FOR ECONOMICALLY ACTIVE MALES (per cent)

	1871	*1901*	*1951*	*1971*
Manufacturing, mining,	43	43	47	33
'General labour'	16	15	—	—
Dealing, distribution, financial services	11	12	15	19
Transport	11	10	12	11
Construction	8	9	9	11
Public & professional services	6	6	13	18
Domestic svcs, agriculture, misc.	5	5	5	9
Total male workforce	49,734	101,544	126,153	118,246

Source: Census of Ireland, 1871, 1901; Census of Northern Ireland, 1951, 1971.

by the continued expansion of the tertiary sector, in distribution, in government and in professional services. Changes in the format of census tables over the years make it difficult to standardise published data of this type in any detail, but table 3:1, necessarily grouping industrial sectors into very broad blocks, indicates the changes in outline, for economically active males. The large category of 'General Labour' was not further identified by the census in the pre-partition period, but we may assume that by far the greater part of it was employed in manufacturing.

Data Sources

Census analysis of industry and occupation by religion is only possible (and then in a very limited way) for Belfast in the period of 1871–1911. This essay is therefore based on samples of manuscript data, drawn from two main sources. For 1901 a simple random sample of 8 per cent of households in Belfast County Borough was drawn from the manuscript census schedules of the Census of Ireland. Data in these tables are based on employed male members of such households. For the Census of Northern Ireland, such data are closed under a 100-year rule. Marriage register data (sampling one in every three marriages on a systematic random basis) have thus been used as the best substitute, so that except where stated in this essay, industrial and occupational data by religion for 1951 are obtained by taking the stated occupations of bridegrooms, together with those of their fathers and fathers-in-law, from the marriage certificates. This may produce some slight distortion, in that single men will of course be totally excluded, while middle-aged men may be somewhat over-represented. When we come to examine occupational mobility between generations, however, the nature of the data will have positive advantages, and indeed data of this type have been widely used in mobility research (Rogoff, 1953). It has also been necessary with the 1951 data to assume that the religion of all parties to the marriages corresponded to the denomination carrying out the marriage ceremony. Civil ceremonies conducted by the Registrar, some 12 per cent of the total for 1951, have been excluded from all tables, but a separate analysis of these data did not suggest that their exclusion would introduce a bias in any particular direction.

Industrial and Occupational Distributions

The use of sample data enables us to make more precise comparisons across time than we were able to achieve in table 3:1.

Table 3:2 shows the industrial distributions of Roman Catholics and Other Demoninations (in practice more than 99 per cent Protestant) for 1901 and 1951, together with ratio figures which indicate the relationship and direction of progress of the Catholic data in relation to the Protestant. The classification is that developed by Charles Booth, as modified by W. A. Armstrong (1972). The phi coefficients (chi-square derivatives which move between 0 and 1 for 2 x n tables), used here as summary measures, indicate the existence of some association between industrial sector and religion, an association which increased slightly over our period. Using comparison of ratios to examine the details, we note that five of the eleven sectors in 1901, and eight of the sectors in 1951, had variations of .3 or greater (i.e. the proportion of Catholics in a sector was 30 per cent higher or lower than the proportion of Protestants found in the same sector). The most extreme case of Catholic under-representation was in that part of the manufacturing sector which included engineering, printing, shipbuilding and metal manufacturing, where the proportion of skilled and highly paid workers was highest (Hobsbawm, 1964:337). This sub-

Table 3:2

INDUSTRIAL SECTOR BY RELIGION. 1901, 1951 (economically active males)

	1901			*1951*		
	RC[1] %	*OD*[2] %	*Ratio RC:OD*	*RC*[1] %	*OD*[2] %	*Ratio RC:OD*
MANUFACTURING						
Engineering, printing, shipbuilding, metal m/f	7	22	0.3	8	20	0.4
textiles & finishing	14	12	1.2	3	4	0.8
other manufacturing	14	8	1.8	9	13	0.7
INDUSTRIAL SERVICES						
Labour	19	13	1.5	33	17	1.9
Finance	3	4	0.8	4	6	0.7
DEALING	13	10	1.3	7	7	1.0
TRANSPORT	9	10	0.9	13	10	1.3
CONSTRUCTION	8	9	0.9	8	9	0.9
PUBLIC & PROFESSIONAL SERVICES	6	6	1.0	7	10	0.7
DOMESTIC SERVICES	4	2	2.0	5	2	2.5
AGRICULTURE, MINING, MISC.	3	4	0.8	4	2	2.0
TOTAL (N)	1707	5673		673	1960	
Chi-square =		266.7			156.6	
Phi =		0.19			0.24	

[1] Roman Catholic

[2] Other Denominations

sector was by far the largest employer of Protestant males in 1901, and still retained a clear predominance in 1951. For Catholics it was of relatively modest importance in their industrial profile. There was little change in the balance between the denominations over the period, notwithstanding a degree of structural change brought about by the rise of electrical engineering. Catholics were over-represented, on the other hand, in the area of domestic, mainly personal, services, and in the much larger sector of industrial services (labour). In both of these sectors there was also a pronounced increase in the degree of Catholic over-representation during the period under study. Other striking features of the table are a very sharp decline in the importance of textiles and clothing in the labour market, affecting both denominations in a broadly similar manner, and a substantial decline in the dealing sector, affecting Catholics more intensely, and bringing them down to parity with Protestants (probably due to a reduction in the number of very small shopkeepers). On a slightly smaller scale came a clear rise in the proportion of Protestants who were in public and professional services, not paralleled on the Catholic side to any considerable extent. A significant element in this was almost certainly the creation at the time of partition of a Northern Ireland Civil Service under Unionist political control, but a more detailed breakdown shows a relative Catholic decline in the professional as well as the public service sub-sector. In transport on the other hand, an opposite trend is apparent, with Catholics increasing their share considerably, while the Protestant proportion remained stable. The two categories where the largest apparent reversals took place, 'other manufacturing' and 'agriculture, mining and miscellaneous', are in fact both residual categories, where we are more likely to be measuring change in the industrial composition of the categories than changes in the religious balance within particular industries. In summary we may say that differences between the industrial distributions of the two denominations were considerable in 1901, and increased to a degree during the first half of the twentieth century.

Differences in industrial distribution may hint at differences in the fortunes of individuals or religious groups, but to establish these at all clearly we need to look directly at occupational structure. The Registrar General's Classification of Occupations, 1970, is the current version of the most widely used system of classification. It is used here in collapsed form, in order to retain maximum confidence in the sample data by keeping cells as large as possible without sacrificing the basic distinctions which the analysis will seek to make. Table 3:3 outlines the general changes in the class structure during the century, and attempts a partial verification of the sample by regrouping the occupational listings from the 1951 published census according to the 1970 classification (the published data for 1901 do not permit a comparable regrouping).

Table 3:3

OCCUPATIONAL CLASS. 1901, 1951 (per cent economically active males)

	1901 sample	*1951 sample*	*1951 actual*
Class I/II professional/intermediate	10	13	12
Class IIIN routine nonmanual	16	10	13
Class IIIM skilled manual	34	40	37
Class IV/V less skilled	39	37	38
TOTAL (N)	7398	2924	134,232

This classification scheme does not allocate members of the armed forces to social classes, and they have been excluded from all the tables that follow. The 1951 sample does not fully reflect the true 1951 data in every respect—Class IIIN is rather too small and Class IIIM too large by a similar proportion. The discrepancies in these instances lie slightly outside the limits at the customary 95 per cent confidence level. The probable explanation is that the inclusion of both fathers and fathers-in-law alongside the grooms has biased the sample slightly towards Class IIIM and against Class IIIN. The latter class, especially, might well have had a high proportion of younger people. The 1901 sample on the other hand is based on a very large household sample, and it is unlikely that the range of error is more than one percentage point for any class.

Remarkably little change, perhaps none at all, took place in the overall balance of manual (Classes IIIM, IV and V) and nonmanual (Classes I, II and IIIN) employment in the city during the half-century. There were, however, some upward movements between classes within the manual and nonmanual sectors. The growth of government, managerial, professional, and teaching employment account for the relative growth of Class I/II. This growth was matched, and possibly outweighed by the decline in the lower nonmanual sector, where the replacement of men by women in many areas of clerical and shop work constitutes at least part of the explanation. In the manual sector there was clearly some degree of increase in the skilled Class IIIM, and probably a slight decline in the proportion of the workforce in the less-skilled Class IV/V.

Table 3:4

OCCUPATIONAL CLASS BY RELIGION. 1901, 1951 (economically active males)

	1901			*1951*		
	RC %	*OD* %	*Ratio RC:OD*	*RC* %	*OD* %	*Ratio RC::OD*
Class I/II	10	10	1.0	11	13	0.8
Class IIIN	14	17	0.8	8	12	0.7
Class IIIM	29	36	0.8	31	44	0.7
Class IV/V	47	36	1.3	50	32	1.6
TOTAL (N)	1686	5645		660	1888	
Chi-square =	60.4			73.0		
Phi =	.09			.17		

How have these changes been distributed between the religious groups? Table 3:4, resting now entirely on sample data, attempts to answer this question. Perhaps surprisingly, Catholics had as large a proportion of their number in Class I/II as did Protestants at the turn of the century. Later tables will explore the character of this balance, by relating it to industrial distribution and poor law valuation. We may be fairly confident that the growth of this class during the twentieth century has benefited Protestants rather more than Catholics. Among the lower white-collar workers of Class IIIN, the evidence suggests a Protestant predominance that has been at least maintained as the relative size of the class has contracted during the century. Amongst manual workers, differences between the profiles of the two religious groups are more pronounced. While there has been little change in the ratio between religions for skilled workers, the pronounced Protestant leadership in this class has been fully maintained. The proportion of Catholics in this class probably increased slightly, but given the overall increase in the size of the class within the occupational structure, Catholic growth was probably insufficient even to maintain the group's relative position. The obverse is true of the less-skilled category. The over-representation of Catholics in this class was pronounced in 1901, and it appears more certain than anything else in the table that this imbalance intensified over the following half-century. If we are prepared to accept an 80 per cent level of confidence we may assert that the proportion of the Catholic workforce which lay in Class IV/V actually increased during the first half of this century. We may be more fully confident (at the 95 per cent level) that the proportion of Protestants in this class declined over the same period.

Occupational classifications of this kind are broad summary measures. Bankers and shipping magnates share the top category with the smallest of corner shopkeepers. Clerks, so described, no matter what their educational attainments and their responsibilities, are classified together with the humblest shop assistants. The cook or the housepainter, however limited his training or experience, is ranked equal to the highly paid, extensively-trained carpenter or plater from the shipyards. Even where levels of training or skills are more closely comparable, levels and regularity of pay may vary considerably. The next two tables seek to illuminate further certain aspects of the basic occupational profiles of the religious groups.

Table 3:5 offers some explanation for the otherwise surprisingly strong Catholic position in Class I/II revealed above. Almost a full two-thirds of the Catholics in this top grouping worked in the dealing sector, with no more than marginal change between 1901 and 1951. Of Protestants in the same class however, less than half were in dealing in 1901, falling away to less than a third by 1951. By the latter year then, Catholics were more than twice as dependent on dealing as were Protestants for their representation in the top echelon. The other interesting aspect of the distribution of Class I/II is the public service and professional sector, where similar proportions in 1901 had become differentiated, probably quite considerably, by 1951. The same trend is true in the lower nonmanual category, Class IIIN, where the proportion of Catholics who were in public service or professional work actually declined at a time when the proportion of Protestants in this sector was increasing. In the same class the religious balance of the dealing sector (mainly shop assistants) was brought closer together over the period by a decline in the proportion of Catholics. The most pronounced shift in Class IIIN, however, was the very considerable increase in the size of the sub-sector of industrial services (finance), i.e. commercial clerks and travellers, insurance and other commission agents, etc. Here the proportion of Catholics trebled while that of Protestants did not quite double, thereby balancing out the Catholic decrease in the public and professional sector of the same class.

In Class IIIM the only trend of any real significance is in that sector of manufacturing which included the higher-paying industries of engineering, shipbuilding, metal work and printing. Here we see that, even when controlling for occupational class as we are, the

Protestants still dominated in this relatively attractive area of employment, and that predominance was significantly greater in 1951 than it had been in 1901. The other interesting figure in Class IIIM is that for skilled construction workers where, in contrast to the trend in engineering and related trades, the Catholic position probably improved in relation to the Protestant.

Table 3:5

CLASS BY SELECTED INDUSTRIES AND RELIGION. 1901, 1951 (per cent economically active males)

	1901		*1951*	
	RC %	*OD* %	*RC* %	*OD* %
Class I/II				
Dealing	62	44	65	30
Public/professional	18	17	14	25
TOTAL (N)	148	533	51	214
Class IIIN				
Industrial services: finance	19	22	56	41
Public/professional	27	20	14	26
Dealing	36	26	30	27
TOTAL (N)	236	859	50	210
Class IIIM				
Engineering, shipbldg, etc.	22	34	26	42
Construction	18	21	24	17
TOTAL (N)	516	2143	194	827

Put another way, the strong Catholic position in construction work, widely acknowledged in more recent years, is a feature which has only emerged during the twentieth century. Building activity fluctuated widely during our period, with a great expansion at the very beginning of the century, followed by a very long period of little activity to 1945, and a steadier expansion since then (Jones, 1960; Birrell et al., 1971). In the short-term, however, construction work is more vulnerable to seasonal and other fluctuations. In a period of relative expansion, such as the years after World War II therefore, while engineering and other trades with strict apprenticeship entry remained largely Protestant preserves, it became easier for Catholics to move into the construction sector at the skilled level, where the system of apprenticeships was less rigid and the typical size of individual firms much smaller. In other words, the expansion of engineering or shipbuilding meant the same few firms taking on many more men, but through the same formal and informal recruitment networks, whereas expansion in construction meant more small firms coming into existence, as well as numerous existing firms growing larger. Class IV/V is not analysed in this table, because in this least-privileged part of the occupational structure less significance is attached to differences in industrial distribution.

Table 3:6

OCCUPATIONAL CLASS BY PLV AND RELIGION. 1901, 1951
(Mean PLV of economically active male householders)

	1901				*1951*				*Ratio of RC*	
	RC		*OD*		*RC*		*OD*		*mean: OD mean*	
	N	*£ mean*	*N*	*£ mean*	*N*	*£ mean*	*N*	*£ mean*	*1901*	*1951*
I/II	59	15.28	300	24.47	21	29.14	102	35.51	0.6	0.8
IIN	77	9.13	379	12.90	22	15.20	91	21.64	0.7	0.7
IIIM	240	5.97	997	7.99	90	11.57	387	14.83	0.7	0.8
IV/V	362	4.82	1018	5.90	179	10.24	360	10.84	0.8	0.9

Source for PLV data: Special Valuation of Belfast, 1900–01 (PRONI, VAL 7B); 2nd General Revaluation of Northern Ireland, 1956 (PRONI, VAL 4B).

Table 3:6 explores possible religious differentials within the four occupational classes by another means—the poor law valuation of economically active male householders. This is, of course, a fairly crude measure of relative prosperity, but it has the advantage that the data are both hard and specific to individual cases. Because of the intervening general revaluations of Belfast property which took place we cannot compare figures between the two dates, but we can compare ratios between the two religions. Before doing this, however, we should note that even after controlling for occupational class, as we are effectively doing, Protestants in every class, in both years, occupied properties with significantly higher valuations than those occupied by Catholics. This fact stands out far more clearly than any other comparison or trend in the table. By comparison, any changes over the period are relatively minor. Differences between the highest and lowest classes on the Catholic side were somewhat narrower than on the Protestant (and also tended to narrow more over the period), and this becomes more pronounced if we omit the top class. Overall we may note in all four columns wide gulfs between the manual and nonmanual sectors of Class III, amply justifying the distinction between these two classes introduced by the Registrar General in his 1970 Classification of Occupations. In the Belfast case, so far as these data are a guide, the distinction between non-manual and manual within Class III appears to be a more crucial one than that between skilled and less-skilled manual.

Moving more specifically to the religious comparison across time, the trend, weak though it is, is unidirectional. For Class IIIN the relationship between the two means remains the same, but for the other three classes the Catholic means apparently drew a little closer to the Protestant means in all cases. This pattern is the opposite of that detected in our analysis of industrial and occupational distributions, and three factors may be relevant. In the first instance, since we are using PLV as an indicator of prosperity in relation to occupation, we must restrict our sample to household heads. In doing so, however, we may in effect be excluding those sons who worked in the Belfast labour market for some years, but who departed without ever becoming householders. We know that the Catholic differential in out-migration, at least for Northern Ireland as a whole, has been substantial in the twentieth century (Walsh, 1970). It may be, therefore, that at any given time a body of future emigrants would weight the industrial and occupational structure in a certain direction, but would never become householders and so influence the PLV distribution. Householders may have been slightly less differentiated by religion than the male workforce as a whole, and this may have been more the case in 1951 than in 1901. Secondly, we know that the greater propensity of Catholics to have large families is a trend which has emerged only during the twentieth century (Hepburn and Collins, 1981:216). The main impact of this on housing may have been a relative increase in Catholic overcrowding, but it is also likely to have increased the proportion of Catholic householders occupying larger, more highly-rated houses. The third factor is a simpler one. No public housing at all was erected in Belfast until 1917 (Budge and O'Leary, 1973). In 1951 more than 5 per cent of working class householders in the sample occupied such housing, where valuations were significantly higher. The effect was certainly to increase the mean value of working class housing to some extent, and possibly also to even out slightly the religious differentials.

Social Mobility

Analysis thus far has focussed on changes affecting the two religious groups as blocks. It is now time to turn to the question, related but separate, of how the individuals comprising those blocks fared in the labour market from generation to generation. Social mobility has been the subject of systematic study by contemporary social scientists, especially in the United States, for forty years. In the last two decades historians too have begun reconstructing data bases to enable them to attack the problem. Some have considered individual career (intra-generational) mobility as well as movement between the generations (inter-generational), although the nature of our data restricts analysis here to the latter phenomenon. Work has focussed on such questions as the impact of nineteenth-century industrialisation on mobility prospects, the effects of twentieth-century structural changes on this situation, and also the relative fortunes of ethnic and racial minorities in various societies. It is hard to generalise from the results of individual studies—local economic circumstances, demography, and migration patterns are all complicating factors, while the difficulties of standardising the systems of occupational classification, and the points at which generations are compared, are important problems of a different type. One study which has attempted to generalise from historical work concludes that, for the nineteenth century in western Europe and north America, 'even if it should emerge—as expected—that occupational mobility increased in comparison with pre-industrial society, it is most probable that downward mobility predominated' (Kaelble, 1981:22). For the twentieth century, the same study found the picture even less clear. The oldest theory, the American-centred 'blocked mobility' hypothesis, that mobility rates have declined in the twentieth century, now retains little if any credibility. Subsequently the classic contemporary studies of Rogoff (1953) in the United States and of Glass (1954) in Great Britain found little change during the century, and emphasised the stability of mobility rates. More recently-published studies by historians which include the first half of the twentieth century in their analysis reach similar conclusions (Chudacoff, 1972; Thernstrom, 1973; Kaelble, 1981).

Contemporary social scientists surveying the last twenty years have identified a greater degree of mobility, especially in the upper occupational groups, though some, like Goldthorpe et al. (1980), see the development as a structural change rather than the outcome of increased equality of opportunity. Thus the overall twentieth-century pattern is not entirely clear. But evidence for increased mobility does tend to come from studies of the most recent decades. Such consensus as exists suggests that stable mobility rates were the norm in the first half of this century.

Let us now return to the Belfast case. Table 3:7 simply presents

Table 3:7

INTERGENERATIONAL OCCUPATIONAL MOBILITY. 1901, 1951

Son's occupational class by father's class (actual sample numbers)

	Classes	Fathers *I/II*	*IIIN*	*IIIM*	*IV/V*	*Totals*
Roman Catholics 1901						
	I/II	8	3	2	1	14
	IIIN	19	14	14	5	52
Sons	IIIM	18	10	42	12	82
	IV/V	4	4	27	59	94
Totals		49	31	85	77	242
Other Denominations 1901						
	I/II	31	1	7	5	44
	IIIN	59	36	49	43	187
Sons	IIIM	66	47	207	125	445
	IV/V	18	16	65	144	243
Totals		174	100	328	317	919
Roman Catholics 1951						
	I/II	10	1	2	1	14
	IIIN	5	7	4	6	22
Sons	IIIM	11	2	34	35	82
	IV/V	7	5	15	65	92
Totals		33	15	55	107	210
Other Denominations 1951						
	I/II	39	7	9	3	58
	IIIN	18	14	35	15	82
Sons	IIIM	20	26	142	98	286
	IV/V	7	4	42	72	125
Totals		84	51	228	188	551

the raw sample data matrices on which the following analysis will be based. Data for 1901 are for male household heads and for their employed sons (aged 16 and over) living at home. Data for 1951 are drawn from marriage registers, and thus consist exclusively of bridegrooms and their fathers. In all cases, therefore (with the exception of a very few late and second marriages in 1951), we are comparing the occupations of young men with the positions attained by their fathers at a later stage in life. Data for comparing fathers and sons at similar stages in their careers would be very hard to obtain, and in fact marriage register data of this type have been widely used in mobility research by Rogoff (1953) and others. In this case it is important to note that the two religious groups are fully comparable within each year, and are comparable between years to the extent that a sample of fathers and co-resident employed sons and a sample of bridegrooms and fathers are unlikely to differ greatly in any important way so far as occupation is concerned.

Analysis of the mobility matrices begins in table 3:8. The amount of observed mobility, the level of upward and downward movement between classes, changed little between 1901 and 1951. If anything there was a slight decrease in the overall volume of mobility, with the differential between the Catholic and the slightly higher Protestant figure being maintained at the same level. These overall rates of movement for Belfast within a four-class scale are very similar to those found, for instance, by Thernstrom for twentieth-century Boston, and five to ten per cent lower than those found in some German studies of the same period (Thernstrom, 1973; Kaelble, 1981). The figures for Belfast Catholics suggest somewhat lower mobility levels than for Protestants or for those found in other studies.

Table 3:8

INTERGENERATIONAL OCCUPATIONAL MOBILITY AND RELIGION, 1901, 1951

Overall Mobility (per cent)

	1901			*1951*		
	All	*RC*	*OD*	*All*	*RC*	*OD*
a. % observed mobility	53	49	55	50	45	52
b. % 'expected' mobility	71	72	70	68	66	68
c. Ratio of observed to expected (a/b)	0.75	0.68	0.79	0.74	0.68	0.76
d. % structural mobility	20	16	22	16	16	16
e. % circulation mobility (a–d)	33	33	33	34	29	36

'Expected' or 'perfect' mobility is a hypothetical figure, estimating from the structural distributions of the sons' and fathers' occupations the probable mobility figures in the event of perfect mobility. This permits the calculation of a ratio of observed-to-expected mobility, a commonly used indicator in mobility research, which controls for changes in the occupational structure between generations. The index moves between 0 and 1, with a high figure indicating a high level of mobility. Very clearly, there was no change in the amount of Catholic mobility in our period, and only a slight decline in the Protestant level. More significant than any change within a religious group was the difference between them, which remained very clear, narrowing only slightly in 1951. The next rows, *d* and *e*, aim to distinguish mobility which was purely structural, that is the inevitable product of differences between the occupational structures of the fathers' and the sons' groups, from the residual category often termed 'circulation' mobility, which we may interpret as that proportion of mobility brought about by individual fortunes and efforts. The amount of structural mobility within the religious groups showed little change, with the exception of the Protestants in 1901, where the overall difference in the observed mobility of the two groups is shown to have been the product of a greater structural change on the Protestant side. The same observed differential in 1951, however, can now be seen to have been entirely the product of circulation mobility. There was no change in the Protestant structure in 1951, but somewhat more fluidity between its members.

Table 3:9

INTERGENERATIONAL OCCUPATIONAL MOBILITY AND RELIGION, 1901, 1951

(Movement between manual/non-manual and skilled/less skilled categories)

		1901			*1951*	
	All	*RC*	*OD*	*All*	*RC*	*OD*
'Climbers'						
a. % sons from manual background in nonmanual work	16	14	16	13	8	15
b. % sons from less-skilled background in skilled work	35	16	39	45	33	52
'Skidders'						
c. % sons from nonmanual background in manual work	52	45	54	44	52	42
d. % sons from skilled background in less-skilled work	22	32	20	20	27	18
Ratios of upward to downward mobility:						
e. Nonmanual/manual (a, c)	0.3	0.3	0.3	0.3	0.2	0.4
f. Skilled/less-skilled (b, d)	1.6	0.5	2.0	2.3	2.0	2.9

The above measures are concerned only with fluidity of structure and of individual movement. They make no distinction between upward and downward occupational mobility. We now turn, in table 3:9, to measures designed to analyse this distinction. The line between manual and nonmanual is often taken to be the most basic one in industrial societies, and while there are sometimes doubts expressed over the relative status of some skilled manual occupations vis-a-vis some routine nonmanual ones (doubts encapsulated in the Registrar General's Class III nonmanual/manual division), the weight of evidence tends to suggest a higher status for the nonmanual category in most contexts. This is confirmed in the Belfast case by the PLV data displayed in table 3:6. We shall explore another aspect of this question in table 3:10, but for the moment it may be assumed that the movement from manual to nonmanual work represents upward movement, and the reverse downward movement. Overall, the first half of the twentieth century witnessed a slight decline in upward mobility across the nonmanual/manual line, but the decline was very unevenly distributed between the two religious groups (row *a*). While the proportion of Protestants who 'climbed' out of the working class remained virtually the same, the proportion of Catholic sons who were able to make the same move fell by half.

Let us now turn to the distinction between skilled and less-skilled manual work. Although there were clear differences of income and status between different occupations within Class IIIM there can be no doubt that jobs in that class carried higher status and income than all significant occupations in Class IV/V. Table 3:9 suggests considerably more climbing within the working class, across the skill barrier, than took place across the nonmanual divide—more than twice as much in 1901, considerably more than three times as much in 1951 (row *b*). Again Protestants were much more likely to make the climb into the skilled category, with over half the sons of less-skilled workers doing so in 1951. But in this case the Catholic trend was in the same direction, and the Catholic rate of improvement, from a smaller base, substantially greater. Among Catholics in 1951, one-third of sons of less-skilled workers had moved into the skilled class.

When we turn to the case of those who experienced downward mobility, the 'skidders', it is especially important to remember that we are in most cases comparing the occupation of a father near the end of his career with that of a son near the beginning of his. The data in the table are likely to overestimate considerably the objective amount of downward intergenerational mobility in Belfast society, although this is a weakness common to most mobility studies. There was a clear decrease in the overall amount of downward mobility from nonmanual to manual work (row *c*) and a very slight one from skilled down to less-skilled work (row *d*). In the case of descent across the nonmanual divide, Catholic and Protestant trends diverged very considerably. While Protestants were clearly more likely than Catholics to make the descent in 1901, if descent it was, the reverse was true fifty years later. Just as it became harder, as we saw above, for Catholics to climb into the nonmanual category, so it also became easier for them to skid out of it. At the skilled/less skilled barrier, on the other hand, there was a slight decrease in the overall amount of skidding (as compared to the great increase in climbing), brought about mainly by the reduction in the amount of Catholic skidding. It should be noted, nonetheless, that a more pronounced characteristic was still the differential between religions. It was still the case in 1951 that more than one in four Catholic sons, against less than one in five Protestants, slipped from a skilled background into less-skilled work.

The relationships between the categories of 'climbers' and 'skidders' identified in table 3:9 are summarised in the ratio figures for upward/downward mobility given in the same table. It should be noted that none of the data used in table 3:9 make any allowance for the proportion of structural or 'minimum' mobility identified in table 3:8, which accounted for 22 per cent of Protestant mobility in 1901 and 16 per cent of mobility in the other three cases. Bearing this in mind as a limitation on the weight we should attach to any comparison of these ratios across time, we may note that the ratio of upward to downward mobility across the nonmanual/manual divide was consistently adverse, for both years and both religions—upward mobility was seldom more than one-third as common as downward mobility. Part of this at least is to be explained by what we are comparing—old fathers with young sons. More variety is revealed within the working class sector. Protestants were always much more likely to rise into the skilled category than to slide into the less-skilled one, and this was even more evident in 1951 than in 1901. Catholics, on the other hand, had a more mixed experience. In 1901 they were far more likely to experience decline than to rise, but in 1951 they were more likely to rise, although still lagging behind Protestants in this respect.

One aspect of the four-class occupational classification used in this essay which has not been explored in table 3:9 is that of differentiation within the working class in relation to movements across the nonmanual/manual divide. Although the basic assumption must be that class is an ordinal scale in which progression between adjacent rungs is the most likely form of movement, there are some complexities to be borne in mind. They centre on the equivocal position of the skilled manual class in relation to the lower nonmanual sector, and in particular on the related facts that skilled manual workers may quite often enjoy the prospect of greater incomes than lower-grade non-manual workers, while the tight apprenticeship and craft-union structure of sections of the skilled working class are to some extent peculiar to that class, and likely to exert a particular pull of sons into the same occupations as their fathers. For this reason table 3:10 examines in more detail movements into and out of the working class. Thernstrom (1973), in his Boston study, was able to compare the last jobs of fathers and sons, finding far more mobility out of the less-skilled working class than he had expected. In particular he noted that sons of low manual background were far more likely (at any time in the last century) to move into low white-collar employment than into the skilled manual class, and were also more likely to make such a move than were the sons of skilled manual workers. The high level of movement out of the low manual class which he observed, about 60 per cent, was in his view sufficient to overturn the widely-held 'culture of poverty' theory in so far as it portrayed the entire lower working class as trapped at the bottom of the social ladder from generation to generation (Lewis, 1969).

The data for Belfast presented in table 3:10 are more equivocal on

Table 3:10

INTERGENERATIONAL OCCUPATIONAL MOBILITY AND RELIGION, 1901, 1951

(Non-manual, skilled, and less-skilled workers)

		1901			*1951*	
	All	*RC*	*OD*	*All*	*RC*	*OD*
'Climbers'						
a. % of sons from skilled background in nonmanual work	17	19	17	18	11	19
b. % of sons from less-skilled background in nonmanual work	14	8	15	8	7	10
Chi-square =		1.93			1.97	
Phi =		0.12			0.16	
'Skidders'						
c. % of sons from nonmanual background in skilled manual work	40	35	41	32	27	34
d. % of sons from nonmanual background in less-skilled work	12	10	12	13	25	8
Chi-square =		0.01			5.74	
Phi =		0.01			0.26	

this question. Direct statistical comparisons between the two cities mean little in view of the different occupational structures—one would not expect very large proportional movements out of a large Belfast working class into a fairly small white-collar sector. On the other hand the data do suggest, for Protestants but not for Catholics, that a less-skilled background provided almost as good a springboard to nonmanual work as a skilled background in 1901. By 1951 this had ceased to be the case, but the change was balanced by the decreased likelihood of Catholics from the skilled manual class moving into nonmanual work. Thus the phi coefficients for 'climbers' in 1901 and 1951 both indicate a very weak relationship between religion and the presence or absence of a skilled background in providing entry to the nonmanual sector (the significance levels for the chi-square statistic, from which phi is derived, are also far too low for any relationship to be asserted). The data on 'skidders' on the other hand, indicate that the working class was a lot easier to enter than it was to leave, although the overall figures suggest that nonmanual skidders were at all times much more likely to drop to skilled occupations rather than into the chasm of less-skilled work. In 1901 there was no demonstrable religious differential at all on this point. But by 1951 a sharp one had emerged. While Catholic non-manual skidders divided virtually fifty-fifty between skilled and less-skilled classes, Protestants slipped below the skilled level in less than one quarter of cases. The chi-square score is a significant one in this case, while the phi coefficient of .26, though not suggesting a very strong relationship in itself, indicates the existence of a clear degree of association between religion and depth of skidding in 1951 which is not present elsewhere in this table. If we sum the respective column totals of row b in table 3:9 and row b in table 3:10, we find that 49 per cent of sons in 1901 and 53 per cent in 1951 escaped their less-skilled background into skilled and nonmanual work—figures somewhat lower than those found for Boston, but still high enough to indicate a reasonably accessible route upwards for the sons of the less-skilled working class (table 3:11). When we come to look at the individual religions, however, we find a very large differential favourable to Protestants. The Catholic data show the same upward trend, and indeed a faster rate of improvement, but it nonetheless remained the case in 1951 that only two in five Catholics against more than three in five Protestants were able to rise above their origins in the less-skilled working class.

Table 3:11

UPWARD MOBILITY OF SONS FROM LESS-SKILLED BACKGROUNDS
(per cent who were mobile)

	All	*RC*	*OD*
1901	49	24	54
1951	53	42	62

Conclusions

The nature of the data has led to a concentration on certain aspects of employment to the exclusion of others. No discussion of unemployment has been possible, although this is less important for the years in question than it would be for the inter-war period or for the more recent years of high unemployment. Female employment has not been considered, although the proportion of women and girls in the city's labour force was 38 per cent of the force in 1901 and 36 per cent in 1951. The role of female earnings in the family economy was clearly an important one, but the data on religion and female employment for 1951 are extremely patchy, while for the earlier period it is clear that religious differentials in female employment were narrower than for men. Catholic women in the late nineteenth century were more likely to work than Protestant women, although it is likely that this was less a direct function of religion than of the occupational class of their fathers or husbands (Hepburn, 1980). A third limitation of our analysis lies in its restriction to the Belfast county borough area. It was the case, however, that the city accounted for almost one-third of the entire six-county population, and almost two-thirds of its urban population. To that extent, developments in the city would be central to any study of employment in the Province. A final limitation of the data which must be recalled is the non-equivalence of the 1901 and 1951 data sources, referred to above. It is certainly possible that some of the findings may be affected slightly by the use of marriage register data as a substitute for census data in 1951—causing an over-representation of older men and, perhaps more important, a total exclusion of single men. On the other hand there is no likelihood of the manuscript census data for 1951 becoming available to researchers for another seventy years. Table 3:3 indicated that the degree of bias introduced by the use of this source is slight, and probably limited to Social Class III.

It is clear from our analysis that major differences existed in the employment profiles of Catholics and Protestants at the beginning of the century and that they did not, in general, narrow during the ensuing fifty years. The disadvantageous position which Catholics had increasingly slipped into during the second half of the nineteenth century was not alleviated during the first half of the twentieth. The basic difference in industrial distribution widened slightly during our period, with Catholics gaining only in the less attractive areas of industrial labour, transport and domestic services. In Class I/II Catholics owed a full two-thirds of their position to dealing (predominantly retail shopkeeping and licensed victualling). In Class IIIM they did not share in the advances made by Protestants in the postwar years, making some ground in construction work but losing even more in engineering, shipbuilding, printing, etc. The proportion of Protestants who were in Class IV/V declined, while that of Catholics probably increased, so that an already substantial differential between the religious groups widened significantly over our period.

The individual analysis of intergenerational mobility by religion conforms to this general picture. Belfast remained a predominantly working-class city, with nonmanual employment hard to climb into, and relatively easy to skid out of. But again Catholics were increasingly likely to make unfavourable moves across this divide, whereas the Protestant position showed no deterioration. While the gradient from less-skilled to skilled was becoming easier to scale, Catholics only made a slight inroad on the Protestant lead here while, as we have seen, their gains tended to be in the less attractive or more volatile areas of the skilled working class. While Catholics born into the less-skilled class increased their capacity to rise out of it at a faster rate than did Protestants, the Protestant capacity for making that advance remained considerably greater. It also remained the case that Catholics were much more likely to skid into the less-skilled class, either from nonmanual or from skilled backgrounds. Whether the earlier Protestant trend to skid from a nonmanual background into skilled manual work really represented a downward movement in 1901 must be questioned. Certainly it was a movement in conflict with all other major trends. While it had become easier, by 1951, for individual Catholics to rise out of the less-skilled class, they were replaced there in more than full measure by other Catholics, so that individual mobility did not have the effect of raising the overall group profile. Upward mobility for working-class Catholics appears to have been particularly precarious.

It must not be forgotten that in a city which was three-quarters Protestant, a substantially higher Catholic *proportion* in the less-skilled class still left a higher *absolute* number of Protestants in that class. To say that the Protestant community had nearly all the plums is a long way from saying that nearly all the Protestant community had plums. Leaving entirely aside any degree of sectarian feeling arising out of the conflict of nationality, this fact alone would have made it hard to secure the level of consensus in favour of measures to ameliorate the minority's status which was attained in affluent, white America during the 1960s and 1970s.

But these findings nonetheless offer little sign of any narrowing of the gap between the two communities during the first half of the twentieth century. On the contrary, the evidence leans more towards the 'dual labour market' interpretation which has been applied by more pessimistic observers to the race relations question in Britain (Rex and Tomlinson, 1979). Although there was a high degree of class overlap between Catholic and Protestant, it did appear that the Catholic position was a less favourable one at every level. There was a high proportion of Belfast Catholics in the less-skilled working class, and a bigger gap between them and the dominant community in that respect, than that found a quarter of a century later by Rex and Tomlinson (1979:279) for West Indians and Asians in relation to native whites in Birmingham. While this parallel does not hold for the white-collar sector of the labour market, where Belfast Catholics enjoyed substantial representation, it has to be noted that this latter position was based heavily on over-representation in the dealing sector, and on a full and protected share of teaching employment. To a very considerable extent, it was a position which derived such strength as it had from separate and segregated districts and institutions.

4. Religion and Occupational Mobility

R. L. Miller

Since the end of the Second World War, empirical studies of social mobility have made up an important area of research within the general sociological analysis of stratification. Opportunity and the relative chances for social mobility of different groups has been a common, if sometimes secondary, concern of the analysis of social mobility. Furthermore, some researchers, most notably those working in the United States investigating the relative mobility chances of non-whites, have applied social mobility analyses directly to the examination of discrimination (Blau and Duncan, 1967; Featherman and Hauser, 1978). In a Northern Irish context, the relative mobility chances of Protestants and Roman Catholics would be a relevant area of study. This chapter will avail itself of some of the analytical tools, techniques and insights developed through the study of social mobility elsewhere. Specifically, it will apply the technique of log-linear modelling to occupational mobility data collected by a major study of Protestant and Catholic men in Northern Ireland.

E. A. Aunger, in chapter 2, documented 'major variances between Protestants and Catholics, both at the manual and non-manual level'. The first research paper of the Fair Employment Agency for Northern Ireland, following Aunger's original article (1975), stated in its summary that 'the occupational profile of Protestants and Roman Catholics revealed a distribution of Roman Catholics towards unskilled occupations' (Fair Employment Agency, 1978). The present author (Miller, 1978:17), also writing in an Agency publication, observed:

> As the report points out the difference in the proportionate distributions of Protestants and Roman Catholics cannot be taken as proof of religious discrimination. Events in the past have produced the present observed inequalities between Protestants and Roman Catholics. Once these inequalities exist they will tend to reproduce themselves over time, even in a situation of complete equality of opportunity. For example, as

> has been demonstrated by numerous studies of occupational mobility conducted throughout the world, a child is more likely to inherit the social position of his parents than he is likely either to move up or down. The child of a skilled manual worker is more likely to become a skilled manual worker himself rather than anything else . . . this pattern will reproduce itself across generations . . .

So, a current, unequal, occupational distribution could be due to simply a passive replication of a pattern of inequality already existing in previous generations. This chapter will investigate this possibility within the occupational sphere.

The Data and Analysis

The data used come from information collected as part of a major investigation into occupational and social mobility in Ireland. The project, set up in 1971 to study the 'Determinants of Occupational Status and Mobility in Northern Ireland and the Irish Republic' comprised a number of surveys based in the Department of Social Studies of the Queen's University of Belfast. The major part of the 'Irish mobility study' consisted of an interview survey carried out in both parts of Ireland which collected information on the demographic, educational and occupational life histories of its respondents, the educational and occupational attainments of members of the respondents' 'extended families', and the responses of the sample to a comprehensive set of attitude questions. This main interview survey, conducted in late 1973 and early 1974, covered the uninstitutionalised male populations aged 18 to 64 of both Northern Ireland and the Irish Republic using an almost identical research instrument and design developed and elaborated through previous research. Only results for Northern Ireland will be presented here. The valid response totalled 2,416 for Northern Ireland, corresponding to a response rate of 73.4% of the sampled population.

Other publications arising from the study contain discussions of various characteristics of the sample broken down by religion to which the reader may wish to refer (Jackson, 1979; Miller, 1979, 1981). While it would be redundant to attempt to summarise those discussions here, one may note that '. . . of the 2,416 respondents in the total sample, 1,523 (63%) are Protestant, 849 (35.1%) are Roman Catholic, and only 44 (1.8%) either are non-Christian or could not be placed into a religious category' (Miller, 1978:8). Since the survey relied on personal interviews rather than postal contacts, almost all respondents could be '. . . classified into a religious group (of the 44 not identified as Protestant or Roman Catholic only 13, or one-half of a per cent, could not be given any religious classification'. This is of significance as a reliable, virtually complete, categorisation by religion is rare in Northern Irish data. Many social research publications on Northern Ireland ignore religion altogether. Authors who do include religion in their system of categorisation often must rely on secondary indications of a person's religion, such as the school he attended or the area in which he resides. Even the census falls liable to these problems, with modern censuses up to 1971 not including religion in their tabulations and with almost a tenth of the population declining to state their religion on the optional question in 1971. At the date of writing an even greater amount of non-response to the 1981 census religion question seems likely.

One should also note that the sample, covering only males aged 18 to 64, excludes all women and the very young and the old. The career experiences and opportunities of women differ radically from those of men and require additional sampling and analytic procedures that were beyond the resources of this survey. Similarly, the situations of the very young, having just embarked on their careers or having not yet entered the active labour force, and the old, many of whom have left the labour force, constitute problems for analysis that are unique unto themselves. Therefore, the focus of this survey on males of working age, while unfortunate in some respects, does not necessarily originate from a sexist or age-related bias but rather from the main concerns and practical demands placed upon the original study.

The main portion of this chapter consists of a presentation and discussion of a log-linear analysis of the occupational mobility of Protestants and Roman Catholics. Very briefly, log-linear analysis is a technique that allows one to construct a model of the interactions between a number of categorical variables. A model is specified by allowing a combination of variables to 'interact' or to be associated with each other. The result of an analysis predicts the numbers that should appear in each individual cell of a multi-dimensional cross-tabulation. In a model that has been adequately specified the permitted associations will predict well the numbers in the cells of the cross-tabulation tables. If it does so, the model 'fits'. If it does not do so, one may try another specification of associations. 'Goodness of fit' can be measured by chi square. The usual goal is parsimony; that is, to find the simplest possible set of associations that produces a good 'fit'. One may then assume that the associations left out are unnecessary for describing the interactions between the variables in the model—they are assumed to be artifacts of the 'real' associations.

Log-linear analysis has been frequently applied in recent years to the analysis of social mobility tables (Hauser, 1978; Goldthorpe, 1980). It has several advantages for the analysis of social mobility. Researchers may be unable or unwilling to impose an ordering upon the variables in their analysis. A sociologist working with occupational categories, for instance, may be reluctant to make the assumption that one class or occupational strata should be placed between two other groups even if that 'intermediate' group falls between the other two on indices like income or freedom from supervision. Similarly, it may not be clear as to how two distinct groups, such as clerical workers and small proprietors, should be ranked relative to each other. Log-linear analysis needs only to assume distinct categories so the problems of ranking do not have to arise. Secondly, occupational distributions change, either between generations or over time within a single cohort or generation. One will, therefore, expect to find some observed mobility apparently resulting inevitably from these changes in distribution. In the table in the appendix to this chapter, for example, the proportionate sizes of the 'service' categories have increased in the respondents' generation relative to those of their fathers, leading one to anticipate mobility into these categories from other groups. This has given rise to the breaking down of 'gross' mobility into so-called 'structural' mobility and net or 'exchange' mobility (Bland, 1980). The effects of marginal distributions become more complex when one works with multi-dimensional cross-tabulation tables where different individuals will appear in different mobility tables with differing occupational distributions. This can lead to real problems in the interpretation of the tables. A log-linear model will break down the observed mobility into a number of distinct marginal and interaction effects. These effects are independent of each other so it is possible to distinguish between mobility that could be said to arise from change over time in occupational distributions and true or net mobility. As well, in a multi-dimensional case it is possible to distinguish the independent effects of interaction between some or all of the variables. In the case below, one can control for the effect of varying occupational distributions and then look independently at the interaction between religion and the distribution of occupations among the respondents and among their fathers and also at the interaction between the occupational distributions of the respondents and their fathers (net mobility). Any interactions that persist once one has developed the 'best' model, the simplest, meaningful model that continues to fit the data well, may be interpreted as real associations independent of any others existing in the model. Related to this, the results of a log-linear modelling exercise do constitute in themselves a powerful description of the data. Intuitively more obvious methods of presentation such as tables of cell frequencies, 'inflow' or 'outflow' percentages, or indices of association may in many cases be appropriate, especially in reports designed for a non-academic readership. The matrices of log effects, however, are interpretable and also avoid the not inconsiderable obstacles to an accurate interpretation that are given above.

Log-linear modelling can be sensitive to the classification systems applied to variables. As Reynolds (1977:79) notes:

> Log-linear analysis provides a sophisticated method for dissecting cross-classifications . . . Contrary to the impression received from reading the literature describing these techniques, one cannot stop worrying about the level of measurement simply because he has a technique that appears to be developed exclusively for categorical data. In particular, it is always necessary to maintain as much precision . . . in one's variables as possible. Arbitrarily collapsing a variable into a few categories throws away valuable information and may lead to false conclusions.

With this note of caution in mind, the occupations of respondents to the Irish mobility survey were aggregated into the seven class scheme based on the Hope-Goldthorpe occupational scale developed by the Social Mobility Group of Nuffield College, Oxford for their 1972 inquiry into social mobility in England and Wales. As Goldthorpe (1980: 39–42) states, the classes are aggregates of occupations,

> . . . whose incumbents will typically share in broadly similar *market* and *work* situations which . . . combine occupational categories whose members would appear, in the light of the available evidence, to be typically comparable, on the one hand, in terms of their sources and levels of income, their degree of economic security and chances of economic advancement; and, on the other, in their location within the systems of authority and control governing the process of production in which they are engaged, and hence in their degree of autonomy in performing their work-tasks and roles.

The scheme is as follows:

(1) Class I, the 'Upper Service' class, consists of 'all higher-grade professionals, self-employed or salaried; higher-grade administrators and officials in the central and local government and in public and private enterprises (including company directors); managers in large industrial establishments; and large proprietors'.
(2) Class II, the 'Lower Service' class, is made up of 'lower-grade professionals and higher-grade technicians; lower-grade administrators and officials; managers in small business and industrial establishments and in services; and supervisors of non-manual employees'.
(3) Class III, the 'Clerical' class, represents those who are 'routine non-manual—largely clerical—employees in administration and commerce; sales personnel; and other rank-and-file employees in services'.
(4) Class IV, the 'Small Proprietor' class, is those who are 'small proprietors, including farmers and smallholders; self-employed artisans; and all other "own account" workers apart from professionals'. This group, especially in its agricultural components for the fathers' generation, is much more numerous in the Irish samples.
(5) Class V, the 'Technical and Manual Supervisory' class consists of 'lower-grade technicians whose work is to some extent of a manual character; and supervisors of manual workers'.
(6) Class VI, the 'Skilled Manual' class is 'skilled manual wage-workers in all branches of industry, including all who have served apprenticeships and also those who have acquired a relatively high degree of skill through other forms of training'.
(7) Class VII, the 'Unskilled Manual' class consists of 'all manual wage-workers in industry in semi and unskilled grades; and agricultural workers' (see Goldthorpe 1980: 39–42, and Goldthorpe and Hope, 1974 for more discussion of the seven classes and of the Hope-Goldthorpe occupational scale).

Since the Hope-Goldthorpe scale is ultimately based on the Registrar General's occupational group and economic status classifications and the Irish data had been coded into these classifications, it was possible to convert the Northern Irish occupational data into an exact representation of the seven class scheme. The seven classes thus make up a conceptually meaningful classification system designed to address the kind of issues of concern in this volume; reward, opportunity, and power. Furthermore, by using the Hope-Goldthorpe classification, the way is open for an analysis in the future directly comparing mobility in the two parts of the United Kingdom.

Results

Table 4:2 gives the results of a log-linear analysis of the intergenerational occupational mobility of the two religious groupings in Northern Ireland. At first glance, especially to the uninitiated, the interpretation of the table appears difficult. Referring back to the above discussion, however, the results *are* capable of interpretation and they avoid the serious pitfalls of other methods. The raw frequencies used to develop this model are given in table 4:1. Glancing briefly at it, the difficulties immediately become apparent. The marginal distributions for fathers and sons for both Protestant and Roman Catholic samples are different. One can observe that the numbers in the non-manual classes have risen for both religions but it is not immediately clear whether or not the changes have been equivalent for both. For the 'Unskilled' class there is an apparent difference with the number of Protestants in the group falling in the respondent's generation while for Roman Catholics the number has risen. Even the diagonal effect of more people being located in their class of origin than elsewhere does not show clearly due to some groups, such as 'Small Proprietors' and the 'Skilled' and 'Unskilled Manual' classes, being much larger than others, such as the 'Manual Supervisory' group, so that these larger groups sometimes contribute larger numbers of individuals to the smaller classes than the small classes do themselves. Percentaging or constructing indices would help presentation vastly but would not solve all problems. For these reasons, we return to the log-linear model.

The results shown in table 4:2 are of a model hypothesizing two-way interactions between all three variables: father's occupation with respondent's occupation, religion with father's occupation and religion with respondent's occupation. The model gave a good fit ($X^2 = 30.8$ with 36 degrees of freedom, $p = .50$). The addition of the three-way interaction of father's occupation with respondent's occupation with religion was therefore unnecessary. The exclusion of any of the two-way interactions resulted in a statistically significant loss of fit. Log-linear models are 'hierarchical', so the inclusion of an interaction between two variables means that the gross ('structural') effects of the numbers in the categories of both variables are also automatically included. Before looking at the table itself, the specification of this model tells us quite a bit. The two-way interaction between father's occupation and respondent's occupation means that the origins and present occupational standings of the respondents are linked, a result obviously expected. The two-way interactions of religion with father's occupation and respondent's occupation means that the occupational distributions of Protestants and Roman Catholics differ both in the present and in the father's generation. These relationships exist independently of any effect of occupational distribution stemming from father-to-son mobility, which is also in the model, and are independent of each other. That is, the difference in the occupational distribution by religion at present cannot be explained as the passive replication of a difference in the past.

The lack of a three-way interaction between the variables means that the mobility of the two religious groupings is equivalent, once one has controlled for their different occupational distributions of origin and destination. This is not to say that the mobility experiences of the two groupings are the same. On the contrary, equivalent mobility within different occupational distributions will mean that mobility experience will not be identical. To put it another way, if it was the case that the Roman Catholic group had the occupational distributions of the Protestants, their experience of mobility would have been the same as the Protestant grouping. The interactions of religion with occupational distribution demonstrate, however, that this is not the case. Similarly, if Protestants had the Catholics' distributions of origin and destination, their group experience of mobility would be the same as the Roman Catholics; but, again, this is not the case.

The table itself provides information as to the form the interactions with religion take. The far right-hand column gives the relative size of each of the seven classes in the fathers' generation and the bottom row gives the relative sizes of the classes for the respondents' occupational distribution. Taking a value of 0.0 for the upper number in a cell as indicating that the number of individuals in that class is about what one would expect to find if people were equally distributed among the classes, a negative sign indicates fewer cases than expected and a positive value indicates more cases than expected. One can confirm this by a quick summation of the marginals in the two tables presented in the appendix. For fathers, the value of 1.1 for Classes IV and VII, 'Small Proprietors' and 'Unskilled Manuals' indicate that these classes are the most numerous; Class I, 'Upper Service', with a value of —1.3 is the least numerous. One can easily observe the expansion

Table 4:2

LOG EFFECT, FATHER'S OCCUPATION BY PRESENT OCCUPATION WITH RELIGION[1]

Father's occupation	*Present occupation class* I	*II*	*III*	*IV*	*V*	*VI*	*VII*	*Father's interaction with religion*[2]	*Size effect of father's occupation*
	1.5	0.6	0.2	—1.2	—0.3	—0.1	—0.7	0.2	—1.3
Class I	5.2	2.2	0.6	—1.5	—0.5	—0.4	—1.8	1.0	—6.7
	0.5	1.0	0.1	0.0	—0.5	—0.8	—0.3	—0.1	—0.4
Class II	2.1	6.3	0.2	0.1	—1.2	—3.0	—1.6	—0.6	—3.5
	0.2	—0.1	0.8	0.1	—0.9	0.2	—0.3	—0.1	—0.6
Class III	0.5	—0.3	3.4	0.4	—1.7	0.9	—1.1	—0.7	—4.9
	—0.8	0.4	—0.1	0.9	—0.2	—0.4	0.2	—0.2	1.1
Class IV	—4.0	4.0	—0.8	5.1	—1.0	—3.3	1.4	—2.6	16.8
	—0.1	—0.4	—0.5	0.0	0.8	0.2	—0.1	0.1	—0.4
Class V	—0.2	—1.5	—1.4	0.1	2.8	0.8	—0.4	1.2	—3.9
	—0.4	—0.8	—0.3	0.0	0.6	0.5	0.3	0.0	0.5
Class VI	—1.9	—4.4	—1.4	0.2	2.8	4.2	2.5	0.5	6.9
	—0.9	—0.8	—0.2	0.0	0.6	0.4	0.9	—0.1	1.1
Class VII	—4.4	—3.7	—1.2	0.1	3.0	3.7	8.1	—0.8	16.2
Present interaction with	0.4	0.1	0.1	—0.3	—0.2	0.0	—0.2		
Religion[2]	4.1	1.3	0.8	—1.6	—1.0	—0.3	—1.9		
Size effect of present	—0.1	0.5	—0.2	—0.6	—0.8	0.5	0.7		Grand mean
occupation	—1.0	6.2	—2.1	—3.7	—5.0	6.4	7.7		effect = 2.3

1. The top number in each cell is its effect; the bottom number is a standardized value of the relative size of the effect. A negative sign indicates a cell frequency is less than would be expected on average.
2. For interactions with religion, a negative number means Roman Catholics are more frequent than average in the cell.

and shrinkage of classes by comparing values in the column with their equivalent cells in the bottom row. The sizes of the two 'service' classes have grown, the 'Unskilled Manual' class has shrunk, and the 'Small Proprietor' class has decreased radically.

By moving in one column and up one row, concrete interpretations of the associations of religion with the fathers' and respondents' occupational distributions may be obtained. In these cells, a negative number means that more Catholics than expected by chance are located in a given class. The lower numbers in the cells are also of significance here since they reflect the actual number of cases in a class. For instance, in the interaction between religion and fathers' class, the top value of 0.2 for Class I, the 'Upper Service' class, indicates Protestants are more numerous there; similarly, the value of —0.2 for Class IV, 'Small Proprietors', indicates Catholics are proportionately more numerous there. Class IV, however, is much larger than Class I in the fathers' distribution so one needs an indicator of the greater numerical significance of 'Small Proprietors'. The standardised value of —2.6 for 'Small Proprietors' compared to 1.0 for the 'Upper Service' class reflects the greater size of Class IV. Looking down the whole column, one observes that the primary source of the interaction with religion for the fathers comes from the Roman Catholic predominance in Class IV, followed by a Protestant predominance in Class V, 'Technical and Manual Supervisory', then the Protestant dominance of Class I and more Catholics than expected among 'Unskilled Manuals'.

Moving to the next to bottom row, which gives the interaction of religion with present occupation, and comparing it with the column, one observes a radical shift in the pattern of the interaction. Protestants predominate in all of the clearly non-manual classes, most markedly in the 'Upper Service' class, where the values are 0.4 and 4.1. Proportionately more of the 'Small Proprietor' class, which includes farmers, are now Catholics but the main source of the interaction with religion for present occupation, from a Catholic point of view, comes from their predominance in the large 'Unskilled Manual' class. The proportionate amount of dominance by one religious grouping or the other in the seven classes is higher, as indicated by the generally larger top values and, from the higher standardised values for the respondents' occupational distribution, this division seems to be more significant. These results lead one to conclude that an association of religion with occupational distribution does exist. Furthermore, the association is not a static one but rather one that is changing over time. The change is one of a widening split between occupational classes, with Protestants predominating in non-manual classes, most especially in the 'service' classes, and Catholics predominating in the manual classes, most especially the 'Unskilled' class.

The balance of table 4:2, the seven by seven matrix, gives the concrete form of the interaction between fathers' and sons' occupations. This is the 'mobility matrix' common to both religious groups with the effects of the differing sizes of the occupational distributions in the respondents' and fathers' generations controlled. While the purpose of this chapter is to discuss the mobility experiences of the religious groupings this matrix does merit comment. The meanings of the values in the individual cells are similar to the effects covered above. Positive values indicate more in a cell than would be expected by chance; negative values indicate less. The standardised values are an indication of how significant an individual cell's deviation from a value of zero is. The diagonal of cells running from the upper left-hand to the lower right-hand corner shows those respondents who fall into the same occupational category as their fathers (the 'inheritors'). The well-documented 'diagonal effect' shows clearly with the values in these diagonal cells being larger and more significant than those around them. The highest positive values indicating the strongest inheritance after the effects of shrinkage between generations (in Class VII) or expansion (in Classes I and II) have been controlled appear at the extremes of the diagonal. The 'Unskilled Manual' class has the highest proportionate amount of inheritance, followed by the two 'service' classes, the only exception to this rule being the small Class V, 'Technical and Manual Supervisors', where more of its present occupants have come from Class VI and VII origins than from within itself. Short-range mobility predominates with the highest proportions of the mobile tending to come from adjacent classes. A notable exception is the 'Small Proprietor' class, which has experienced the most drastic shrinkage in numbers between generations. Those who have left their origins in Class IV have tended, proportionately, to move more to Class II, the 'Lower Service' class (but *not* to the 'Upper Service' class) and to the 'Unskilled Manual' class. Congruent with the predominance of short-range mobility, long-distance mobility occurs relatively rarely. Aside from the lack of mobility of those of 'Small Proprietor' origin into the 'Upper Service' class, the most negative values in the mobility matrix (which, again, indicate less mobility than one would expect to find by chance once the effects of changes in occupational distributions between generations have been controlled for) occur in the lower left-hand cells that signify mobility from the 'Skilled' and 'Unskilled Manual' classes to the service classes and in the upper right-hand cells that indicate mobility from service origins to manual classes. At a general level, the father-son mobility depicted in table 4:2 closely resembles data for the Republic of Ireland (also collected by the Irish mobility study) and the recent results for England and Wales reported by the Nuffield mobility study (Goldthorpe, 1980). Short distance mobility between adjacent categories or straight inheritance are the norms with long distance mobility occurring relatively rarely. The non-manual classes and the manual classes make up two relatively closed systems of mobility. Congruently, the majority of cells with negative values are located in the portions of the table that stand for mobility across the manual/non-manual divide.

Summary

Viewed globally, the mobility results for Northern Ireland do not differ radically from those found in other industrialised nations. Looking at religion, the net mobility patterns of Protestants and Roman Catholics are not significantly different. So, given similar origins and equivalent occupational distributions at present, the mobility experiences of the groupings would be the same. That is, there is nothing inherent about being either Protestant or Roman Catholic that in itself predisposes one towards better or worse chances of mobility. However, the interactions with religion show clearly that the occupational distributions of the two religious groupings are not equivalent. For fathers, the distribution works somewhat to Protestants' advantage but with this advantage being largely counter-balanced. Protestants predominate in the 'Upper Service' class but Catholics are more numerous than chance would expect in the other non-manual classes. Protestants predominate among 'Technical and Manual Supervisory' workers, the distributions in the 'Skilled Manual' class are proportionately equal, and Catholics are found more often than chance would dictate in the 'Unskilled Manual' class. If this pattern was just being passively replicated, the present occupational distribution would tend to resemble that of the fathers. The classes of origin which Catholics dominate, as shown by the 'net' mobility portion of the table above, do not do that badly in comparison to the classes dominated by Protestants. It is the case, however, that in comparison with each other, the present occupational distributions of the religious groupings differ radically. Protestants now clearly dominate all non-manual classes with the exception of the 'Small-Proprietor' class; Catholics are now located disproportionately in the manual classes and most disproportionately in the 'Unskilled Manual' class. Considering that slightly over thirteen per cent of the Catholic sub-sample is unemployed (and thereby excluded from this analysis), compared to only slightly over four per cent of the Protestant sub-sample being unemployed, the distributions of those who have occupations underestimates the size of the considerable advantage enjoyed by Protestants in the present generation. These results indicating a widening, not shrinking or stable, disparity in the occupational distributions of Protestants and Catholics are congruent with more historical analyses reported by others,[2] (Hepburn, chapter 3, in the volume; Bew, Gibbon, and Patterson, 1979).

So, while the results above show that the 'net' mobility of the two religious groups is the same, it is only really the same as long as one artifically assumes that there are no differences in the Protestant and Catholic occupational distributions. In terms of the actual group experiences of mobility, the Catholic experience has been realised in a situation of somewhat of a disadvantage in origin exacerbated by a widened and clarified disadvantage in the present. The origins of this widening cannot be attributed to either a poor or an exceptional mobility performance by either group but must be sought elsewhere. What the above results convincingly indicate is that it would be inaccurate and foolish to assume that present-day inequities are only legacies from the past that will somehow gradually fade into oblivion of their own volition. On the contrary, the assumption must be that present-day inequities will most likely remain or even intensify.

Notes

1. The total number of individuals in table 4:1 fall below the sample size of 2,416. There are several reasons for this. A small proportion of the sample was neither Protestant nor Roman Catholic or could not have religion assigned in coding. Even though the sample was of adult males, some were still in education and/or had never worked. About seven per cent of the sample were unemployed at the time of the interview. For similar reasons, the occupational information for fathers is also sometimes missing.
2. One should be careful to note that the distribution of fathers' occupations given in this chapter does not equal the real occupational distribution of a generation ago. For a 64-year-old respondent 'father's job at the time of your first full-time job' would refer to the occupational structure of sixty years ago. For an 18-year-old respondent who just began full-time work, 'father's job at the time of your first full-time job' would refer to the occupational structure of the 1970s. Similarly, men who worked a generation ago but who never sired male

children or those whose male offspring have emigrated from the Province would obviously not appear in the distribution of fathers. That is, while one may be able to speak of structural mobility, at least part of that structure is an artificial construct.

Appendix

Table 4:1

FATHER'S OCCUPATION BY PRESENT OCCUPATION

Protestants

Father's occupation	*Present occupation class* *I*	*II*	*III*	*IV*	*V*	*VI*	*VII*	*Total*
Class I	31	17	6	0	1	8	2	65
Class II	18	52	10	3	1	8	13	105
Class III	14	12	16	4	0	15	6	67
Class IV	26	114	32	43	14	40	84	353
Class V	14	16	4	5	7	25	17	88
Class VI	26	25	17	10	21	81	62	242
Class VII	25	36	28	22	31	116	183	441
Total	154	272	113	87	75	293	367	1,361
				Catholics				
Class I	3	4	0	0	0	1	3	11
Class II	9	18	2	4	2	3	6	44
Class III	0	6	4	2	1	8	10	31
Class IV	6	62	14	46	8	33	63	232
Class V	2	2	3	2	6	5	8	28
Class VI	3	5	6	10	9	34	39	106
Class VII	5	14	16	13	20	59	123	250
Total	28	111	45	77	46	143	252	702

5. Religion and Unemployment: Evidence from a Cohort Survey

R. L. Miller and R. D. Osborne

In recent years the main source of information on unemployment and religous affiliation has been the 1971 population census. In 1971 the figures were as shown in table 5:1:

Table 5:1

RELIGIOUS UNEMPLOYMENT RATES, 1971 (per cent)

	Male	*Female*	*Total*
Protestant	6.6	3.6	5.6
Catholic	17.3	7.0	13.9

Source: Northern Ireland Population Census, 1971

Generally, a much higher rate of unemployment has been experienced by Catholics, both male and female. Further analysis of the census revealed that Catholic males experienced higher rates of unemployment in all areas of Northern Ireland (measured on the basis of the twenty-six district council areas) irrespective of whether Catholics form a minority or a majority, (Osborne, 1978, 1980b).

Since 1971 *both* communities have suffered significant increases in unemployment. Figure 5:1 gives the unemployment figures reported by the Department of Manpower Services (DMS).

These are aggregate data; the monthly unemployment figures produced by DMS are disaggregated by sex and for young school leavers but not by religion. This precludes detailed assessment of trends in unemployment rates and patterns of unemployment such as those undertaken for ethnic minorities in Britain (Showler, 1980). Despite the absence of unemployment data broken down by religion there is no doubt that an informal assessment is often done as the areas of traditionally high unemployment tend to be areas with a larger proportion of Catholics in the population. A study that has sought to examine the relationship between unemployment and religion by the ecological correlation of census data with a sample drawn from the unemployment register in Belfast in 1972, was undertaken by Doherty (1980). While this study, together with Osborne (1978, 1980b), establishes the higher aggregate experience of unemployment by Catholics, nothing has been reported on the

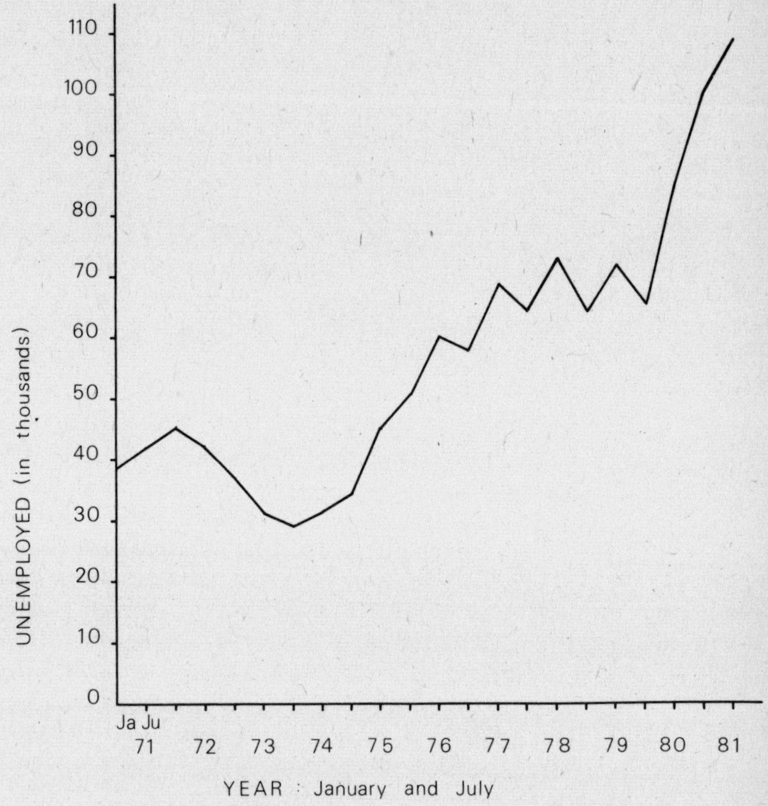

Figure 5:1 Unemployment in Northern Ireland, 1971–81.

characteristics of the unemployed or the *processes* of unemployment in terms of religion. This chapter seeks to begin to fill this gap.

The Survey

This chapter reports some initial analyses of data originally collected and examined by a Department of Manpower Services conducted survey. The Cohort Survey of the Unemployed (CSU) was designed to examine aspects of the *flow* on and off the register rather than a survey of the *stock* of those registered at any one time. The relevant distinctions between the two types of survey lie in the longitudinal character of the flow survey and in the different groups of the unemployed who may be included in each. In this instance the design of the CSU excludes some groups as set out below. There are three main components of the CSU: (i) a sample of adult males drawn from all parts of Northern Ireland who registered as unemployed during January-March 1976 after a previous period of employment. These individuals were asked to complete a questionnaire designed to elicit information on previous labour market activity, previous occupation, socio-economic conditions, work attitudes and so on; (ii) details of individual state benefits were obtained from the Department of Health and Social Services; (iii) employment office clerks were asked to provide estimates of individual job attitudes and prospects. The labour market behaviour of these individuals was then monitored over the next twelve months. The survey recorded an effective sample size of 3,676 although full work records were not available for 376 of those. The main purposes of the survey were to identify the long-term unemployed and to establish whether any variables could be identified as predictors of long-term unemployment. The survey report (DMS, 1979) discusses the findings in these two areas, concluding that the high level of unemployment rendered identification of the long-term unemployed, other than in terms of long established individual characteristics, relatively unfruitful. While the questionnaire included a question seeking religious affiliation, eliciting a 91.6 per cent response, the DMS report did not include this variable in its analysis. Of those indicating a religious affiliation 51.9 per cent (1,749) indicated a Protestant affiliation and 48.1 per cent (1,619) declared themselves as Catholics.

Included in the CSU are adult males registering after a period of employment. Not included in the survey are women, school-leavers or the pre-existing long-term unemployed who constitute part of the stock of unemployed. The longitudinal nature of the survey, however, enables the identification of a long-term unemployed group, defined here as those who remained unemployed throughout the twelve-month period.

Two final points to note are: (i) The CSU was conducted at a time of increasing unemployment in Northern Ireland (Figure 5:1). While the level in 1976–77 was less than that of the early 1980s it is more representative of current conditions than a survey conducted, for example, in 1973–74 when unemployment was uncharacteristically low in Northern Ireland. (ii) The final point concerns the appropriateness of the CSU design for a discussion of religion and unemployment. It could be argued that an initial attempt to penetrate beyond the aggregate figures would be best made with a *stock* survey (such as that undertaken by Smith (1981) to examine unemployment and race in Britain) and in general we would concur with this view. However, the very absence of such a survey in Northern Ireland provides ample justification for the full utilisation of the CSU for basic description, quite apart from the specific advantages of the longitudinal dimension of the survey.

This analysis of the CSU comprises two parts. The first is a basic description of the survey sample and a discussion of the essential findings in terms of religious affiliation. The second part focuses on the role of the employment offices in relation to those gaining employment and those remaining unemployed.

Sample description[1]

(i) Age, marital status and dependents

In keeping with the pattern in the wider population the mean age of Protestants in the sample is higher at 31.7 years than that of Catholics at 30.6 years. A larger proportion of Catholics falls in the prime working age group of 18–30, 63 per cent, than of Protestants, 58.9 per cent. Statistically significant differences exist between Protestants and Catholics in terms of marital status with 61.5 per cent of Protestants married while 53.2 per cent of Catholics have the same status. Only 2.8 per cent of Catholics are divorced, separated or widowed compared with 6.6 per cent of Protestants. For those married, Catholics had a higher mean number of dependent children (3.1) than Protestants (2.0) with the bulk of this difference accounted for by the higher proportion of Catholics with 3 or 4 children and to a lesser extent by those with 5 or more children.

(ii) Qualifications

The overwhelming majority of the sample report no formal qualifications (80.7 per cent). Although a statistically significant difference exists between Protestants and Catholics the difference is small with 78.7 per cent of Protestants without qualifications and 82.9 per cent of Catholics unqualified. Of those with qualifications more Catholics have a degree or equivalent while more Protestants have 'A' levels than Catholics.

Table 5:2A

CATEGORICAL VARIABLES BY RELIGION[1]

Variable name	*Categories*	*Protestants*	*Roman Catholics*	*Significance level* (X^2)
Marital status	Married[2]	61.5	53.2	0.001
Academic qualification	Degree or HND	0.9	1.2	
	A-level or ONC/OND	1.5	1.1	
	O-level	2.7	2.4	
	CSE, 4 or more	3.0	3.7	0.01
	City and Guilds	10.4	6.4	
	Other	2.6	2.3	
	None	78.7	82.9	
Previous occupation	Professional and intermediate	3.6	3.5	
	Skilled non-manual	4.6	3.4	
	Skilled manual	41.3	43.6	0.001
	Semi-skilled	31.3	35.4	
	Unskilled	13.9	11.2	
	Armed forces	2.7	0.4	
	Inadequately described	2.6	2.6	
Occupation sought	Professional and intermediate	2.5	2.5	
	Skilled non-manual	5.1	4.2	
	Skilled manual	42.7	46.0	N.S.
	Semi-skilled	25.1	24.7	
	Unskilled	7.8	7.7	
	Armed forces	0.6	0.2	
	Inadequately described	16.2	14.6	
Trade union membership	Yes	34.8	24.6	0.001
Vehicle ownership	Yes	36.8	30.9	0.001
Father unemployed when respondent was at secondary school	Yes	18.5	26.6	0.001
Number of times registered unemployed	First time	19.9	11.4	
	Two to four	52.3	52.0	0.001
	Five or more	27.8	36.6	
ESO assessment of attitudes to work	Keen	47.3	45.8	
	Reasonable	49.5	51.5	
	Problems	2.5	2.5	N.S.
	Near retirement	0.8	0.4	

Table 5:2A (*Continued*)

Benefits compared to previous pay	Benefits more	2.2	3.5	
	Benefits equal or not less than £5 of previous pay	4.8	4.7	0.05
	Benefits between £5 and £10 less than previous pay	9.9	11.7	
	Benefits at least £10 less than previous pay	83.0	80.0	
Time prepared to spend travelling to work	Up to 15 mins	12.3	10.9	
	Up to 30 mins	45.4	45.2	0.05
	Up to 1 hour	29.2	27.3	
	Over 1 hour	13.1	16.6	
Distance prepared to travel to work	Up to 5 miles	37.4	37.9	
	Up to 10 miles	30.5	25.8	0.05
	Up to 20 miles	18.1	18.3	
	Over 20 miles	14.0	18.1	
Live away from home to find work	Yes	34.4	39.7	0.05
Move house to find work	Yes	25.8	24.5	N.S.
Job opportunities restricted due to "Troubles"	No	38.3	37.7	
	A little	32.6	23.4	0.001
	A lot	29.1	38.9	
Concern at being out of work	Very concerned	70.6	73.9	
	Quite concerned	18.1	16.5	N.S.
	Not very concerned	11.3	9.6	
Harder to get jobs in recent years	Yes	29.6	43.3	0.001
Reasons for leaving last job	Redundant	30.4	33.8	
	Dismissed	15.7	10.2	
	End of contract	10.1	14.6	
	Health reasons	5.8	6.3	0.001
	Left voluntarily	20.4	14.8	
	Other	17.6	20.2	

1 All proportions are column proportions.
2 'Married' includes separated, divorced, and widowed.
Source: CSU

(iii) Previous occupation and occupational aspirations

Statistically significant differences exist in the occupations held prior to becoming unemployed. Protestants are more likely to have

Table 5:2B

VARIABLES AVERAGED BY RELIGION

Variable name	*Protestants*	*Roman Catholics*	*Significance level (F)*
Age	31.7	30.6	0.01
Dependent children[1]	2.0	3.1	0.001
Frequency of unemployment in previous 3 years	1.8	2.1	0.001
Age when first registered as unemployed	22.8	20.6	0.001
Number of job submissions	1.15	0.84	0.001
Total benefits (£)	15.82	16.15	N.S.

[1] Average based on married men only.
Source: CSU

been in a non-manual occupation (8.2 per cent) than Catholics (6.7 per cent) but slightly more Catholics (43.6 per cent) than Protestants (41.3 per cent) were in the skilled manual category. Similarly, a larger proportion of Catholics (35.4 per cent) were semi-skilled than Protestants (31.3 per cent) leaving 13.9 per cent of Protestants and 11.2 per cent of Catholics in the unskilled category. In broad terms this represents a slight over-representation of Catholics in the skilled manual category and an under-representation in the unskilled group when compared with the distribution suggested by Aunger (see chapter 2). Unfortunately no information was collected from the sample on the type of industry in which they had been employed and this hampers the discussion of the labour market position of the two groups (see below).

In terms of the type of job being sought, no statistically significant differences were recorded but for both groups there was a tendency for a higher proportion to be seeking skilled manual work than had previously been employed in this category.

(iv) Trade Union membership

A number of studies of unemployment have suggested that unemployment can be higher amongst those who are not union members, (Hill et al, 1973; Daniel, 1974). This, however, is strongly related to industry, with some industries markedly less unionized than others. For our sample more Protestants are union members (34.8 per cent) than Catholics (24.6 per cent), a difference which is statistically significant.

(v) Reasons for leaving last job

Statistically significant differences emerged on the reasons for leaving last job. Catholics were more likely to have been made redundant (33.8 per cent as against 30.4 per cent for Protestants) or as a result of coming to the end of their contract (14.6 per cent as against 10.1 per cent). Protestants were more likely to have been dismissed (15.7 per cent as against 10.2 per cent) or to have left voluntarily (20.4 per cent as against 14.8 per cent). Other reasons included poor health, moving house and so on, which evidenced few differences between Protestants and Catholics.

(vi) Previous experience of unemployment

A higher proportion of Catholics reported their fathers as being unemployed whilst they were at secondary school, 26.6 per cent for Catholics compared to 18.5 per cent for Protestants. Catholics also record a lower average age for the first experience of unemployment than Protesants (20.6 years to 22.8 years) with this difference holding across age categories. A further indicator of experience of unemployment is the frequency of unemployment in the previous three years. While 11.4 per cent of the Catholic sample are registering for the first time some 19.9 per cent of Protestants are doing so. On the other hand, 27.8 per cent of Protestants have been unemployed on five or more occasions compared with 36.6 per cent of Catholics. In summary, Catholics are more likely to record their fathers as unemployed, to have registered unemployed for the first time at a younger age and to have a larger number of previous periods of unemployment. These indications of a greater experience of unemployment by Catholics are congruent with the aggregate patterns of Table 5:1 and, as is suggested below, suggest differences between Catholics and Protestants which are perhaps best understood in terms of dual labour market theory.

(vii) Attitudes to job situation

Protestants (29.6 per cent) were significantly less likely than Catholics (43.3 per cent) to agree with the suggestion that it had become harder to obtain work in recent years, while similar proportions of Protestants and Catholics reported themselves to be either 'very concerned' or 'quite concerned' at being unemployed with only 10 per cent of Protestants and Catholics reporting themselves as 'not very concerned'. The pattern of responses generally sustain Daniel's (1974) findings on the retention of the 'work ethic' amongst the unemployed and also those of Miller

(1978) who has argued a basic similarity in the commitment to the 'work ethic' by Protestants and Catholics in Northern Ireland.

(viii) Geographical mobility

The potential geographical mobility of the unemployed has attracted comment by politicians and has also been examined in other studies of unemployment, (Sinfield, 1981). The CSU included a range of questions concerned with mobility. While equal proportions of Protestants and Catholics were prepared to move house to find work, more Catholics (39.7 per cent) were prepared to live away from home than Protestants (34.4 per cent). Despite a higher proportion of Protestants being car owners more Catholics were prepared to travel over ten miles on a daily journey to work than Protestants, although the modal category for both groups was 0–5 miles. Some significant differences were reported, however, to the question of whether the 'troubles' had restricted access to jobs. While a similar proportion of Catholics and Protestants indicated this not to be the case, for those who suggested the 'troubles' had inhibited job access, Catholics were more likely to say 'a lot' than Protestants. Whether this indicates a potential or a real inhibition of travel to work patterns is unclear. In general terms, however, few differences were observed in stated willingness to travel for work.

(ix) Benefits[2]

An area of particular social and political controversy has been the relationship between the social benefits available to the unemployed and wage levels, with some arguing that the level of benefits is such as to curb the incentive to work. Deacon (1981), however, has pointed out that the more extreme 'scrounger' assertions tend to be made particularly in periods of rising unemployment, although there is a continuing concern with the effects of benefits on work incentives. In Northern Ireland, it has also been argued that because benefit is linked to family circumstances, Catholics, through having, on average, larger family size, are more likely to receive benefits approximating to, or in excess of, previous wages.[3]

In the sample as a whole only some 2.8 per cent are in receipt of benefit in excess of previous pay. This breaks down into 2.2 per cent of the Protestant sample and 3.5 per cent of Catholics. A further 4.8 per cent of the sample receive benefit equal to previous take home pay or within £5 (per week) of that sum. This group represents 4.8 per cent of the Protestant sample and 4.7 per cent of the Catholic sample. In the next category, that between £6 and £10 of previous weekly wages, a further 10.8 per cent of the sample is located, representing 11.7 per cent of the Catholic and 9.9 per cent of the Protestant samples. Altogether, two-thirds of the sample receive benefit which is £15 or less of previous net weekly take home pay.

Returning once more to the two categories of those receiving benefit in excess of previous wages and those in receipt of a sum within £5, we can examine the extent to which those with large families (defined as five or more dependent children) fall into these potential 'scrounger' categories. Of those receiving excess benefit, only 22.6 per cent have five or more children and over half of this category (54.9 per cent) is represented by those with 0–2 dependent children. Some 13.8 per cent of those with five or more dependent children fall into the excess benefit category, and comprise 16.7 per cent of Catholics and 8.3 per cent of Protestants with families of this size. Similarly, for the 'within £5' category comprising 4.8 per cent of the sample, only 10.4 per cent have large families representing 10.9 per cent of the large family group. Some 8.9 per cent of the Catholic and 14.6 per cent of the Protestant large families fall into this category.

In summary, then, two points can be made. The first is that with less than 3 per cent of the sample receiving more benefit than take home pay and with less than a further 5 per cent receiving within £5 of previous pay, the relatively small size of this *potential* 'scrounger' group can be seen in a realistic light. Further, the insignificance of large families in these two groups points towards explanations of the apparently limited 'scrounger' problem being located within the labour market structure and, in particular, with the problems of low pay (Black, et al, 1980).

(x) Experience during the year

The strength of CSU lies especially in its longitudinal construction; we can trace the experience of the cohort for a year after registering unemployed. Four important aspects can be considered: the submissions made by the Employment Offices of individuals for jobs; the average number of days before obtaining a job; final employment status at the end of the year; and, the long-term unemployed, defined as those who did not obtain a job during the year.

The provision of job information and the attempted linking of individuals with job vacancies has been one of the state's primary mechanisms for intervening in the labour market. As such, it is appropriate to consider its operation notwithstanding the extent to which informal networks may outscore the formal mechanisms linking individuals to jobs, (Showler, 1976). In the CSU the average number of submissions for Protestants was 1.15 and for Catholics 0.84, a difference of around one-third. Some care should be taken in interpreting these figures as the relationship between submissions and gaining employment is not straightforward. On the one hand, a larger number of submissions could represent a higher marketability of Protestants to employers, although in terms of education and previous skills alone this would not seem to be the case. On the other hand, a larger number of submissions could imply relative failure in the labour market resulting in many unsuccessful submissions to employers. Assistance in interpreting this situation can be gained from considering the average number of days taken to the first job obtained. This can be calculated in two ways, as shown in table 5:3:

Table 5:3

AVERAGE NUMBER OF DAYS TO FIRST JOB

	(a) *All*	*(b)* *Those obtaining a job*
Protestant	156.4	88.1
Catholic	193.4	100.1
Source: CSU	(X^2 significance 0.001)	(X^2 significance 0.01)

Column (a) includes all in the sample,[4] while column (b) includes only those who obtained a job during the year. On either calculation, Catholics spend approximately 25 per cent longer on average before gaining a job. This difference holds across age categories (with the 51 + group showing the smallest difference) and geographical regions (with the difference smallest in the West). On this evidence the larger number of submissions of Protestants is a function of labour market opportunity rather than labour market failure.

Final employment status also shows some significant differences, as is shown in table 5:4:

Table 5:4

FINAL EMPLOYMENT STATUS

	Unemployed	*Employed*
Protestant	45.5	54.5
Catholic	61.8	38.2
All	53.5	46.5

(X^2 significance 0.001)

Source: CSU.

Overall, a majority of the sample was unemployed at the end of the year, but while just under half of the Protestant sample were unemployed virtually two-thirds of the Catholic sample were without work. Once again this difference applied to each age category (with the 51 + group virtually the same). The 22–30 age group, those of prime working age, recorded the largest difference. The pattern for the different regions is shown in table 5:5:

Table 5:5

FINAL EMPLOYMENT STATUS BY REGIONS IN NORTHERN IRELAND
(Per cent)

				Regional Representation (sample)		
		Protestant				
	Employed	*Unemployed*	*Total*	*Protestant*	*Catholic*	*Total*
Belfast Region	55.1	44.9	100	61.2	38.8	100
West	37.1	62.9	100	25.5	74.5	100
North	59.2	40.8	100	69.0	31.0	100
South	61.3	38.7	100	46.6	53.4	100
		Catholic				
Belfast Region	38.1	61.9	100	61.2	38.8	100
West	29.5	70.5	100	25.5	74.5	100
North	56.0	44.0	100	69.0	31.0	100
South	51.6	48.4	100	46.6	53.4	100

(X^2 significance 0.001)
Source: CSU.

Once again, for each region, a higher proportion of Catholics are unemployed at the end of the year. The largest difference is in Belfast which contains over half (52.6 per cent) of the sample as a whole. It is interesting to note that Catholics fare less well than Protestants even in areas where they form the majority of the sample.

The long-term unemployed

The final part of this descriptive assessment focuses on the long-term unemployed defined, in the survey, as those who did not obtain a job during the year and were unemployed at the end of the period. They represent 53.5 per cent of the total sample; 44.1 per cent of the Protestant cohort and 55.9 per cent of the Catholic. Catholics are thereby over-represented in the long-term unemployed. Comparing Protestants and Catholics in the long-term unemployed there are no statistically significant differences in previous jobs held, in trade union membership, in the proportions with educational qualifications or in the preparedness to move or live away from home to find work.

Catholics are statistically more likely to report an unemployed father, to record their first period of unemployment at a younger age, to have been unemployed more frequently in the previous three years and for the duration of that unemployment to have been longer. Catholics are statistically more likely to report jobs being harder to find in recent years but not to indicate that job opportunities were restricted by 'the troubles'. Catholics are more likely to be concerned at being out of work. There are no statistically significant differences in the proportions of Protestants and Catholics receiving benefit in excess of previous income, or within £5 of that income (previously defined as the potential 'scrounger' categories). Indeed, of those who became long-term unemployed, only 8.3 per cent fell into these two categories, providing further evidence of the unimportance of 'scroungers' in this large scale sample of the unemployed. Within the long-term unemployed those with large families (five or more dependent children) constitute 10.2 per cent of the group compared with 5 per cent of the sample as a whole, so those with large families are somewhat over-represented. Catholics with large families are slightly but not significantly more likely to become long-term unemployed than Protestants, but it should be stressed that the bulk of those in this category do not have large dependent families.

The quite high proportion of the whole sample who at the end of the year could be defined as the long-term unemployed is indicative of the extent to which the general rise in unemployment levels has meant not only more people registering as unemployed but also an increase in the average duration of unemployment. In this situation the traditional variables of age and skill level, used to identify the long-term category, became less significant (see DMS, 1979). Nevertheless, when religion is considered, Catholics are over-represented in this group, just as they have been on each measure of unemployment experience in this survey. At a time, therefore, of rising unemployment and increasing duration of unemployment, Catholics are more likely than Protestants to become long-term unemployed. This evidence questions those who have predicted that the general rise in unemployment will tend to even out the religious differential (Byrne, 1980), although it must be acknowledged that the most dramatic increase in unemployment rates has taken place since 1978 (Figure 5:1).

In summarising the evidence we can note the basic similarity between Protestants and Catholics in terms of their characteristics:

in terms of skill levels (previous occupation), education, type of job being sought, preparedness to travel to work, concern about being out of work and so on. Some differences were observable in age structure and number of dependent children. Protestants and Catholics differed quite markedly, however, in previous experience of unemployment both in frequency and duration and age first registering as unemployed. Moreover, further significant differences in the labour market experiences during the year covered by the survey emerged with Protestants more likely to be employed generally and across each region, to record more job submissions, to record a shorter average time to first job and to be under-represented amongst the long-term unemployed. For the sample as a whole, the proportion receiving benefit equal to or above previous take home pay was small and on a similar scale for Protestants and Catholics. Having a large family is not a good predictor of those falling into these categories for either Protestants or Catholics.

The Role of Employment Sub-Offices (ESOs)

The descriptive analysis of the 'Cohort Survey of the Unemployed' will now be augmented by an evaluation of the effects of the working of the ESO offices upon the sample's ability to find employment. The interaction of religion with the offices' functioning will be considered while controlling for the effects of some of the correlates of unemployment established above and in the original report by the Department of Manpower Services.Up to this point the secondary analysis of the survey has been largely descriptive, covering the association of religion with the response to specific questions asked of the unemployed and with the information subsequently returned by the ESO offices during the period of the survey. Aside from grouping the results into bodies of related information no attempt has been made yet to parcel out the strength of interactions with religion. Similarly, the longitudinal nature of the survey has not been exploited through looking at the effects of the working of the ESO offices over the survey period. To demonstrate that religion associates significantly with a variety of correlates of unemployment does not demonstrate that the link results solely from a person's religion. Some of the association of religion with correlates of unemployment derives at least in part from indirect effects of other variables. For instance, proportionately more of the Roman Catholic part of the sample lived in the west of the Province. Since the west in general shows higher rates of unemployment at least some of the higher Catholic rate of unemployment is an artifact of geographical location. What one needs to do to consider realistically links between religion and unemployment is demonstrate whether or not religion remains significantly associated with unemployment and its correlates after the effects of other salient variables have been controlled.

A log-linear modelling exercise will allow one to evaluate the controlled associations of religion in a model of unemployment. As noted above the effect of the state upon the parameters of unemployment, through the actions of the ESO offices, is doubly relevant since its actions are hopefully non-sectarian and, in any case, are more open to modification than other factors such as traditional methods of recruitment or the structure of job opportunities in an area, that may also affect patterns of unemployment. By including activities of the ESO offices into the model (the number of submissions for employment made by the offices' and clerks' assessments of the prospects and attitudes of the unemployed) the model also becomes an assessment of the activities and significance of ESO offices. Log-linear modelling has been discussed by Miller in chapter 4. That discussion will not be repeated here though one point should be reiterated. The model bases itself on the idea of control; so any relationships that persist once one has developed the 'best' model (that is, the simplest model that continues to 'fit' the data well) are real associations independent of any others existing in the model. For example, pre-empting the results below, a significant interaction between (1) religion and final employment status when (2) area and final employment status and (3) area and religion are also allowed to interact means that the effect of religion on employment status is not an artifact of geographical religious distribution. That is, the effect of religion is a unique effect, distinct from the effect of geographical location on employment status.

Log-linear models do not assume causality. By exploiting the longitudinal nature of the CSU, however, one can work out a temporal sequence of events and thereby know which half of an association had to have occurred first. 'Final employment status' by definition applies to the end of the fifteen-month data collection period. 'Number of submissions' accumulated during the fifteen months of data collection. The ESO clerks' assessments of 'employment prospects' and 'attitudes to work' occurred at the beginning of the survey period when individuals first signed on.

'Number of submissions' and the two assessments taken together are the three variables that directly concern the operation of the ESO offices. The balance of information included in the model below: 'frequency of unemployment in previous three years', 'geographic area', 'social class of previous job', 'age', and 'religion' existed immediately prior to the beginning of the study. Figure 5:2 gives a representation of the results of the analysis. Lines indicate interaction; no lines indicate no significant interaction. The model depicted in the figure is the simplest that still gives a 'fit' with anticipated cell frequencies not significantly different from actual cell frequencies.

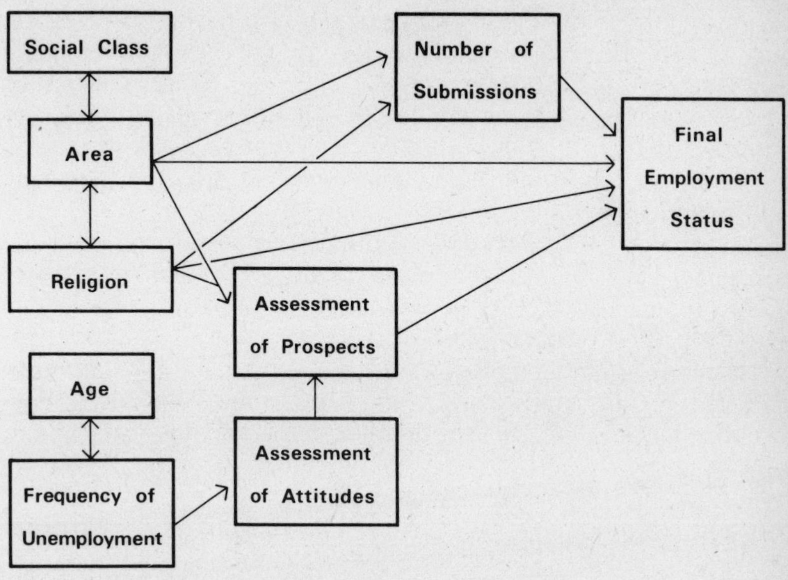

Figure 5:2 A model of unemployment.

Final employment status is significantly associated with two of the variables relating to the performance of ESO offices and with area and with religion. In the model, those who received no submissions are significantly more likely to be unemployed at the end of the survey period. For the half of the sample that had received no submissions, 55.3 per cent were unemployed at the end of the survey period. Compared to this, 49.9 per cent of those who had received from one to three submissions were unemployed at the end of the survey period. One should note the caution attached to this link in the original Manpower Services report where it was noted that the minority who received a relatively large number of submissions were more likely to be unemployed than those who had received only a few. For instance, of the six per cent who had received four or more submissions, 63.9 per cent were unemployed at the end of the survey period. The area in which an office is located associated significantly with the eventual employment outcome of its clients. The West showed the worst employment outcome, with 68.4 per cent being unemployed at the end of the year. The North showed the best outcome with 42.4 per cent unemployed followed by the South (45.0 per cent) and then the Belfast area (51.3 per cent). The association of religion and final employment status takes the form of more Protestants being employed at the end of the year; 54.5 per cent of Protestants are employed compared to 38.2 per cent of Roman Catholics. (These results for religion appear in table 5:4 above.)

The number of submissions an individual received varied by region and by religion independently. People in the South and North did the best, averaging slightly over one submission each. People in the West received, on average, the smallest number of submissions (.71 each). Protestants averaged more submissions than Roman Catholics, receiving slightly over one on average (1.15) compared to slightly less than one (0.84) submission for Catholics. Both results are statistically significant at the .001 level. Protestants received, on average, more submissions than Catholics in all four areas.

Table 5:6

NUMBER OF SUBMISSIONS BY RELIGION FOR EACH REGION

Region	*Protestant*	*Catholic*	*All*
Belfast	1.15	0.86	1.04
West	0.81	0.69	0.71
North	1.28	0.87	1.15
South	1.35	1.16	1.26
All regions	1.15	0.84	1.00

Source: CSU.

There was no link between social class of previous job and submissions, although perhaps a finer measure of previous occupation incorporating industry might demonstrate a link with number of submissions. Once these effects of religion and area are controlled, no unique relationship between number of submissions and assessment or employment prospects by the ESO clerks remains.

The clerks' assessment of the employment prospects of their clients was found to be most strongly linked to the clerks' own assessment of their clients' attitudes to work. For instance, over 80 per cent of those assessed by clerks as having good prospects were also assessed as having keen attitudes to work. Similarly, those with 'reasonable' attitudes to work had 'fair' prospects and those whose attitudes to work were assessed as problematic were more likely than anyone else to have 'poor' employment prospects. While assessment of prospects does not link in the model with number of submissions or with final employment status, the ESO clerks' assessments do appear to be reasonably valid since they correlate with the final employment status of clients with more of those assessed as having 'poor' prospects being unemployed at the end of the survey period and more of those assessed as having good prospects being in employment.

Prospects were also significantly and independently linked to a composite effect of religion and area. That is, the ESO clerks' assessment of prospects varied by the religion of the person who signed on and this variation itself was not the same in each region. In the most populous Belfast area Protestants were more likely to receive a good assessment of prospects, the West and North showed no significant difference between the religious groups in the assessment of employment prospects, and in the South, Roman Catholics were more likely to receive a 'good' assessment of prospects (table 5:7).

Table 5:7

ESO ASSESSMENT OF PROSPECTS BY REGION AND RELIGION

	REGION							
	Belfast		*West*		*North*		*South*	
Prospects	*Protestant*	*Catholic*	*Protestant*	*Catholic*	*Protestant*	*Catholic*	*Protestant*	*Catholic*
Good	33.3	24.4	15.6	17.9	36.8	32.2	23.9	43.1
Fair	59.2	61.9	74.5	74.4	59.2	58.9	68.6	46.4
Poor	7.5	13.7	9.9	7.7	4.0	8.9	7.5	10.5
TOTAL	100.0	100.0	100.0	100.0	100.0	100.0	100.0	100.0
(N)	(1,045)	(672)	(192)	(559)	(250)	(112)	(201)	(239)
Significance level X^2	0.001		N.S.		N.S.		0.001	

Source: CSU

As covered in the descriptive section above, the Catholic portion of the sample was slightly, but significantly, younger. Roman Catholics made up a majority, 51.8 per cent of those aged twenty-one or younger. One should remember that the sample was of those who became unemployed in a three-month period after being in work. It therefore excludes school-leavers who have never worked and who will tend to be younger than average, and will under-represent the long-term unemployed who will tend to be older.

Religion also linked significantly with geographic area as shown in table 5:5 above. Three-quarters of those entering the unemployment rolls in the West were Roman Catholics. In the Belfast area and the North region, Protestants predominated. Eight of the twenty-seven ESO offices had Protestants making up over 70 per cent of the sample for those who stated religion. These offices were: Antrim (76.7 per cent Protestant), Ballymena (76.6 per cent), Bangor (91.8 per cent), Carrickfergus (91.0 per cent), Coleraine (72.5 per cent), Larne (80.0 per cent), Lisburn (72.9 per cent), and Newtownards (87.6 per cent). Ten offices had Roman Catholics making up over 70 per cent of the sample: Armagh (78.6 per cent Catholic), Downpatrick (87.1 per cent), Enniskillen (73.6 per cent), Limavady (70.2 per cent), Londonderry (86.1 per cent), Magherafelt (74.2 per cent), Newcastle (76.3 per cent), Newry (94.9 per cent), Omagh (74.4 per cent), and Strabane (70.3 per cent). Belfast was not broken into regions and hence it is only possible to give figures for the city as a whole (56.5 per cent Protestant, 43.5 per cent Catholic).

Two general results come out of the model. Religion, even when the independent effects of a variety of other variables are controlled, exhibits a multiplicity of significant associations. It shares this pervasiveness with only one other variable, geographic area. Putting in even more additional variables, while not feasible for the computing routines that produced this model, would not be likely to increase significantly its explanatory power. As has been noted many times before (Heath, 1981; Blau and Duncan, 1967; Pearson, 1914), attempting to reduce variance in social science models by continuing to add in new variables while retaining the old, fast approaches redundancy, not 'cumulation'. That is, the new variables, if they are associated to some degree with a few or all of the originals, have little in the way of additional information to contribute; they will, therefore, tend to obscure rather than augment a model.

While religion does not significantly associate with the ESO clerks' assessment of their clients' attitudes, it does associate with their assessment of prospects and with the number of submissions received. This is a clear indication that the performance of the ESO offices does vary depending upon the religion of the person signing on. This is relevant since both the assessment of employment prospects and the number of submissions do link significantly with final employment status. Attaching an interpretation to this is more difficult. The clerks may well be reacting to their perception of varying chances of employment. If in different regions, such as the Belfast area and the South, the clerks feel that the prospects of one denomination is not as good as the other, their evaluation may be their realistic judgement of chances and does not necessarily imply behaviour that is directly sectarian on their part. Geographic area seems to play an independent role in the model similar to that of religion, linking with the same variables. Different denominations are seen as having better prospects in different regions with this regional assessment of prospects fitting broadly with the final employment status of individuals of different denominations. The original Department of Manpower Services report, when it looked at the variations in number of submissions received by the sample as a whole, noted that, 'These variations merely suggest that registrants are submitted on the basis of compatibility with the requirements of employers'. Similarly, when one notes that the Protestant unemployed receive more submissions than the Catholic, this does not inevitably mean direct discrimination on the part of the ESO offices; realistic employment possibilities for Protestants may appear to the clerks to be better than those for Roman Catholics. For instance, it was not possible from the CSU data to look at the industrial or skill background of the unemployed in any detailed manner. A study of these factors at a more disaggregated level might go some way towards explaining the differences in the number of submissions received by Protestants and Catholics. One must conclude, however, that direct or indirect, and actively discriminatory or not, the offices do appear to behave in a manner which acknowledges the structure of the labour market since the religion of the unemployed persons entering the rolls does relate to the subsequent behaviour of the offices.

DMS policy in relation to ESOs and religion expressly forbid personnel to ask registrants for their religious affiliation although, as DMS accepts, this does not mean that religious affiliation cannot be ascertained, with a reasonable level of accuracy, from other information. DMS policy also prevents ESO offices from accepting job vacancies which stipulate a particular religious affiliation. DMS also argue that changes of procedure since the CSU was conducted 'tend to eliminate the effects of any conscious or unconscious discrimination (if it exists) by ESO personnel in submission behaviour'.[5] This has been achieved, according to DMS, by the development of Job Markets, which, through an open display of job opportunities from which an individual can select and submit themselves, thereby reduces the ESO clerks' role. Other offices are also adopting these 'self-service' procedures.

Discussion

A theoretical model which seems to offer some assistance in the understanding of the Protestant/Catholic experiences of unemployment revealed in this survey is that of the 'dual labour market'. This model, while still requiring full empirical verification, seeks to explain the structure of labour markets in advanced economies. According to Blackburn and Mann (1979:21–23) the dual labour market model:

> asserts that the labour market is increasingly divided into primary and secondary sectors. Into the primary sector go the monopolies; capital-intensive, highly profitable and technologically advanced firms and industries. Into the secondary sector go small, backward firms located in competitive markets—in retail trades, services and non-durable manufacturing such as clothing or food processing. The primary sector is high wage, highly unionized and contains internal labour markets... In the extreme forms of the internal labour market only the lowest manual jobs are filled from the outside. The remainder are filled by promotion from within . . .

While the primary sector is looking more than ever for the stable worker and workforce, the secondary sector needs to use labour turnover and redundancy to adjust employment levels to unpredictable product markets. Thus secondary employers abandon the 'queue' and look for unstable employees—women, ethnic minorities and other marginal and relatively docile groups.

From what has been shown of aggregate differences in unemployment by the census (table 5:1), the contrasting experience of unemployment discussed above, and from what is known of industrial distributions (chapter 2) and recruitment patterns of young school leavers (chapter 8), then it is probable that Protestants benefit to a greater extent from the primary labour market while Catholics rely more on the secondary market. This duality in labour market structure, therefore, may significantly coincide with the Protestant/Catholic division.

The evidence from this longitudinal survey, conducted at a time of increasing unemployment, provides important confirmation of the saliency of religion in the process of unemployment. Becoming unemployed in the early part of 1976 and the experiences of the following year involved major variations between Protestants and Catholics; generally to the disadvantage of Catholics. Differences in such things as skill level, geographical mobility, motivation, levels of benefit received and benefit in relation to previous income, and so on, could not readily account for these differences. Geographical location does play a part but in several important ways location does *not* 'explain' or subsume observed differences between Catholics and Protestants. This survey has provided a first opportunity to penetrate in a significant way behind the aggregate figures. With unemployment set to rise to even greater heights it is clear that further detailed work is a priority to enable an accurate and up-to-date appreciation of the contrasting experiences of unemployment between the two communities in Northern Ireland.

Notes

1. A summary of the variables used and their significance levels in this descriptive section is shown in Table 5:2.
2. The CSU gathered information on previous take home pay (net) and total benefits payable when unemployed. Information was not obtained, however, on receipt of benefits whilst in work, such as Family Income Supplement and various rebates. To this extent available resources whilst at work (pay + FIS, etc) are underestimated. This, however, can only act to reduce the proportions in the sample receiving benefit close to or in excess of resources available when at work.
3. Discussions of this issue use two measures of wage levels. The first is previous take home pay and the second is 'minimum acceptable pay', that is, the wage level for which individuals would be prepared to return to work. The latter measure may be more valid over a long period of time with high inflation, depending on when the question is asked. Since this survey was conducted, at the start of the period of unemployment, previous (net) wage level is used in this analysis. Benefit available to the unemployed varies through time. It is at its peak shortly after registration as unemployed when an earnings related supplement is payable (abolished in 1982). When, however, first this supplement is exhausted and eventually unemployment benefit also, the individual relies solely on supplementary benefit payable at the lower scale rate for the unemployed. In this survey, benefit is measured at its maximum.
4. Those gaining no job during the year allocated 365 days.
5. Letter to the authors from DMS, 15 February 1982.

6. The Role of Women in the Northern Ireland Economy

J. M. Trewsdale

Since the end of the second world war the structure of industry in Northern Ireland has changed in a way unequalled since the Industrial Revolution of the nineteenth century. The change has been a reflection as well as a consequence of the structural shift of industry in Great Britain and the industrial world. The heavy engineering industries such as shipbuilding and the traditional textile industries such as linen have diminished in importance by comparison with the man-made fibres and service industries. This change of emphasis has affected the whole labour force, both male and female; however, the repercussions in the female labour market have been particularly noticeable.

Female participation rates in the Province's labour force have traditionally been lower than those of other regions in the United Kingdom or the United States due to the strong social and religious influences which maintain that 'a woman's place is in the home'. Although the actual number of women employed in Northern Ireland did increase during the 1960s and 1970s the participation rate has remained at around 40 per cent, compared to figures of 45 per cent and more for the United Kingdom as a whole.

The increase in the total number of female employees in the Province over the past two decades masks a substantial movement away from full-time into part-time employment. In 1971 19 per cent of the female labour force was officially classified as part-time,[1] by 1978 the proportion had risen to 32 per cent. There are now, however, signs that the economic recession of the early 1980s has resulted in a slight decrease in the numbers of females employed part-time. This does not detract from the fact that during the 1970s the increase in the total numbers of employees in employment (male and female) in Northern Ireland was due solely to the increase in the female part-time labour force.

In common with working females in the rest of the western world, the majority of female employees in Northern Ireland are to be found working in poorer paid industries and employed in low status occupations. Differences however do exist and, as with many such national differences, the origin lies in part in the traditional religious and social structure of the Province. A simple example is the entry or rather re-entry to the labour force of married women after the age of 35. In both Great Britain and the United States the participation rates for all women aged 35–49 have been higher than those in the 20–24 group for the past twenty years. In Northern Ireland this development has not taken place. The married Northern Ireland female shows a much greater propensity to leave the labour force permanently on the birth of her first or second child, than her contemporaries in Great Britain and the United States (Hakim, 1979).

It is against this backdrop that the role of women in the Northern Ireland economy will be considered. The main data source for information on religion is the Census of Population (NI) 1971, the latest and most comprehensive analysis available. This involves a problem in that the data refer only to one day in 1971 and that there are no other data points of comparable accuracy with which they can be compared.

The aim of this chapter is to attempt an analysis of the religious breakdown of the female labour force in Northern Ireland. To this end only data referring to females have been used and the broad distinction between Roman Catholics and non-Roman Catholics[2] has been made. Hence, as the data are primarily given in percentages, where it is appropriate only the Roman Catholic figure is presented. The hypothesis which is being examined is that any significant difference which can be found in the employment of Roman Catholic and non-Roman Catholic women in the Northern Ireland economy (1971) can be attributed to the geographical distribution of the population and to social practice rather than directly to any form of religious discrimination.

The Standard Industrial Classification (SIC) 1968 contains tweny-seven industrial orders which in their turn are broken down into over two hundred sub-sections. The Classification of Occupations 1970 is of similar magnitude. To simplify the analysis only those industrial and occupational orders which relate directly to females are considered. For example, the industrial breakdown of the 1971 Census of Population (NI) data showed that 75 per cent of all female employees were to be found in only five of the twenty-seven industrial orders. They were in descending order of numbers employed: Professional and Scientific Services, Distributive Trades, Miscellaneous Services, Clothing and Footwear, and finally Textiles. Information collected by the Department of Manpower Services suggests that by June 1980 the overall percentage had not changed but Distributive Trades had moved into third place behind Miscellaneous Services. Thus the industrial pattern of female employment had remained fairly static, despite the changes in the relative importance of certain industries.

The occupations in which the majority of females work and within which women often form the majority of workers are: assemblers, leather workers, textile workers, clothing workers, clerical workers, shop assistants, service, sport and recreation workers. Table 6:1 presents a detailed breakdown of the proportion of female workers in each occupation, and the proportion of the female workers who were Roman Catholics. The data which are presented in table 6:1 confirm the proposition made earlier that the actual jobs women carry out within a given industry were of the semi-skilled and unskilled manual type. There were only three

Table 6:1

OCCUPATIONS OF FEMALES BY RELIGION, NORTHERN IRELAND 1971

Order	*Females in order %*	*Roman Catholic females in order %*
Assemblers (electronic and electrical)	79	28
Leather workers	55	40
Textile workers	52	29
Spinners, doublers	45	37
Winders, reelers	79	27
Weavers	59	28
Clothing workers	89	43
Hand and machine sewers	97	44
Food, drink and tobacco workers	34	24
Telephone operators	82	24
Clerical workers	69	22
Shop salesmen and assistants	74	26
Service, sport and recreation	66	32
Administrators and managers	7	16
Professional, technical	45	37
Nurses	90	43
Primary and secondary school teachers	63	38
Social welfare and related	64	22
Females in labour force	35	
RC females in female labour force	30	

Source: Census of Population (NI) 1971

occupations which are classed as 'professional' in which women were in the majority: nursing (90 per cent), primary and secondary school teaching (65 per cent), social welfare and related services (64 per cent). These three groups taken together accounted for less than fifteen per cent of all female employees in 1971. A fact which is worth noting at this stage and which will be discussed in detail later in the chapter was the high proportion of Roman Catholic females in both the teaching and nursing professions.

Having established the type of industries and occupations in which the majority of women worked in 1971 we can now move on to consider the role played by religion in the female labour market. In 1971 the potential female labour force were those women in the population aged 15–59;[3] of those women 33 per cent stated they were Roman Catholic. Of those females actually in employment in 1971, 30 per cent stated they were Roman Catholic. This three percentage point difference between the potential supply and the actual demand for Roman Catholic female labour can be explained by the substantial difference in the participation rates of Roman Catholic married women compared to their non-Catholic counterparts. This point is discussed in detail later in this chapter. The overall aggregate supply and demand proportions in the two religious categories were not significantly different in 1971. As can be seen from table 6:2, however, there were significant differences in the representation of the two groups in particular industrial orders. Industries such as Leather, Leather Goods and Fur, Clothing and Footwear, Professional and Scientific Services and Miscellaneous Services had an above average proportion of Roman Catholics while others were well below the overall average of 30 per cent. What then is the explanation of these differences? Why should nearly half the female workers in Clothing and Footwear be Roman Catholic compared with only 18 per cent of those in Insurance and Banking?

Neither the supply side nor the demand side of the female labour market is perfectly mobile. The average female worker is probably even less free than the average male worker to move or travel long distances in search of work. Her home environment and relative economic position frequently force her to seek work close to home. In 1971 approximately half the female labour force of Northern Ireland was married and in the majority of cases it would have been the husband's place of employment which determined the geographical area in which the wife would seek work. Single women,

Table 6:2

FEMALE EMPLOYEES IN EMPLOYMENT BY STANDARD INDUSTRIAL CLASSIFICATION, NORTHERN IRELAND 1971

SIC Order	*Total*	*Percentage of Roman Catholics*
Manufacturing		
Agriculture	2,235	21
Mining	83	23
Food, drink and tobacco	9,105	21
Coal and Petroleum products	17	—
Chemicals and allied industries	302	17
Metal manufacture	52	17
Mechanical engineering	1,545	11
Instrument engineering	787	22
Electrical engineering	5,634	22
Shipbuilding	306	5
Vehicles	933	10
Metal goods	825	21
Textiles	17,714	26
Leather goods	251	46
Clothing and footwear	21,538	46
Bricks, pottery, glass etc.	485	35
Timber, furniture etc.	518	18
Paper, printing, publishing	2,279	16
Other Manufacturing industries	1,530	27
Construction	1,820	22
Services		
Gas, electricity and water	846	15
Transport and communication	3,507	25
Distributive trades	31,750	32
Insurance, banking etc.	5,544	18
Professional and Scientific	47,184	34
Miscellaneous services	24,514	34
Public admin. and defence	9,423	25
TOTAL	190,994	30

Source: Census of Population (NI) 1971.

although in theory more mobile, are more inclined to live in the parental home until marriage or death than their counterparts in Great Britain or the United States.

The other side of the equation can be regarded as being equally immobile in that manufacturing industries in particular tend to be located in relatively large units in specific geographical areas. In Northern Ireland, as elsewhere, the location of an industrial unit is the result of many varied and complex decisions; those decisions will not be analysed in this chapter.

Although Roman Catholics account for approximately one third of the population of Northern Ireland their distribution across the Province is not uniform. The traditional geographical dividing line is the River Bann. Roman Catholics tend to be in the majority to the west of the river although there are some areas east of the Bann which are predominantly Roman Catholic, e.g. West Belfast. This historic distribution of the religious denominations in the Province has been well documented (Compton, 1978) and, when combined with the known geographical location of certain key industries, results in an important insight into the few religious differences in female employment which existed in 1971.

In order to simplify the analysis the District Councils as listed in the Census of Population (NI) 1971 have been grouped into the thirteen Travel-to-Work-Areas as defined and used by the Department of Manpower Services (NI) (see figure 6:1). The two sets of

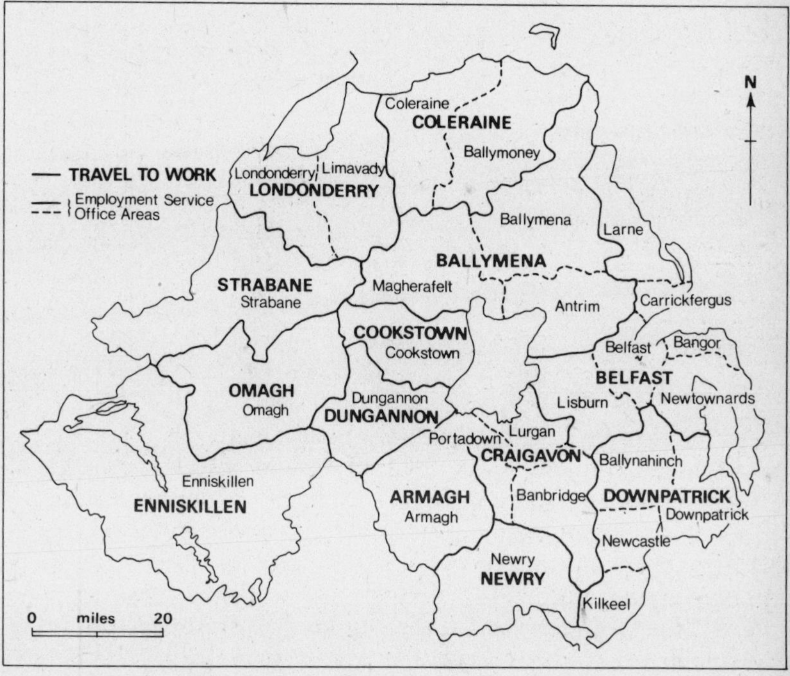

Figure 6:1 D.M.S. travel to work areas and employment service office areas.

administrative boundaries were devised for different reasons; one mainly social, the other economic. They are not completely geographically compatible: the population is allocated to district councils by domestic residence, the Travel-to-Work-Areas are local labour markets defined as being areas within which the vast majority (on average 93%) of the residents work. The two do not fit together exactly; however, any overlaps or omissions which do exist are relatively small and allowances have been made in the calculations. The results of the analysis are set out in table 6:3,

Table 6:3

PROPORTION OF ROMAN CATHOLIC FEMALES AND WORKERS BY TRAVEL-TO-WORK-AREAS, NORTHERN IRELAND 1971

	Female Roman Catholics as % of female population aged 15–59 years	*Female Roman Catholic employees in employment as % of all female employees in employment*
I *East of the River Bann*		
Ballymena	23.3	25.3
Belfast	23.4	21.0
Coleraine	27.0	23.2
Craigavon	31.7	28.3
Downpatrick	51.2	45.0
II *West of the River Bann*		
Armagh	41.4	45.0
Cookstown	44.3	41.0
Dungannon	45.7	43.8
Enniskillen	50.3	46.6
Londonderry	59.0	58.2
Newry	69.7	75.7
Omagh	57.7	57.6
Strabane	54.3	56.0

Source: Census of Population (NI) 1971.

where the proportion of Roman Catholic females of working age (15–59) in the population is compared with the actual proportion of Roman Catholic female employees for each of the thirteen areas.

Two things stand out clearly from the data. First, there was the wide variation in the proportion of Roman Catholics in the potential female labour force which as one would have expected reflected the variations in the distribution of all Roman Catholics throughout the thirteen areas, the two extremes being the Belfast and contiguous Ballymena area which recorded 23 per cent and Newry which reached nearly 70 per cent.

Second, and of particular relevance in the context of alleged discrimination, there was a very close correspondence between the proportion of Roman Catholics in the potential labour force and the proportion of Roman Catholic females in employment in the various Travel-to-Work-Areas. Only in Downpatrick and Newry was there any substantial divergence between the two proportions; in Downpatrick the proportion of Roman Catholics in employment was 6 percentage points below the proportion in the potential labour force; in Newry the reverse was the case.

In the other areas, the employment of female Roman Catholics matched closely what might have been expected from the population structure. There was no evidence from the geographical data that any significant difference existed between Roman Catholic and non-Roman Catholic females in terms of overall opportunities for employment.

If employment opportunities are equal, the next question which must be asked is whether there are any differences in the type of job carried out by the females from the two main religious groupings in the Province? From table 6:2 only those industries which employed more than 2,000 females (more than one per cent of the total female work force) and which also employed a percentage of Roman Catholics which deviated markedly from the 30 per cent average will be analysed in detail.

Of the traditional manufacturing industries 'clothing and footwear' was the main employer of women in 1971 employing over 11 per cent of all female employees in employment in the Province. Of those employed nearly half were Roman Catholic. A detailed breakdown of the industry showed that 'overalls and men's shirts' centred on Londonderry, Belfast and Ballymena; 'millinery' centred on Cookstown and the dress industry (not elsewhere specified) also centred on Cookstown: each recorded a percentage of Roman Catholic female employees at least thirteen percentage points higher than the figure for the whole area. Hence in the industry which employed more women than any other, Roman Catholic females were over represented, even after having made allowances for the differences in the geographical location of the Roman Catholic population.

In contrast the 'textile' industry, which employed just under 10 per cent of all female employees in 1971 had a distinct bias towards non-Roman Catholic employees, with only 26 per cent of its female work force classified as Roman Catholic. However, within this industry there were only five sub-groups which differed significantly from the working population average. The only category in which a greater proportion of Roman Catholics were employed was 'hosiery and other knitted goods'. The difference can be attributed to the geographical location of the main centre of this sub-group, namely Strabane, where 56 per cent of all female employees were Roman Catholic. The two groups which fell well below the average for the Province were 'carpets' and 'textile finishing' with only just over 11 per cent in each. The main areas of carpet production in 1971 were Craigavon and Belfast, predominantly Protestant towns. The 'production of man-made fibres' and 'weaving of cotton, linen and man-made fibres' make up the five groups, with 23 per cent in each.

The production of man-made fibres was centred on Carrickfergus and Antrim and, as a result, over three-quarters of the female workers in this industry were included in the Belfast and Ballymena Travel-to-Work-Areas. The proportion of Roman Catholic female workers in the man-made fibre industry in the Ballymena area was close to the proportion for that whole area. In Belfast it was nine percentage points lower than the percentage for the area as a whole. The sub-area of Carrickfergus, however, had a proportion of 14 per cent Roman Catholic women in the local workforce, which was closer to the Belfast figure for the production of man-made fibres.

This part of the analysis has been overtaken by events. The man-made fibre industry in Northern Ireland has since collapsed and as a result the total number of females working in the textile industry had fallen by 41 per cent by June 1980. Since June 1980 there have been further closures announced, e.g. I.C.I. and Courtaulds in Carrickfergus. The argument that the man-made fibre industry was predominantly non-Catholic, albeit due to geographical location, is no longer valid. The same is also true of the closely related 'weaving of cotton, linen and man-made fibres', with its traditional centres of Belfast, Ballymena, Craigavon and to a lesser extent Armagh.

The third largest employer of females in the manufacturing sector was the 'food, drink and tobacco' industry. Of the nine thousand females employed in this industry in 1971, just over one half were involved in the production of tobacco. The vast majority of those employees were to be found in the County Borough of Belfast and in the Ballymena Rural District Council area. The two tobacco firms of Gallahers in Belfast and Ballymena, and Carreras in Carrickfergus, made up the tobacco industry in Northern Ireland. The siting of the firms and the tendency for females to work close to their homes would have accounted for the low proportion of Roman Catholics in the industry. Ballymena Rural District Council had, for example, only 16 per cent of its potential work force classified as Roman Catholic; Carrickfergus 14 per cent. The four thousand female employees in the tobacco industry not so far accounted for were to be found in the Belfast area which had an overall average of 21 per cent.

Thus, what at first sight seemed a fairly substantial difference of nine percentage points below the Northern Ireland average of 30 per cent can be attributed to the geographical location of three large factories.

Of the other half of the industry (food and drink) over two thousand were employed in Belfast within the sub groups 'bread and flour confectionery', 'bacon curing', 'animal feedstuffs' and 'milk products'. As with the other geographical areas the proportion of Roman Catholics was in line with the area average.

Of the females employed in the electrical engineering industry in 1971, 22 per cent were Roman Catholic. However, nearly three-quarters of all the female employees in the industry were to be found in Belfast where 21 per cent of all the female work force were Roman Catholic. Within this sector only 5 per cent of the females assembling 'electronic computers' and 17 per cent of those manufacturing 'telegraph and telephone apparatus and equipment' in Belfast were Roman Catholic. As was the case with the tobacco industry the manufacture of computer equipment was centred in an area of small Roman Catholic population. Thus the 5 per cent employment figure should be viewed in the context of a potential Roman Catholic female labour force of only 9 per cent. By exactly the same argument the 17 per cent involved in the manufacture of telegraph and telephone equipment should be compared with the 15 per cent potential Roman Catholic female labour force which was to be found in Newtownabbey. The only other area where any sizeable number of females were employed in this sub-category was Enniskillen. In that area 43 per cent of the females employed in the telegraph and telephone industry were Roman Catholic compared to an average of 47 per cent for the work force in that area.

The only remaining manufacturing industry which had more than two thousand workers and which employed less than the overall average of Roman Catholics was 'paper, printing and publishing'. Of the 2,279 workers in this industry over 1,700 were located in Belfast and of those the majority were to be found in 'packaging products' and 'other printing, publishing etc.'. The first sub-group employed 21 per cent female Roman Catholic labour, the average for Belfast. However, 'other printing etc.' employed only 10 per cent. Printing and publishing like tobacco production and the computer industry is controlled by two or three firms where traditional methods of recruitment by word of mouth and family contacts tend to perpetuate any imbalance which might exist (see chapter 8).

In 1971 the 'services' sector of the economy employed 64 per cent of all female employees in the seven categories listed in table 6:2. Of those categories only one, 'gas, electricity and water', employed less than two thousand people. Of the remaining six, three industries employed an above average number of Roman Catholics, three a below average.

The traditional service industry known as 'distributive trades' covers all aspects of wholesale and retail distribution and in 1971 employed 16 per cent of all female employees. The proportion of Roman Catholic females was just two percentage points above the average for the Province. A detailed analysis of the geographical distribution of the workers showed that no areas existed where the proportion of Roman Catholics employed was statistically different from the average for that area. Similarly within the industry there was no sub-group where the difference was worth noting. This should come as no surprise; service industries by their very nature involve relatively small units spread across the Province following closely the main centres of population. Distributive trades is a classic service industry and was the one industry of all 27 which was the closest to the overall average of 30 per cent for Roman Catholic female workers.

The industry which employed the largest number of females was the 'professional and scientific' industry, employing as it did in 1971 one quarter of all female employees in employment. This industry includes educational services, medical and dental services, religious organisations and research and development services. It has already been established that the majority of employees in nursing and teaching were women, and therefore it follows that this industry should have employed the largest single proportion of females in the economy. As with Distributive Trades, it is an industry which is spread throughout the Province according to the same pattern as the geographical location of the centres of population. It does, however, have an above average proportion of female Roman

Catholics, namely 34 per cent. If geographical location cannot go some way to explain the difference, what is the explanation?

The two major components of female employment within the industry are 'maintained primary and secondary schools' and 'hospital and consultant service'; in 1971 these two sub-groups accounted for over 70 per cent of the females employed. Within these two groups the proportion of Roman Catholics was 35 and 37 per cent respectively.

The educational system in Northern Ireland at primary and secondary school level is made up of two main sectors; the state schools, similar to those found in the rest of the United Kingdom, to which children of any religious affiliation may go, and the Roman Catholic schools run by the Church but which are state supported and attended by Roman Catholic children. It is a natural corollary to this that for all practical purposes the teaching staff in the Roman Catholic schools are themselves Roman Catholic. With this form of segregation built into the educational system by the Church the demand for Roman Catholic teachers is naturally held high and is accentuated by the relatively high number of Roman Catholic children of school age. Hence in each of the Travel-to-Work-Areas, except Londonderry and Strabane, the proportion of Roman Catholic females in those groups was above the average for that area, and even in those two areas the difference, although below the average, was not statistically significant.

As with schooling, the hospital and dental service industry is distributed throughout the Province according to the centres of population, with all the areas but Londonderry and Strabane having returned a proportion of Roman Catholic female employees above the average for the area. The explanation of this difference again lies in the concept of medical and dental care for the community by members of that community. There is, however, no inbuilt segregation by the Roman Catholic Church as in the case of education; the distinction is one of social and traditional habit which have developed over the years and is in no way peculiar to Northern Ireland.

An occupational breakdown of the medical and related category showed that although women accounted for three quarters of the employees the majority of them (88 per cent) were classified as nurses and only just over 3 per cent were medical practitioners. Of the 12,500 females in the order 40 per cent were Roman Catholic, well above the average for the Province, but of those 93 per cent were nurses compared to 85 per cent of other denominations. Within the overall small number of female medical practitioners only 20 per cent were Roman Catholic. In all other categories except physiotherapists, the percentages were so small as to involve less than 50 people (Ditch and Osborne, 1980).

The difference which exists is due in part to the attitude to scientific education at school level of females in the Province. To enter medical school a high grade is required in the major science subjects. In common with many all girls' schools throughout the United Kingdom, opportunities in the science subjects were not up to the standard of those in mixed or boys' schools during the 1950s and 1960s. As the majority of Roman Catholic secondary schools in Northern Ireland are single sexed, in contrast to the high proportion of mixed state schools, the Roman Catholic school girl would have had fewer opportunities to study the necessary science subjects to enter the medical profession, other than at the lower levels (see chapter 7).

The third largest employer of women in 1971 was the 'catch all' category of 'miscellaneous services', accounting for 13 per cent of female employment; this had actually increased to 16 per cent by June 1980. The industries included are entertainment, hotels, restaurants, hairdressing, private domestic service, laundries etc., all areas where female employment has traditionally played an important role. As with other service industries so far covered, Roman Catholic females were represented in a proportion which was slightly above the average for the Province. The explanation lies partly in the wide and diverse nature of this category and the broad geographical distribution of the sub-industries.

The remaining three service industries between them accounted for 20 per cent of female employment in 1971. Transport and communication was the smallest of the three with just under two per cent of all female employees of which one quarter were Roman Catholics. As with other service industries the pattern of employment tended to follow the population centres. The majority (64 per cent) worked in the Belfast area and of those workers exactly 21 per cent were Roman Catholics, exactly the same proportion as for the Belfast area. Within the remaining twelve Travel-to-Work-Areas no significant difference existed between numbers of Roman Catholics employed and those in the potential work force.

In 1971 Public Administration and Defence employed 5 per cent of all females in employment, of which one quarter were Roman

Catholics. As with Transport and Communication the main centre of Public Administration in the Province is the capital, Belfast, where 61 per cent of the females in this category were employed. Of those 6,000 women 22 per cent were Roman Catholic, one percentage point above the overall average for the area.

The two main sub-groups of the industry are 'all other government departments and establishments excluding armed forces and defence' and 'other local government services excluding police and fire service'. The first sub-group which employed the majority of females had a proportion of 29 per cent Roman Catholic women; of the majority centred on Belfast 24 per cent were Roman Catholic. There were no significant differences worth noting in any of the other Travel-to-Work-Areas. The second sub-group accounted for two thousand of the grand total of women in the industry, 19 per cent were Roman Catholic and in every Travel-to-Work-Area except Newry the percentage of Roman Catholics fell well below the average for that area. The residual which worked outside the Belfast area was so small that the problem of 'small numbers' makes the analysis statistically unsound: for example, in Strabane one additional Roman Catholic female employee would have increased the percentage by four points.

Finally in this industrial analysis of the female labour force we turn to 'insurance and banking', which as mentioned at the beginning of the chapter employed only 18 per cent Roman Catholic females. This figure was 12 percentage points below the average for the whole Province.

As would be expected, the centre of the Insurance and Banking industry is situated in Belfast and hence over 73 per cent of the female work force in this industry were employed in this area; of those 14 per cent were Roman Catholics. In all the other Travel-to-Work-Areas the proportion of Roman Catholic females fell well below the average for that particular area; Newry recorded the smallest difference, which was six percentage points.

Splitting the category into its two main components of 'Insurance' and 'Banking and Bill-discounting': within Belfast the Insurance sector employed only 11 per cent Roman Catholic females whereas the Banking sector employed 19 per cent, only two percentage points below the Belfast average of 21 per cent. Throughout the remaining twelve areas the Insurance sector was well below the average for that area, and although the Banking figures were also low, it was by a much smaller margin, in other words it was the

Insurance sector which was pulling the overall average down. Studies carried out since 1971 have shown that recruitment for the Insurance industry had traditionally been centred on a few state schools which had unwittingly perpetuated the bias towards non-Catholics. This practice has since been amended.

A conclusion to be drawn from the analysis to date is that, assuming one accepts the basic premise that the average female worker seeks work close to home, then differences in the proportions of the religious denominations employed within the industries discussed, be they in favour of or against Roman Catholics, can in the first instance be explained by the traditional demographic and industrial pattern of the Province. Traditional methods of recruitment through word of mouth by friends and family, methods which are to be found in any western industrial society, naturally play an important part (see chapter 8).

We return to the basic difference of three percentage points in the potential Roman Catholic female work force and the actual numbers employed in 1971.

In 1971, of all Roman Catholic females aged between 15 and 59, just over 60 per cent were married, widowed or divorced, and of those non-single women only 26 per cent were economically active (definition includes those seeking work as well as those in employment). The comparable figures for the other denominations were 72 per cent and 38 per cent respectively. Thus, although fewer of the potential work force of Roman Catholic women were married, nearly half as many again of non-Catholic married women considered themselves available for employment. These two simple 'participation rates' for married women had a significant effect on the pool of women from which employers were able to recruit their labour force.

One of the main factors affecting the economic activity of married women is the number and age of any children she may have and this in itself is closely allied to the religious affiliation of the mother. Historically Northern Ireland has always recorded the highest number of children per family of any region in the United Kingdom. This tendency towards larger families coupled with the tradition of older marriages results in the average female being approximately ten years older than her mainland counterpart when her family is completed. This in itself is a natural disincentive to return to the labour force.

Table 6:4 sets out the relevant data for 1971 and compares only

Table 6:4

ECONOMIC ACTIVITY BY RELIGION BY NUMBER OF CHILDREN AGED 16 OR UNDER FOR NON-SINGLE WOMEN, NORTHERN IRELAND 1971

	Roman Catholic	*Other Denominations*
	Economically Active	
Average number of children per female	2.4	1.5
	Economically Inactive	
Average number of children per female	3.1	1.9

Source: Census of Population (NI) 1971.

those women who could have been regarded as the potential labour force, i.e. those aged between 15 and 59.

Within each of the two economic categories the difference between the Roman Catholics and other denominations was approximately one child. However, the difference between the economically active and inactive Roman Catholic mother was 0.7 of a child compared with 0.4 for the other denominations. There can be little doubt that the larger the number of children a woman has to care for, the less likely she is to be able to work, especially in a society where there are strong social pressures on married women to stay at home. (In Northern Ireland until the early seventies a woman had to resign her post on marriage in the Civil Service and the Banking sector.) The most interesting information to emerge from these data was the different threshold at which mothers in the two religious communities take the positive decision to become economically inactive. The differing attitudes to family size and economic activity of married females is deeply rooted in the religious and social structure of the society in the Province and hence in itself has a very definite effect on the pattern of female employment.

The final section to be considered in this chapter is female unemployment. The study of female unemployment in Northern Ireland has always been hampered by the lack of reliable data (Trewsdale 1979, 1980). This problem is not unique to the Province nor indeed to the United Kingdom. The regulations concerning unemployment benefit are such that there is little if any financial incentive for the married woman to register. As a result she is lost to the official labour market statistics, which are based solely on the registered unemployed. The Census of Population figures for the female unemployed include the unregistered but unfortunately they also include the out of work sick, and hence cannot be compared directly with other official unemployment data, which deal only with the able-bodied seeking work.

The Census of Population data showed that in 1971 the overall female unemployment rate was 4.7 per cent and, of those females who were unemployed, 46 per cent were Roman Catholic. The denominational unemployment rates were 7 per cent for Roman Catholic women and 4 per cent for women of other denominations. The difference between the two female unemployment rates was less pronounced than that of the male equivalent in 1971. Osborne (1978) showed that the male rate was twice as high for Roman Catholics in all areas of Northern Ireland and discussed in detail a number of factors which may underpin the differences.

One of the reasons for the difference in the female rates is again based on the geographical distribution of the Roman Catholic female labour force. Areas east of the river Bann (table 6:3) where the proportion of Roman Catholic females was relatively low have traditionally experienced lower rates of total unemployment than those areas west of the Bann. In July 1981 when the overall registered unemployment rate for the Province was 18 per cent, Belfast recorded a figure of 15.3 per cent compared with 36 per cent for Strabane.

The female unemployment rate in an area will naturally reflect the lack of job opportunities in that area. There were however certain areas in the Province where females in general and Roman Catholic females in particular found it easier to get jobs than their male counterparts. The shirt-making firms of Londonderry employed a predominantly female labour force in an area where Roman Catholics were in the majority.

The lack of reliable comprehensive data results in any analysis of female unemployment being primarily hypothetical.

It is perhaps an interesting conclusion and a reflection of the attitudes which prevailed in the Province until quite recently that any detailed analysis which has been carried out on the labour force in Northern Ireland had been exclusively concerned with men. It is only in the past few years that the female labour force has been studied in any detail. It is true that the female participation rate had never equalled that of the rest of the United Kingdom, but with the shift towards part-time employment women are making increased inroads into the economy of Northern Ireland.

Differences which did exist in the female labour market of Northern Ireland in 1971 could be attributed to sex rather than religion. Apart from a small minority of teachers and medical personnel the average working female was, and indeed still is, in a low-paid unskilled or semi-skilled occupation. This description applied to women as women regardless of whether they were Roman Catholic or members of any other religious denomination in Northern Ireland.

Notes

1. The Department of Manpower Services (NI) defines part-time employment as 30 hours or less per week.
2. All data quoted on religion in this chapter have been calculated *excluding* the 'not stated' category. This category accounted for 9 per cent of the total population and was considered by Aunger (1975) and others to be distributed evenly across all denominations.
3. In 1971 the statutory school leaving age was 15 and the female retirement age 60. In 1972 the school leaving age was raised to 16.

7. Educational Qualifications and Religious Affiliation

R. C. Murray and R. D. Osborne

The possession of certain educational qualifications, usually obtained in secondary schools, is a precondition for entry to an increasing number and range of better rewarded and higher-status occupations and to further education, which in turn is necessary for access to other occupations. Even where qualifications are not mandatory it is likely that people with them will find it easier to get better jobs than those without. If, then, it is felt to be important, for whatever ideological or other reasons, that equality of opportunity of access to the more-favoured occupations and positions in society should prevail amongst different social groups it is necessary, at the very least, that children's chances of leaving school suitably qualified should not be related to social characteristics such as race, class, sex or religion. Researchers have demonstrated, however, that this is not what happens. Girls, children from working class homes, and children of ethnic minorities, for example, all have a significantly lower chance of leaving school with good formal qualifications. Similarly, women, people from working class backgrounds, and members of ethnic minorities are significantly under-represented amongst the better-rewarded and higher-status occupations.

It has long been asserted, at least by Catholics, that in Northern Ireland there has been and still is a marked under-representation of Catholics not only in higher-status occupations but also in whole sectors of employment, and that this is the result of discriminatory policies by Protestant employers. Unfortunately this subject has shared in the general lack of critical social research in Northern Ireland in the past, a problem exacerbated by the absence of any tabulations of employment measures by denomination from census reports prior to those for the 1971 population census. Thus, until recently, there has been no systematic and extensive appraisal of Catholic and Protestant occupational patterns. The few studies that were undertaken (Boehringer, 1971; Barritt and Carter, 1962;

Campaign for Social Justice, 1969; Donnison, 1973) were confined mainly to limited areas of the public and private sectors. It was only with the availablity of information from the 1971 population census that detailed analyses were undertaken, first by Aunger (1975) (see chapter 2) and then by the Fair Employment Agency for Northern Ireland (1978).

These two studies looked at the relative proportions of Catholics and Protestants in the different fields of employment, at the distribution of Catholics and Protestants across the different occupations within the construction and engineering industries, and at the social class composition of the Catholic and Protestant occupations. Their findings were summarised in the Fair Employment Agency (1978:14) report thus:

> The industrial profiling of Protestants and Roman Catholics demonstrates major areas of Roman Catholic under-representation, most notably Engineering, the Utilities and Insurance, Banking, Finance and Business Services and the unhealthy over-dependence of Roman Catholic males on the Construction Industry (which is particularly prone to high levels of unemployment). Extending the industrial profile to consider wages it was observed that there was a tendency for those industries which had the highest weekly manual wage in 1971 to be predominantly Protestant, a tendency which was more marked for women.
>
> The occupational profile of Protestants and Roman Catholics revealed a distribution of Roman Catholics towards the unskilled occupations. The modal Protestant male is a skilled manual worker whereas the modal Roman Catholic male is unskilled. When occupations were matched with industry, which was only possible for construction and engineering, there was a tendency in construction for Roman Catholics to be employed in lower status occupations while in engineering, a higher status industry, there was a general under-representation of Roman Catholics in most occupations, particularly marked at managerial level.
>
> Overall, a Roman Catholic middle class exists. Its size (which is proportionately smaller than the Protestant), however, seems to be largely a product of meeting the demands of a segregated society rather than through performing a more general role as does the Protestant middle class.

One interpretation of these findings is that they reflect the operation of widespread discrimination in both the public and private sectors with predominantly Protestant employers giving preference to Protestants for the better jobs. Another hypothesis that has been advanced, however, (mainly as a complementary explanation rather than as an alternative to the discrimination argument) is that these patterns relate to differences in levels of education. The sectors of the economy in which Catholics are especially under-represented (including Public Administration, which was not mentioned in the Fair Employment Agency summary) are those which generally require a minimum standard of formal qualifications above the average level, or qualifications of a specialized nature, or both. If Catholics tend to have lower levels of educational attainment or lack qualifications in certain areas then this may contribute, in some degree, to the patterns of employment observed in the 1971 census.

An obvious starting point for a test of this hypothesis is an examination of the patterns of educational levels revealed by the same 1971 census. Amongst the tables published in the census reports is one on persons with 'A' level qualifications (the highest school examination) or their equivalent and those with higher qualifications; these are disaggregated by sex and denomination for all persons aged 18–69. From this table we have extracted the information presented in tables 7:1 and 7:2.[1]

These tables indicate that Catholics are probably slightly under-represented amongst persons with these levels of qualifications but the pattern is not a straightforward one because of sex differences. Amongst the 'A' level group the Catholic shortfall is entirely due to the low proportion for women whereas in the higher qualifications group it is due to the low proportion for men; if anything, Catholic women appear to be over-represented in the latter group. On the whole, however, since males predominate in the employed population these figures tend to support rather than contradict the hypothesis that Catholic under-representation in certain occupations is in part attributable to their under-representation amongst that section of the population who are suitably qualified.

For those persons with higher qualifications the census also provides information on the general subject area in which they were obtained and tables 7:3 and 7:4 summarize those data. They demonstrate, very markedly for males, the degree to which Protestants are over-represented amongst those qualified in science and technology; in the latter area there are more than seven Protestants for every Catholic with the appropriate qualifications. The figures essentially reinforce the conclusion of Aunger (1975) and the Fair Employment Agency (1978) that middle-class Catholics tend to be concentrated in occupations—notably education and health—that service their co-religionists, whereas middle-class Protestants are more widely spread across the range of occupations. One study undertaken also of the adult male population has been reported by Boyle (1977).

Boyle's study, based on a postal questionnaire (response rate of 59.3 per cent) administered to males aged 17–63, was designed to examine the factors influencing educational attainment and subsequent occupational achievement with particular reference to religion. Boyle (1977: 99) concluded that 'while Catholics suffer no educational disadvantage as such, they are nevertheless caught in a cycle in which lower occupational status leads to lower educational attainment which leads to lower occupational status and so on'. While these comments should be borne in mind it should be noted that Boyle's study related to adult males and not to the current output of the education systems.

If we are concerned with the issue of recruitment to occupations and in particular with the role of education in that process then the census figures, interesting though they may be, have two shortcomings which render them inadequate for our purposes. First, the people who make up these tables represent only a residue; we have no information on those people who were educated in Northern Ireland but who have subsequently left the province. If better-qualified Catholics have found it more difficult than Protestants to obtain employment commensurate with their talents within Northern Ireland, they may well have migrated in disproportionately high numbers. Alternatively, a general lack of opportunities for well-qualified people in the Province, due to its peripheral position and relative economic under-development, may have initiated high levels of emigration of both Protestants and Catholics.

Secondly, many of the qualifications covered in the two categories of these tables are obtained not at school or even in full-time higher education but in the course of employment, through either on-the-job training or various sandwich courses. This applies particularly to technological qualifications which are usually attained in the course of apprenticeships in the engineering and similar industries; such qualifications may be equivalent to 'A' levels or to higher qualifications. A similar opportunity to acquire further qualifications of a specialised, vocational nature exists in many white-collar occupations. Thus the patterns revealed in the census tables are not only a possible *cause* of employment patterns but also an *effect* of them. For example, the low proportion of Catholic males with technological qualifications may be attributable in part to their lack of success in gaining apprenticeships, regardless of their qualifications at the time of applying.

If, then, we wish to test the hypothesis that the over-representation of Protestants in certain occupations and strata is partly attributable to differences between Protestants and Catholics in the quantity or quality of their educational qualifications then it would seem better to look at the qualifications of school-leavers rather than adults. This would avoid the two problems with the census data discussed above. It would enable us to assess how well-equipped Catholic and Protestant pupils are to enter various occupations or to proceed to some form of higher education.

Although of necessity there is some blurring of division in a few rural areas, there exist *de facto* in Northern Ireland two separate educational systems at both the primary and secondary levels. The state ('controlled') system is attended by Protestants, with a number of voluntary grammar schools also attended predominantly by Protestants. Catholics attend schools which have varying management structures and financial support, but which are all voluntary (as opposed to state controlled and financed). Voluntary schools receive differing levels of state grants for recurrent and capital expenditure. Those voluntary schools having 'maintained' status receive one hundred per cent grants for recurrent costs and eighty-five per cent of capital costs on building and alterations. Voluntary grammar schools (both Protestant and Catholic) receive varying levels of grants for current and capital costs, from fifty per cent upwards. Remaining costs for all categories of voluntary schools must be met from church and community resources. This bipartite system long predates the present constitutional arrangements in Ireland. The first Education Act passed by the new Northern Ireland parliament in 1923 attempted to replace church schools of whatever denomination with a single, unified system in which there would be no denominational slant in organization, administration, staffing, or curriculum. The Act, however, was vehemently rejected by all churches, Protestant and Catholic, and was soon replaced by another which provided for denominational education, with religious instruction in schools, church representatives on the management committees of schools in both systems, and the effective selection of teachers on religious grounds (Akenson, 1973). This pattern still largely prevails today.

Any organised education system has a variety of obvious and not-so-obvious effects, some intended and others incidental, on the children who pass through it. The controversy over the attempted secularization of schools in Northern Ireland arose because the churches believed that the schools should deliberately attempt to instil certain religious values and convictions through the curriculum. Most of the unease that has been engendered by the presence of the two education systems arises from the fear that this perpetuates and even strengthens the wider social and political divisions within the Province. This may come about not just through differences in the teaching of subjects such as history but as a result of the whole environment of the school.

Most of the research on education in Northern Ireland, particularly since 1969, has reflected this anxiety and has looked at differences between the two systems in the contents of their curricula and in the attitudes and values held by their pupils. Some concern has also been expressed about the possibility of differences in educational standards. The different methods of funding the two systems may result in lower standards of provision in the Catholic system, such as larger classes or fewer grammar school places, which may be reflected, in turn, in lower overall levels of educational achievement amongst their pupils. This issue, however, has attracted very little attention from researchers.

Darby (1976:132), for example, concluded that 'no evidence substantiates the occasionally expressed view that Catholic schools are academically less successful than state'. However, the evidence he was able to advance in support of this statement, while consistent, was extremely limited: an observation by Kennedy (1970) that Catholics win a disproportionate share of scholarships at Queen's University, Belfast, and an undergraduate dissertation (Graham, 1962) which surveyed grammar school pupils and found no significant differences in educational performance between Protestants and Catholics.

It must be emphasised at the outset that the research reported below is concerned not with differences between Protestant and Roman Catholic pupils but with differences between pupils attending state and voluntary schools. The distinction is necessary because although our data relate to individuals we have no information on the particular religious affiliation of any individual; all we know is their sex, the type of school they attended, and the school system to which it belongs. It is known that a small number of pupils attend the 'wrong' school (usually because there is no school of the appropriate system sufficiently near their home) but neither ourselves nor any other researchers can specify, for Northern Ireland as a whole, the likely numbers that are involved or have been involved at specific points in the past. It is accepted however that for all *practical* purposes differences between the two systems constitute valid measures of the differences between Protestants and Catholics.

The measures of educational attainment that we have used are passes in the 'O' (Ordinary) level and 'A' (Advanced) level examinations of the General Certificate of Education (GCE). These examinations, which are usually taken at the ages of 16 and 18 respectively, are the standard recognised examinations within Northern Ireland as well as England and Wales (Scotland has its own system). They comprise separate papers in each subject, for example, English Language, Mathematics, Physics, Religious Education, etc, and an individual pupil may sit for one paper or several. The examinations are organized by a number of separate Boards and it is up to each school to choose for which Board's examinations it will enter its pupils. In Northern Ireland the great majority of pupils in both the state and voluntary systems are entered for the papers set by the Northern Ireland Board but there are also those who gain their passes from other Boards; this practice has created certain problems for our research, but we discuss these at the appropriate point in our analysis. In recent years another examination, the Certificate of Secondary Education (CSE) has been gaining ground. This is of a lower standard than the GCE 'O' level and was introduced so that the less academically-able pupils might nevertheless have the opportunity of leaving school with some formal qualification. As will be seen, however, this had made little impact in Northern Ireland in the period we have examined and it is not considered in any detail in this study.

For this study of differences in educational attainment between the two school systems we have analysed two separate aspects of the examination passes. First, the quantity of passes at each level expressed as a percentage of pupils within each system who achieve a specified number of passes; for example, we have looked at the proportion with two, and three or more 'A' levels as these are the minimum standards for higher education admission. Entry to certain occupations and higher education courses, however, requires not only that the individual possesses a certain number of passes but also that these include passes in specified subjects. It may be that pupils from the two systems have the same quantity of passes but differ in the subjects in which these are obtained. It has been suggested, for example, that pupils from the state system are more likely to have passes in the science subjects and that this may be a factor in the over-representation of Protestants in engineering occupations. The second dimension we examined, therefore, was the proportion in each system with passes in each subject.

In order to test our hypothesis that there will be differences between the two systems in one or both of these indicators of educational attainment it is sufficient to simply look at the overall proportions for each system. If we wish, however, to consider possible explanations for any differences we find or to examine other aspects of educational inequality then it will be useful to introduce two additional factors. One is the type of schooling. Both systems in Northern Ireland, unlike most areas of the United Kingdom, still maintain two types of secondary school: grammar schools, which are intended to provide an academic education for the more able pupils, and secondary schools which are supposed to cater for the remainder, who are generally regarded as not capable of passing GCE examinations. (There are a very few 'comprehensive' schools which combine both features; for simplicity these have been classified as secondary for the purposes of this study.) Pupils are assigned to one type of school or the other mainly on the basis of tests at the end of primary school, although many grammar schools will admit a proportion of pupils who fail these tests if their parents pay their fees; overall, the pupils in grammar schools tend to come from middle-class homes, those in secondary schools from working-class homes. This distinction between grammar and secondary schools is important because in general the former have curricula which prepare their pupils for the GCE examinations; a growing number of secondary schools now do this but still only on a small scale. Pupils in grammar schools, therefore, have a considerably greater opportunity of obtaining the type of qualifications with which we are concerned here. The difference between the two types of school is reinforced when we consider 'A' levels as, in order to sit these examinations, pupils usually need to stay on at school beyond the statutory minimum leaving age of 16; they also require a higher standard of teaching. In both respects the differential between the two types of school is more marked than for the 'O' level examinations. If the two school systems differ in ratio of grammar/

secondary places, or in the proportions staying on at school, we would expect a corresponding difference in the overall levels of educational attainment.

The other factor we have included in the analysis is that of sex. This may be particularly important in considering our second indicator, passes in specific subject areas, as research in Britain and the USA has shown that boys and girls tend to follow different curricula in some respects; in general, girls tend to be over-represented amongst pupils doing arts subjects and under-represented on the science side. As the value system of the Roman Catholic church is often supposed to foster a more traditional view of the female role, this stereotyping may be more marked in the voluntary schools. These same values may also lead to a higher proportion of girls in voluntary schools leaving at 16 rather than staying on at school to prepare themselves for higher education and a subsequent career, and this in turn would tend to lead to a lower proportion of 'A' level passes within the voluntary system.

There is one other factor, the most significant of all, that leads us to expect that there may be differences in levels of educational attainment between the two school systems and that is the social class composition of the two groups of pupils. We have already noted that the 1971 census demonstrates that among adults a higher proportion of Roman Catholics than Protestants are found within the working class. As Catholics tend to have larger families than Protestants, and working class couples generally have larger families than middle-class couples, this disparity will be even more marked among school-children. As the inverse relationship between social class and educational attainment has been thoroughly documented we would anticipate that on their social class backgrounds alone Roman Catholic children would not perform as well as Protestant children, regardless of any differences between the two school systems in terms of funding or organizations; indeed, such a difference in social class could be expected to lead to a weaker performance among Catholics even in a single integrated school system. Unfortunately, just as we have no information on the affiliation of individuals, we do not know the class backgrounds of pupils and thus cannot control systemically for this factor.

The output of the two systems was investigated with information on the qualifications of all pupils who left school in 1971 and 1975 with data derived from the Northern Ireland Department of Education and the Northern Ireland GCE Board.[2]

As students can obtain their final count of 'O' and 'A' level passes at more than one diet of examinations the figures for school leavers provide a better basis for comparing the two school systems than the alternative of looking at the results of one year's examinations. Moreover, this information covers all passes regardless of the Board by which they were awarded. Thus we have a complete profile of the pupils of the two systems at the time they are available for entry into employment or higher education. The relevant figures are presented in tables 7:5 and 7:6 disaggregated by sex of pupil and school system.

For the present we will confine our attention to a comparison between the overall proportions in the two school systems (table 7:5). This shows that in both years the pupils leaving the state system were slightly better qualified than those from the voluntary system; a higher proportion of the former had 'A' level passes, particularly with 3 or more 'A' levels, and a slightly higher proportion had 'O' levels, but not 'A' levels. Between 1971 and 1975 there was an overall increase in the proportion of pupils leaving school with formal qualifications, due mainly to the introduction of the CSE examinations. The relative position of the two systems shows a convergence—noticeable in terms of the proportion of leavers with 'A' levels and those without qualifications. Another way of examining these data is to look at the relative proportions of pupils from the two systems within the total pool of school leavers with specific qualifications; this indicates the probability of an individual with a given level of attainment being from one system compared to the other. The results in table 7:7 reinforce the suggestion that pupils from voluntary schools are under-represented in those with qualifications. The scale of this under-representation is not large, however, and it is clear that we are not dealing with a level of apparent under-attainment demonstrated by West Indian school leavers in Britain, or anything like it (Little, 1981).

These results, however, tend to confirm our first hypothesis: pupils leaving voluntary schools had a slightly lower level of educational attainment, in the years studied here, than those leaving state schools; the difference is mainly due to the higher proportion of state pupils with 'A' levels. This study was not designed to investigate possible causes of any differences that might be found, but an examination of the figures disaggregated by sex and by type of school, as well as pointing up the existence of other bases of inequality in educational attainment, suggests some reasons for the difference between the two educational systems. As expected the tables show that girls were less likely than boys to leave with 'A' level passes, although the difference was not marked, and more likely to have 'O' levels; this is in line with the situation in England and Wales where researchers have demonstrated that this pattern is mainly a result of fewer girls than boys staying on after the age of 16. Such differences as do exist between boys and girls are insignificant, however, by comparison with those between grammar and secondary school pupils. Regardless of whether they are boys or girls, in the voluntary system or the state system, pupils who are allocated to secondary schools have almost no chance of leaving school with any 'A' levels (the very small number who do manage this tend to attend the 'comprehensive' schools) and little chance of obtaining 'O' levels. Even the introduction of the CSE examinations was not sufficient to prevent the majority of secondary pupils leaving school without any formal qualifications at all (at least in 1975).

Earlier, in justifying the disaggregation by sex and by type of school, we argued that this could throw light on two possible features of the school systems that might contribute to any differences between them. One was the ratio of grammar school to secondary school places. The other was the extent to which girls sat for examinations. We have also referred to a third: the proportion of pupils who stay on at school beyond the age of 16; as the main difference between the two school systems is in the proportion leaving with 'A' levels, which are only sat for by older pupils, this is probably a key factor. These possibilities can be assessed by seeing what happens to the differences between the two school systems when we control for sex of pupil and type of school, separately and together. For example, if the two systems differ in the proportion of pupils who attend grammar schools, the differences in educational attainment should disappear when we hold the type of school constant, if school type is the critical factor rather than system.

Table 7:8 shows the figures for 1975, and indicates that this is the case for both boys and girls. The proportion of boys from voluntary grammar schools who leave with 'A' levels is virtually identical to the figure for boys from state grammar schools. Thus the higher overall proportion of leavers with 'A' levels amongst boys from state schools must arise because a higher proportion of them attend grammar schools, or stay on at them beyond the age of 16. The same observation can be made and the same argument applied in the case of the girls. Part of this conclusion is supported by the figures on the type of school attended by the leavers (table 7:9) and these show that for boys and girls more of those in the state system will have attended a grammar school than those in the voluntary system. There does not appear to be any readily available firm evidence on the ratio of grammar school to secondary school places within the two systems; Barritt and Carter (1962) noted that in the late 1950s there were fewer voluntary grammar school places than would have been expected from the Roman Catholic share of the appropriate age group, but Osborne and Murray (1978) estimated that in 1975 approximately the same proportion of pupils secured grammar school places in each school system. If the latter conclusion is correct (although the methods of estimation were problematic) then the most likely explanation that reconciles the different figures we have discussed so far is that fewer pupils stay on after the age of 16 at voluntary grammar schools.

Although we do not know the social class of individual pupils we can be sure that a significantly higher proportion of children attending voluntary schools will come from working class homes; this was the major ground for our expectation that the level of attainment in voluntary schools will be lower than in state schools. This means, if our assessment of an equal proportion of grammar places in the two systems is correct, that it is likely that more working class pupils attend grammar schools in the voluntary system. Yet the tables above show that for grammar schools in the two systems there is little or no difference between the proportions of boys who obtain 'O' level passes. The likely explanation is that working class pupils in the voluntary system do better than their counterparts in the state system, at least at this level (even if a smaller proportion of the former stay on at school). Boal (1978), in demonstrating a better pass rate at the 11+ qualifying examination for voluntary primary schools in Belfast in 1975 also suggested that working class children are doing better within the voluntary system. It is interesting that Payne and Ford (1977:91) from their study of a cross-section of adults in Scotland—where the schools are organised into two systems on the same basis as in Northern Ireland—also concluded that 'the Catholic system's record of achievement for the sons of manual families is in fact *better* in the same respects than the non-Catholic'.

The second hypothesis concerned with educational qualifications that was tested in this study was that there would be differences between pupils in the two systems in the proportions obtaining passes in the various subject areas. Again, we have used data on school leavers in 1971 and 1975 as this information includes passes from all the examination Boards; the results are shown in table 7:10 for 'O' level passes and table 7:11 for 'A' level passes. For both 'O' levels and 'A' levels we find the same pattern emerging. More than twice as many pupils from voluntary schools have 'O' levels in Languages than pupils from state schools (this is largely due to the numbers in the former who have an 'O' level in Irish and, to a lesser extent, in the Classics) whereas the proportion of pupils in the state schools who have an 'O' level in the Sciences is half as high again as the proportion in the voluntary schools. A very similar pattern is found for passes in the different subject areas at 'A' level. These patterns show relatively little change over the admittedly short time span covered by these tables.

As with the earlier analysis of the number of passes obtained we can look at these figures for subject passes in terms of the relative proportion of passes in each year that were held by pupils from voluntary schools and from state schools; these figures (for just boys in this instance) are contained in table 7:12 ('O' levels) and table 7:13 ('A' levels). These emphasise the points already made. To take, for example, boys with 'O' level passes in 1975, we observe that pupils from voluntary schools make up a majority of those with a pass in a Language (59 per cent) but a much smaller proportion (29 per cent) of those with a pass in a Craft; the figures for boys with 'A' levels in the same year are almost identical. Thus, on the 1975 figures, a position, such as an apprenticeship or further education place in engineering which requires a qualification in a Craft subject is about three times as likely to be filled by a boy from a state school as one from a voluntary school, *other things being equal.* It should be pointed out, however, that the figures for boys in 1971 reveal a very different picture for Craft subjects with roughly equal numbers from the two school systems.

When we examined the various sub-groups, disaggregated by sex and type of school, we observed, as with the similar breakdown of numbers of 'O' and 'A' levels, that marked inequalities do not only reside in the differences between voluntary and state schools; a boy from a voluntary school may have less chance of gaining the necessary qualifications for entry to a scientific or technological occupation than his counterpart in a state school but he has a vastly greater opportunity of doing so than a girl, whatever school system she attends. Despite the presence of these other sources of inequality, however, the overall pattern of subject differences between the voluntary and state systems generally repeats itself whenever we compare similar sub-groups between the two systems.

It seems likely to us, although we have no supporting evidence for these views, that these differences in subject passes are the result of a number of factors, to which we wish to draw attention as an indication of the direction subsequent research might take. Firstly, the Science and Craft subjects generally require more expensive facilities for their teaching (in the form of specialised rooms and equipment) than the Arts and Humanities, and the voluntary schools, being dependent to some extent on raising their own funds, may have been less able to finance such facilities. These subjects also require teachers with particular qualifications in them and since fewer pupils leave the voluntary schools with the 'A' level passes that will enable them to acquire the appropriate degrees or other qualifications in Science or Technology this creates a vicious circle because of the practice in Northern Ireland that both school systems are staffed almost entirely by people of the appropriate denomination, usually people who are themselves the products of the system. In the last thirty years the growth of high technology occupations throughout the advanced economies have provided many alternative and better-paid opportunities for those with a suitable background. Thus, even if the schools have laboratories or workshops they may be unable to recruit sufficient qualified staff to teach in them. (It should be stressed that this problem is not unique to Northern Ireland, let alone the voluntary schools; for some time now education authorities in England and Scotland have been reporting shortages of teachers in these subjects. For the reasons we have outlined, however, the position of the voluntary shools in Northern Ireland may be more acute; Payne and Ford (1977) draw attention to similar problems in Scotland.)

A second factor concerns the general ethos and aims of the school, related to their role in mediating broader social values. As their histories show both systems have been concerned, perhaps more consciously and deliberately than their counterparts elsewhere, with transmitting not only the culture of which each is part—Irish in the voluntary schools, British in the state schools—but also a complex of religious values. It seems, however, that the voluntary system may place more emphasis on its pupils' cultural heritage than does the state system and therefore attaches more importance to those subjects which embody it: History, Irish Language and

Literature. Moreover, it is possible that the influence of Roman Catholic values within the voluntary system tends to render it more sympathetic to the Arts and Humanities in general, less sympathetic to the Physical and Biological Sciences with their emphasis on rationalism (see O'Brien (1966) arguing the same point in relation to the curricula in Catholic schools in England).

Despite some problems already indicated we are satisfied, particularly because of the fact that our data are based on entire populations and not on samples, that the figures presented in the tables are sufficient grounds for concluding that, in the years studied, Roman Catholics, overall, left school slightly less well qualified than Protestants; most notably they were less likely to have obtained passes at 'A' level although we also noted a trend towards convergence. We can also conclude that Roman Catholics were less likely than Protestants to leave school with qualifications in Science or Craft subjects at 'O' or 'A' level. Thus the two specific hypotheses that guided this study are both sustained. Although we have drawn attention to possible reasons for these differences, and have speculated on others, it was not our intention to account for our observations; that task we must leave for other researchers. We are concerned in this chapter, however, with the differences and their possible consequences for employment and social stratification.

Consequences for Employment

First, there is the obvious point that, although this study was generated, in large measure, by the earlier analyses of the 1971 census data on occupational structure undertaken by Aunger (1975) and the Fair Employment Agency (1978), our findings cannot, in themselves, explain the 1971 patterns. The full study (Osborne and Murray, 1978) also included material (omitted here for reasons of space) on pupils who sat 'O' and 'A' level examinations, set by the Northern Ireland Board alone, in 1967, and when this was compared with similar information for 1971 and 1975 it showed that the differences we have noted above were even more marked in that year. When we consider the 1971 occupational patterns, however, we are dealing with a population of persons who entered employment (or unemployment) since about 1925. We have no way of telling whether our results, even from 1967, can be extended back in time in this form. In particular, we cannot infer that the differences between the two groups were even more marked the further back we go; as our tables show (and the full study shows even more clearly) the educational levels of both groups—and of the sub-groups within them—have generally improved even over this limited period and it is possible that at some point in the past the two groups were roughly level but Protestants initially improved faster than Catholics. The 1971 census material on the educational qualifications of adults is not inconsistent with our findings but we have already pointed out the deficiencies in those data, and in the sample study analysed by Boyle (1977) which produced similar conclusions.

Let us suppose, however, that the general pattern presented by these two sources and by projecting our results is broadly correct and that for many years now there has been a lower level of educational attainment among Roman Catholics in Northern Ireland, not only overall but also in specific subjects; as we noted earlier the former at least would have been reliably predicted on the basis of social class differences alone. Would it then be valid to conclude, as many people did after the original report on this study was published (Osborne and Murray, 1978), that these differences in education can account, in whole or in part, for the different occupational patterns observed for Catholics and Protestants in 1971, or earlier? In other words, what relationship is likely to hold between educational and occupational attainment?

This question, of course, is by no means unique or original. As a recent survey of research and theorizing on social mobility (Heath, 1981) makes clear, it has been an intrinsic feature of work in this area, particularly of post-war British studies. This work, and contemporary American research, was predicated on the assumption that was outlined in the first paragraph of this chapter, and was summed up by Little and Westergaard (1964:303): 'As professionalisation, bureaucratisation and automation of work proceed, so access to occupations of the middle and higher levels increasingly demands formal educational qualifications.'

Given this belief, most research has tended to concentrate on demonstrating the persistence of class differences in educational attainment, despite reforms that were intended to bring about equality of opportunity, and on identifying their causes. For a long time it was assumed that people with formal qualifications would gain access to the better occupations, particularly those created in the post-war expansion of the economy, while those without such qualifications would not manage this, and that in both cases the individual's social class background would play little or no part in the process, nor would practical experience or competence in employment compensate for the lack of formal qualifications.

These assumptions, combined with the clear demonstration of differences in educational attainment between social classes, similar to those we have found between Catholics and Protestants, led British social scientists in particular to the almost unanimous conclusion that children from working class homes would continue generally to be excluded from middle-class occupations because of a lack of formal educational qualifications. In other words, the route to social mobility lay through the attainment of qualifications and, therefore, the key to increased levels of social mobility for working-class children was to improve their educational opportunities so that all able children had an equal chance of achieving success, regardless of their backgrounds. There seems, on the face of it, no reason why a similar argument should not be put forward regarding Protestants and Catholics in Northern Ireland, an argument that would indeed conclude that differences in occupational patterns in the past (and probably for some years to come) were attributable to differences in eduational attainment.

There are, however, certain flaws in such an argument as Payne et al (1977) and Goldthorpe and Llewellyn (1977), among others, have pointed out for the British case. It rests on two links—background to education and education to occupation— both of which may be problematic and require separate analysis. In particular, they point out that the strength of the association within each pair will vary over time because of changes in the educational system, in the case of the former, and in the structure and state of the economy in the latter. We have already observed that in Northern Ireland in the 1970s the link between social class and educational attainment may have been less close in the voluntary sector than in the state sector.

Perhaps more importantly, the relationship between education and occupation is not fixed, in particular because there are changes over time in both the output of the educational system and the demands of the economy for skilled and/or qualified manpower. In Britain since the war there has been a considerable increase in the number and range of middle-class jobs which must be filled somehow. This argument is developed by Payne et al (1979) through the use of diagrams, two of which we reproduce in figure 7:1.

In the first situation there are more 'desirable' jobs than there are people with high qualifications; as a result a high proportion of people without these qualifications will be recruited to the good jobs on the basis of some other criteria. In the second situation there are more people with high qualifications than there are 'desirable' jobs; in this case people with low qualifications will have little chance of getting a 'desirable' job.

Payne et al (1979) argue that post-war Britain most resembles the first diagram, with the supply of non-manual jobs exceeding the

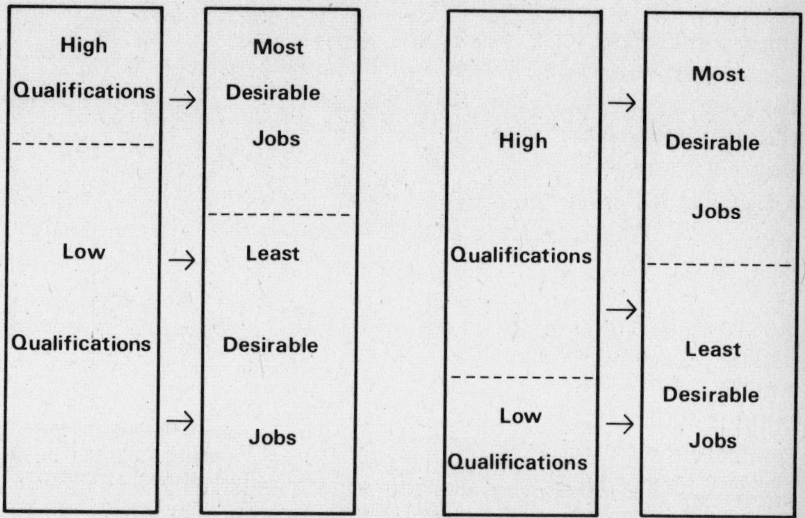

Figure 7:1 Relationships between education and jobs.

output of people with high educational qualifications. The net result, as they demonstrate with survey data from Scotland, and Goldthorpe et al (1980) have shown for England, is that while possession of formal qualifications is generally a sufficient condition for access to non-manual occupations, regardless of class background, it is not a necessary condition; many people manage to obtain such jobs, particularly in industry and commerce, even in the absence of qualifications. This means that the emphasis in explaining class differences in occupational mobility in such a situation no longer lies in the education system, but in the labour market. As Payne et al (1979:19) suggest:

> Control over occupational access lies *within* large organisations in both the private and state sectors. Recruitment, selection and promotion determine mobility; these are the weapons of the personnel manager and the managing director. Recruitment, selection and promotion are

> centrally mechanisms of employer control, so that if we wish to understand mobility—and in more general terms, social stratification—then we must look to the study of organisations as one new locus of explanation.

This point has been well taken by researchers seeking to understand the occupational locations of ethnic and racial minorities. Although the development of employment patterns in Northern Ireland since the war has differed in some respects from the rest of the United Kingdom, it seems that the general situation is not significantly different from that in Britain, as regards the balance between jobs and qualifications. Certainly a comparison between the figures for qualified persons in 1971 and those for the number of persons in middle class occupations shows clearly that a large proportion of the latter were not particularly well-equipped with formal educational qualifications. Thus, although our findings regarding passes in the Science and Craft subjects may account for part of the Catholic under-representation in specific occupations, the overall differences in educational attainment cannot be the cause, probably not even the major cause, of the over-representation of Protestants in middle-class occupations. In Northern Ireland employers must have used other criteria than education as the basis for recruitment and promotion. In Northern Ireland, as elsewhere, the key to the removal of differences in occupational patterns lies not so much in improvements to the education system— indeed, this study suggests that one proposed reform, integrated education, might well work to the detriment of working-class Catholic boys in some respects—but in changes in the processes of recruitment and promotion in the private and public sectors.

Notes

1. Any analysis of material from the 1971 census by religious affiliation is faced with the immediate problem that the census question on religion has always been a voluntary one and in 1971 a higher than usual proportion of the population—9.4 per cent—did not answer it. In our analyses of census data we have used only those who gave a religious affiliation.
2. The original study on which this chapter is based included data from passes from the Northern Ireland Board only for 1967, omitted here for reasons of brevity. The choice of the years 1967, 1971 and 1975 was dictated by the availability of data.

Table 7:1

POOL OF PERSONS WITH HIGHER QUALIFICATIONS BY DENOMINATION (per cent)

	Qualified		*Total Population (18–69)*	
Roman Catholic	24.0		28.4	
Male		8.9		13.7
Female		15.1		14.7
Presbyterian	30.4		28.3	
Male		15.1		13.6
Female		15.3		14.7
Church of Ireland	21.1		23.0	
Male		11.0		11.2
Female		10.1		11.8
Methodist	5.1		5.0	
Male		2.7		2.3
Female		2.4		2.7
Other Denominations	7.3		6.2	
Male		3.6		2.9
Female		3.7		3.3
Not Stated	12.2		9.1	
Male		6.8		4.7
Female		5.4		4.4
TOTAL	100.0		100.0	

Table 7:2

POOL OF PERSONS WITH 'A' LEVELS BY DENOMINATION (per cent)*

	'A' Levels		*Total Population (18–69)*	
Roman Catholic	25.8		28.4	
Male		13.5		13.7
Female		12.3		14.7
Presbyterian	30.2		28.3	
Male		16.0		13.6
Female		14.2		14.7
Church of Ireland	20.4		23.0	
Male		11.2		11.2
Female		9.2		11.8
Methodist	5.5		5.0	
Male		3.0		2.3
Female		2.5		2.7
Other Denominations	6.6		6.2	
Male		3.7		2.9
Female		2.9		3.3

Table 7:2 *(Continued)*

Not Stated	11.4		9.1	
Male		6.8		4.7
Female		4.6		4.4
TOTAL	100.0		100.0	

* These categories are those used by the census. 'A' level includes those who have obtained qualifications equivalent to GCE 'A' level, including Northern Ireland Senior Certificate, Ordinary National Diploma and Ordinary National Certificate. Higher includes those who have gained qualifications above that required for 'A' level. Such qualifications include higher and first University degrees, and qualifications obtained at 18 and over which are higher than 'A' level.

Table 7:3

SUBJECT AREAS AS PER CENT OF HIGHER QUALIFICATIONS

	Roman Catholic		*Protestant*	
	Male	*Female*	*Male*	*Female*
Education	33.2	37.4	16.2	38.3
Health	18.0	52.3	11.8	41.7
Technology	14.8	1.3	10.2	2.8
Science	7.0	1.3	10.2	2.8
Social Studies	12.5	3.3	18.9	4.9
Language Studies	7.1	2.4	3.5	3.5
Others	7.4	3.0	9.0	7.8
TOTAL	100.0	100.0	100.0	100.0

Table 7:4

POOL OF PERSONS WITH HIGHER QUALIFICATIONS IN SELECTED SUBJECT AREAS

	Roman Catholic		*Protestant*		*Not Stated*		
	Male	*Female*	*Male*	*Female*	*Male*	*Female*	*Total*
Education	10.2	19.5	18.1	41.3	4.6	6.3	100
Health	5.5	26.9	12.9	44.4	2.5	7.8	100
Technology	10.0	0.3	74.7	2.4	12.2	0.4	100
Science	10.3	3.2	54.4	14.7	14.2	3.2	100
Social Studies	10.2	4.7	56.1	14.3	11.6	3.1	100
Language Studies	16.4	9.3	29.9	28.6	9.3	6.5	100
All higher qualifications	8.9	15.1	32.4	31.4	6.8	5.4	100
Total Population 18–69	13.7	14.7	30.1	32.4	4.7	4.4	100
Education	29.7		59.4		10.9		100
Health	32.4		57.3		10.3		100
Technology	10.3		77.1		12.6		100
Science	13.5		69.1		17.4		100
Social Studies	14.9		70.4		14.7		100
Language Studies	25.7		58.5		15.8		100
All higher qualifications	24.0		63.8		12.2		100
Total Population 18–69	28.4		62.5		9.1		100

Table 7:5

QUALIFICATIONS OF SCHOOL LEAVERS FROM THE TWO SYSTEMS, 1971 AND 1975 (per cent)

	1971				*1975*			
	Roman Catholic		*Protestant*		*Roman Catholic*		*Protestant*	
3 or more 'A'	6.6		11.8		7.5		11.8	
2 'A'	5.3		5.8		5.6		5.5	
1 'A'	3.0		3.3		3.3		3.6	
With 'A'		14.9		20.9		16.4		20.9
5 or more 'O'	8.4		9.2		7.0		8.6	
1–4 'O'	7.1		7.7		10.7		12.1	
With 'O'		15.5		16.9		17.7		20.7
5 or more CSE Gr. 1†	—		—		0.8		0.7	
1–4 CSE Gr. 1	—		—		6.6		6.2	
5 or more CSE Gr. 2–5	—		—		3.4		4.3	
1–4 CSE Gr. 2–5	—		—		8.7		6.6	
All CSE		—		—		19.5		17.8
No qualifications	69.6		62.2		46.4		40.6	
	100.0		100.0		100.0		100.0	

* GCE 'O' level grades A–C.
† CSE not introduced in 1971.

Table 7:6

PROPORTION OF SCHOOL LEAVERS, GIRLS AND BOYS, WITH QUALIFICATIONS, 1971 AND 1975 (Per cent)

	Girls				*Boys*			
1971	*Roman Catholic*		*Protestant*		*Roman Catholic*		*Protestant*	
3 or more 'A'	6.4		10.6		6.8		12.9	
2 'A'	5.6		5.8		5.1		5.8	
1 'A'	3.0		3.0		3.1		3.5	
With 'A'		15.0		19.4		15.0		22.2
5 or more 'O'	9.2		8.4		7.7		10.0	
1–4 'O'	8.2		8.6		6.1		6.9	
With 'O'		17.4		17.0		13.8		16.9
No qualifications	67.6		63.6		71.2		60.9	
	100.0		100.0		100.0		100.0	
(Total in thousands)	(5.1)		(6.6)		(5.4)		(6.8)	
1975								
3 or more 'A'	6.5		11.0		8.3		12.7	
2 'A'	6.2		5.7		5.1		5.4	
1 'A'	3.6		3.6		3.1		3.4	
With 'A'		16.3		20.3		16.5		21.5

Table 7:6 *(Continued)*

5 or more 'O'	8.4		9.3		5.8		8.0	
1–4 'O'	12.2		12.9		9.3		11.5	
With 'O'		20.6		22.2		15.1		19.5
5 or more CSE Gr. 1.	1.2		0.7		0.5		0.6	
1–4 CSE Gr. 1.	7.1		6.8		5.8		8.0	
5 or more CSE Gr. 2–5	3.1		4.9		3.6		3.7	
1–4 CSE Gr. 2–5	9.3		7.1		8.1		6.2	
With CSE		20.7		19.5		18.0		18.5
No qualifications	42.4		38.0		50.4		40.5	
	100.0		100.0		100.0		100.0	
(Total in thousands)	(4.9)		(6.7)		(5.5)		(6.7)	

Table 7:7

POOL OF SCHOOL LEAVERS WITH QUALIFICATIONS, 1971 AND 1975
(Per cent)

	1971			*1975*		
	Roman Catholic	*Protestant*	*Total*	*Roman Catholic*	*Protestant*	*Total*
3 or more 'A'	30.5	69.5	100	32.9	67.1	100
2 'A'	41.9	58.1	100	43.9	56.1	100
1 'A'	41.9	58.1	100	41.6	58.4	100
'A'	36.0	64.0	100	37.6	62.4	100
5 or more 'O'	41.7	58.3	100	38.7	61.3	100
1–4 'O'	42.0	58.0	100	40.6	59.4	100
CSE	—	—	—	45.7	54.3	100
No qualifications	57.2	42.8	100	47.1	52.9	100
% of school leavers	43.9	56.1	100	43.7	56.3	100

* GCE 'O' grades A–C.

Table 7:8

SCHOOL LEAVERS AND FORMAL EDUCATIONAL QUALIFICATIONS, 1975 (Per cent)

	Roman Catholic				*Protestant*			
	Grammar		*Secondary*		*Grammar*		*Secondary*	
(i) Boys								
3 or more 'A'	36.2		0.7		38.7		1.0	
2 'A'	18.1		1.5		14.6		1.3	
1 'A'	9.4		1.3		10.6		0.6	
With 'A'		63.7		3.5		63.9		2.9
5 or more 'O'	16.6		2.8		18.4		3.3	

Table 7:8 *(Continued)*

1–4 'O'	13.0		8.3		12.9		10.8	
With 'O'		29.6		11.1		31.3		14.1
5 or more CSE Gr. 1	—		0.6		—		1.0	
1–4 CSE Gr. 1	—		7.7		—		8.1	
5 or more CSE Gr. 2–5	—		4.6		—		5.4	
1–4 CSE Gr. 2–5	—		10.3		—		8.9	
No qualifications	6.7		62.2		4.8		59.6	
	100.0		100.0		100.0		100.0	
(Total in thousands)	(1.2)		(4.3)		(2.1)		(4.6)	
(ii) Girls								
3 or more 'A'	24.4		0.8		33.3		0.5	
2 'A'	21.4		1.0		15.6		1.0	
1 'A'	11.3		1.0		9.6		1.7	
With 'A'		57.1		2.8		58.5		3.2
5 or more 'O'	21.5		4.2		21.9		3.3	
1–4 'O'	14.2		11.5		14.7		12.0	
With 'O'		35.7		15.7		36.6		15.3
5 or more CSE Gr. 1	—		1.5		—		1.0	
1–4 CSE Gr. 1	—		9.4		—		10.0	
5 or more CSE Gr. 2–5	—		4.1		—		7.2	
1–4 CSE Gr. 2–5	—		12.2		—		10.4	
With CSE		—		27.2		—		28.6
Nothing	7.2		54.3		4.9		52.9	
	100.0		100.0		100.0		100.0	
(Total in thousands)	(1.2)		(3.8)		(2.1)		(4.6)	

Table 7:9

PROPORTION OF SCHOOL LEAVERS FROM GRAMMAR AND SECONDARY SCHOOLS

	Roman Catholic		*Protestant*	
1975	*Boys*	*Girls*	*Boys*	*Girls*
Grammar	21.5	23.9	30.9	32.7
Secondary	78.5	76.1	69.1	67.3
	100.0	100.0	100.0	100.0
1971				
Grammar	20.1	28.2	30.1	29.2
Secondary	79.9	71.8	69.9	70.8
	100.0	100.0	100.0	100.0

Table 7:10
SUBJECT DISTRIBUTION OF 'O' LEVEL PASSES, ALL SCHOOLS, ALL BOARDS (Per cent)

	1971				*1975*			
	Roman Catholic		*Protestant*		*Roman Catholic*		*Protestant*	
Subject Grouping	*Boys*	*Girls*	*Boys*	*Girls*	*Boys*	*Girls*	*Boys*	*Girls*
English Language & Literature	23	30	22	26	21	27	22	27
Languages (Latin, Greek, French, German, Irish, Russian, Spanish & Italian).	22	26	10	17	19	20	9	16
Mathematics, (Mathematics, Additional Mathematics, Pure Mathematics).	19	12	21	15	18	11	20	14
Science, (General Science, Physics, Chemistry, Biology, Physics-with-Chemistry, Botany, Zoology),	14	6	21	12	14	8	22	13
History/Geography, (History, Ancient History, Economic History, Geography).	12	13	15	16	14	12	16	16
Art/Music/ Religious Education.	3	6	5	6	9	14	5	7
Crafts, (Woodwork, Metalwork, Technical Drawing, Geometrical & Engineering Drawing).	4	—	5	—	3	—	5	—
Other subjects.	2	7	1	7	2	8	1	6

Columns may not exactly total 100 due to rounding.

Table 7:11

SUBJECT DISTRIBUTION OF 'A' LEVEL PASSES, ALL SCHOOLS, ALL BOARDS (Per cent)*

	1971				*1975*			
	Roman Catholic		*Protestant*		*Roman Catholic*		*Protestant*	
Subject Groupings	*Boys*	*Girls*	*Boys*	*Girls*	*Boys*	*Girls*	*Boys*	*Girls*
English Literature	11	23	8	20	11	23	8	20
Languages	20	27	8	21	17	24	6	20
Geography/ History	22	22	23	23	29	21	23	21
Mathematics	22	9	24	8	14	6	19	8
Science	21	11	33	16	23	10	36	19
Crafts/Domestic Science	2	2	1	5	1	2	3	5
Art/Music/Religious Education	2	6	3	6	5	12	4	8
Other Subjects.	—	—	—	—	—	2	1	—

* Northern Ireland Board only.
Columns may not exactly total 100 due to rounding.

Table 7:12

PROPORTIONS OF 'O' LEVEL PASSES GAINED IN SUBJECT AREAS BY BOYS, ALL BOARDS, 1971 AND 1975 (per cent).

	1971			*1975*		
	Roman Catholic	*Protestant*	*Total*	*Roman Catholic*	*Protestant*	*Total*
English, (Language & Literature)	47	53	100	44	56	100
Languages, (Greek, Latin, French, German, Irish, Russian, Spanish, Italian).	60	40	100	59	41	100
Geography/History, (Geography, Ancient History, Modern History, Economic History, Economics and Political Studies).	33	67	100	40	60	100
Mathematics, (Mathematics, Additional Mathematics, Pure & Applied Mathematics).	34	66	100	38	62	100

Table 7:12 *(Continued)*

Science, (Physics, Chemistry, Biology, Botany, Zoology, Physics-with-Chemistry, General Science).	29	71	100	26	74	100
Crafts, (Woodwork, Metalwork, Technical Drawing, Geometrical & Engineering Drawing).	42	58	100	29	71	100
Art/Music/Religious Education, (Art, History & Appreciation of Art, Music, Music Appreciation, Religious Education).	33	67	100	60	40	100
Proportion of all passes gained.	38	62	100	42	58	100

Table 7:13

PROPORTION OF 'A' LEVEL PASSES GAINED BY BOYS, ALL BOARDS, 1971 AND 1975 (Per cent).

	1971			*1975*		
	Roman Catholic	*Protestant*	*Total*	*Roman Catholic*	*Protestant*	*Total*
English Literature	39	61	100	43	57	100
Mathematics (Pure & Applied Mathematics).	27	73	100	25	75	100
Languages, (Greek, Latin, French, German, Irish, Russian, Spanish, Italian).	55	45	100	58	42	100
Geography/History (Geography, Ancient History, Modern History, Economics & Political Studies, Economic History).	32	68	100	37	63	100
Science, (Physics, Chemistry, Biology, Botany, Zoology).	22	78	100	23	77	100
Crafts, (Woodwork, Metalwork, Technical Drawing, Geometrical & Engineering Drawing).	58	42	100	26	74	100

Table 7:13 *(Continued)*

Art/Music/Religious Education, (Art, History & Appreciation of Art, Music, Music Appreciation, Religious Education).	27	73	100	37	63	100
Proportion of all passes gained.	32	68	100	33	67	100

8. The Transition from School to Work

The two studies in this chapter focus on boys entering the labour market in Belfast, Londonderry and Strabane in 1977–78. As unemployment rose throughout the 1970s it became increasingly noticeable that young people, in particular, were experiencing great difficulty in finding work (MSC, 1978). A survey (Eurostat, 1978) conducted in 1977 revealed that Northern Ireland had the highest rate of male unemployment in the United Kingdom, and by far the highest rate for the 14–24 year old group; both rates were just marginally lower than those recorded in the Republic of Ireland. Hence, the prospects for Irish school leavers looked particularly bleak. However, the plight of young people in Northern Ireland, and in the United Kingdom as a whole, has been recognized in the policies and programmes of recent governments through the Youth Opportunities Programme, and the Youth Training Programme: schemes which provide training of various types in Government run and/or sponsored units. The scale of youth unemployment and the ever-increasing level of involvement of the state in the provision of these and related programmes, suggest that we are witnessing the most significant re-structuring of the transition from school to work since the extension of universal education from the elementary to secondary level (Rees and Atkinson, 1982).

Unemployment differentially affects young people from working-class homes. It is only in the last year, for example, that graduates, predominantly recruited from the middle class, are beginning to experience difficulties in gaining employment (QUB, 1981). As can be seen in chapter 2 and in Miller and Osborne's work on unemployment (chapter 5), unemployment differentially affects the Catholic working class, while Catholics are also over-represented in unskilled work: or those in the 'unskilled/unemployed' category 25 per cent were from the Catholic community compared to only 15 per cent from the Protestant community (chapter 2).

Aunger's analysis in chapter 2 refers to the employment patterns in 1971. Towards the end of the 1970s, with unemployment rising, it became increasingly important to form some idea of the degree to which these patterns were being reproduced. The two projects, reported in this chapter, were designed for this purpose. Girls were excluded primarily because they would have required a different questionnaire taking account of factors peculiar to the experience of women in the labour market. Four schools in Belfast, and four schools and one college in Londonderry and Strabane were matched and selected primarily for the purposes of comparing and constrasting the experiences of Protestant and Catholic school leavers.

While it would be foolhardy to generalise from eight schools and one college in three locations to the whole Province, these two studies, nevertheless, provide important information, not available from other sources, on the experiences of young male school leavers entering, or attempting to enter, a labour market offering very few opportunities. Although there was a considerable overlap in research design these were, however, by no means parallel studies. Each study asked different questions, and pursued issues relevant to their particular locations. Hence, in what follows, the findings from each study are discussed separately.

R.J.C. & R.D.O.

(i) The Belfast Study: Into Work in Belfast*

R. J. Cormack and R. D. Osborne

In the Belfast study, a Protestant and a Catholic secondary intermediate school in the East of the city, and one from each community in the West of the city, were selected. The aim was to interview, both before and after leaving school, all the boys in the fifth form (those approaching school leaving age), from these four schools. We were primarily concerned with the initial labour market experiences of the boys, with the opportunities available to them, and the extent to which their circumstances reflected those of the communities in which they lived.

We begin by reviewing existing evidence on the environment in which the boys in our study were growing-up, going to school, and

* Based on *Into Work* (1980) by the editors and W. T. Thompson.

eventually seeking work: evidence marshalled for Northern Ireland as a whole, and at the level of the school catchment areas. This evidence then allows us to explain and justify the selection of the schools included in the study. This, together with details of the methodological procedures employed, constitutes the second section of what follows.

From the evidence presented it is quite clear that opportunities vary greatly *within* the city. Hence, in section three, we deal with the structure of opportunity in identifiable areas of the city, and the level of, and hindrance to, labour mobility between these areas. In particular we investigate the preparedness of boys to work in different parts of the city. Five to eight months after leaving school we again interviewed the boys from the four chosen schools. By this point they were in one of four locations: in work, unemployed, in a government programme, or they had returned to an educational institution. In section four we deal with the search for work, together with the background, education and experience of the boys in each of the locations noted. The Belfast study ends with a review of the major findings.

The Social Context

The boys, whose early careers we have followed, left school in 1978. In terms of the religious divisions in the Province some indication of the nature of the labour market they were to enter is given in Aunger's analysis of 1971 census data (chapter 2). Aunger notes that '. . . the median Protestant is a skilled manual worker, and the median Catholic is a semi-skilled worker'. The unemployment rates for the two communities recorded in the 1971 census were 17.3 per cent for Catholic males, and 6.6 per cent for Protestant males: a rate for Catholics nearly three times that for Protestants (see chapter 5).

The issue of whether or not Belfast constitutes one or a series of labour markets is taken up below. However, using census data we constructed employment profiles of the catchment areas for each of the four selected schools. Differences in these profiles were immediately noticeable; differences which were not altogether associated with religious divisions. *Both* communities in the East of the city, compared to those in the West, were at an advantage in terms of the quantity and diversity of jobs. Nevertheless, in the East and West of the city, regardless of different levels of opportunity, Catholics were at a disadvantage compared to their Protestant neighbours. In other words, Catholics in the East of the city, living in areas contiguous to major industrial sites within the city, did not apparently gain access to the available jobs with the same facility as did Protestants. Likewise in the West of the city, where there was a dearth of jobs, Protestants gained access to employment opportunities much more readily than Catholics.

Based on these 1971 features of segments of the Belfast labour market, opportunities available to the boys in the study looked distinctly limited. In the two Catholic school catchment areas between one-in-three and one-in-four males were unemployed, while those in employment were heavily dependent on the construction industry and various services. In the Protestant schools' catchment areas between one-in-twenty and one-in-five males were unemployed: a pattern reflecting the markedly different opportunities in the East and the West of the city. In both areas, Protestants appeared to have a much wider choice of employment.

These 1971 data reveal a grim picture. But by 1978, when the boys in this study were leaving school, circumstances had deteriorated. For every 56 unemployed men in 1971 there was one school leaver unemployed; by 1979 for every 10 unemployed men there was one school leaver unemployed. By the end of the 1970s the construction industry had contracted considerably, while parts of the manufacturing sector had shrunk or disappeared altogether.

It is worth stressing that for these boys, predominantly from working-class homes, and regardless of religion, the opportunities available to them were diminishing. Their 'life chances', in the sociological sense of a working career and associated opportunities stretching out in front of them, were perhaps even worse than those of their fathers; and, in Northern Ireland, such prospects would have to be thought of as dismal.

Research Design

As we have seen, the 1971 employment patterns revealed major differences in the spatial distribution of jobs between the East and West of the city. In an attempt to take account of the differential availability of jobs in the city, a Protestant and a Catholic school, one of each, from the East and West of the city were selected. Four boys' secondary schools were selected, which informed opinion and analysis suggested were relatively evenly matched, both in terms of the schools themselves, and in terms of their catchment areas.

The initial population was the total fifth form population of each of the four schools. Two questionnaires were administered in school while the boys were still in their last year of compulsory education, one in December 1977 and one in April 1978. If a boy was contacted in either survey he was included in the population to be looked at in the third post-school survey; moreover, efforts were made to follow up boys who were not in school at the time of the first and second surveys. In all 320 boys or 72 per cent of the population were contacted.

The third survey, which reviewed the situation of the boys at the end of November 1978, was conducted by professional interviewers from Ulster Opinion Surveys at the boys' homes. Attempts were made to contact all 320 boys who had been reached earlier. Completed questionnaires were obtained from 243 boys or 76 per cent of the target population. An analysis of non-response to the survey suggests a small loss of non 'O' level Catholic boys, and a slightly lower level of response from 'O' level boys at the Protestant West Belfast school.

The Structure of Opportunity and Labour Mobility

As American studies have suggested, when particular racial or ethnic groups exhibit patterns of residential segregation, such as are characteristic of contemporary Belfast (Boal, 1982), a primary factor influencing the employment characteristics of these groups is the spatial distribution of job opportunities. Together, the two spatial distributions—of people and of jobs—constitute the structure of opportunity. It is within this structure of opportunity that issues of mobility of labour should be initially located. In addition, the institutional characteristics of the labour market in particular, the ways in which employers recruit employees by informal as opposed to formal mechanisms, circumscribe patterns of individual mobility and should be noted.

In setting out to examine mobility in the study of school leavers we:

(i) gathered data on the structure of opportunity in Belfast;
(ii) examined data on patterns of mobility in the city;
(iii) asked our group of boys where in the city they would be prepared to travel to work;
(iv) gathered information from those school leavers in employment on the location of their jobs.

Data on the way in which individuals found jobs was also collected and these are discussed below.

The structure of opportunity in Belfast was examined by aggregating data from the 1978 census of employment (collected by the Department of Manpower Services (DMS) on a regular basis) into broad geographical units of the city to derive a geography of jobs in the city. This pattern was then compared with the distribution of the population in the same geographical area. These are shown in table 8:1.

Table 8:1

SECTOR DISTRIBUTIONS OF POPULATIONS AND JOBS IN BELFAST (including Central)

	*Proportion of Population**			*Proportion of Jobs†*		
	Male	*Female*	*Total*	*Male*	*Female*	*Total*
Catholic West	28.1	24.6	26.3	9.5	21.0	14.1
Protestant West	9.5	10.0	9.8	2.9	3.6	3.2
East Belfast	24.1	24.7	24.4	30.7	18.2	25.6
North Belfast	20.9	21.7	21.3	8.8	10.5	9.5
South Belfast	16.7	18.3	17.5	23.6	18.7	21.6
Central	0.7	0.7	0.7	24.5	28.0	25.9
	100.0	100.0	100.0	100.0	100.0	100.0

Sources: * Based on data drawn from the Housing Executive Survey 1978 (1979).
† Drawn from the 1978 census of employment.

While some variations are shown, when the type of job is considered, the broad pattern for male jobs is of Central Belfast (which has a minute residential population) having a 'surplus' share of jobs over share of population, while Catholic and Protestant West Belfast, and religiously mixed North Belfast, all have substantial 'deficits' of job shares to population shares. Given this quite marked and uneven distribution of job opportunities, it is important to examine patterns of labour mobility amongst the *existing* labour force. This can be done from data drawn from a recent survey conducted by the Housing Executive, responsible for public housing in Northern Ireland, (Housing Executive, 1979). Critically, Catholic West Belfast and East Belfast show the lowest proportions of those in employment travelling out of the home areas for work, and while, for East Belfast, this is explicable in terms of the high proportion of jobs in the area, this is not the case for Catholic West Belfast. In the latter case the comparison with Protestant West Belfast is revealing: 25 per cent travel to East Belfast but less than 5 per cent from Catholic West make the same journey. In seeking to understand this difference, the existence of a reluctance of Catholics to travel from the West to the East of the city has been advanced, with this reluctance based on fears for personal security. Certainly, the existence of segregated areas and sectarian violence produced a reluctance to travel either through or to areas of the other community—a reluctance varying with time of day, mode of transport, perceived risk, and so on (Burton, 1978). Nevertheless, as a complete explanation of labour mobility this seems unlikely; it ignores other important recruitment factors.

In our survey we examined labour mobility at two points in time: the areas our leavers stated they were prepared to travel to work, and the actual travel to work patterns of those in employment. The boys were asked if they would work in 'Protestant', 'Catholic' or 'Mixed' areas. Predictably, areas designated as that of their own community and 'Mixed' areas were highly favoured. However, half of the Catholics said they would work in Protestant areas, while 40 per cent of Protestants said they would work in Catholic areas. When asked about specific locations, well known in the city, interesting patterns emerged. Reponses to these more precise locations did not fit the stereotyped picture of 'ghettoised' areas, which assumes a virtually complete reluctance to move out of home areas. Indeed, there seems to be a complex interplay of factors influencing preparedness to travel to different parts of the city for work. These include the 'normal' factors of distance and transport available, but also the impact of the 'troubles', particularly with specific locations rather than broadly designated areas. Moreover, separate from Protestant-Catholic differences there was an East-West of the city source of variation in responses.

One other aspect of mobility which deserves note is the response to the question of whether or not boys would leave Northern Ireland if they could not find work. Half of the Catholics indicated they would do so, while a third of Protestants did so. This difference suggests a continuation of the traditionally higher rates of Catholic emigration, but we have no indication of the extent to which these potentially very high rates are being realised.

In the post-school survey we asked for the address of the firm or employer of those boys who had found employment. These actual travel to work patterns show some important features:

(1) The general importance of Central Belfast as a work place location for the Catholic West Belfast school. Some 58 per cent of those in full-time employment work in this area. None of the other

schools record such a high proportion having Central as a work location.

(2) The high proportion, approximately half, of the East Belfast Protestant school leavers who remain in East Belfast—with Island ward (which includes substantial manufacturing industry together with the shipbuilding industry) accounting for a significant proportion of this number.

(3) The geographically diffuse destinations of the East Belfast Catholic school contrasts strongly with that of the East Belfast Protestant school.

(4) Approximately 20 per cent of the West Belfast Protestant school leavers travel into East Belfast for employment and this contrasts quite markedly with West Belfast Catholic leavers. It is, however, a similar proportion to that found in the Housing Executive Survey (1979).

In conclusion, the patterns of leavers' job locations demonstrates the relatively short distances travelled by school leavers to work. Comparing the actual travel to work patterns with the responses from the leavers before leaving school shows a more limited pattern of actual travel than might be anticipated from the indications of preparedness to travel. It is possible to interpret these differences in two ways. The first possible interpretation is to regard the questions on preparedness to travel as being responses to only *hypothetical* questions; however, when confronted with trying to get a job, the viability of some potential work locations was higher than that of others. An alternative interpretation is that the answers to preparedness to travel provide an accurate reflection of mobility, but that for a variety of reasons respondents were constrained from obtaining jobs in different parts of the city: factors involved include command over transport, recruitment practices of employers and so on.

Finally, in terms of labour mobility and the structure of opportunity, it can be noted that recent discussions in government statements, Quigley Report, (1976), Department of Environment, 1978), have tended to discuss mobility with little or no reference to the structural or institutional constraints on individuals. Thus while there are exhortations to individuals to 'become more mobile', to 'get on their bike', there are no similar exhortations to employers to encourage mobility by ensuring that information about all jobs is readily available and that fair competition operates, and can be seen to be operating, in all employment decisions. Undoubtedly, however, the most obvious social objective for public policy in terms of promoting equality of opportunity would be to secure a sound economic base for the city and to ensure, through a more even distribution of jobs, a geographically more equal structure of opportunity.

Into Work?

(a) Current Situation of the Boys

By the time of the post-school interviews less than half the boys had found work. Table 8:2 gives the distribution of the boys interviewed across the various locations. Of the half who had not found employment one-third had returned to full-time education, one-third were found on one or other of the Government training schemes, and one-third were unemployed.

Table 8:2

CURRENT SITUATION OF THE BOYS WHEN INTERVIEWED FIVE TO EIGHT MONTHS AFTER LEAVING SCHOOL (Per cent)

	Employed	*G.T.C. Craft Courses*	*Other Govt. Schemes*	*Unem-ployed*	*Full-time education*	*Total*	*N*
Protestant East	67.6	2.7	4.0	13.5	12.2	100	74
Protestant West	51.8	5.4	19.6	16.1	7.1	100	56
Catholic East	35.4	9.2	1.5	16.9	36.9	100	65
Catholic West	39.6	16.7	6.3	27.1	10.4	100	48
All Schools	49.8	7.8	7.4	17.7	17.3	100	243

Source: *Present Survey*

Two major differences between the religious groups emerged when the current situation of the boys was studied. First, many more Protestants (60.8 per cent) than Catholics (37.2 per cent) were in jobs. Second, more Catholics (12.5 per cent) than Protestants (3.8 per cent) were in Government Training Centre (GTC) craft courses. There were also four important school-based differences in the current situation of the boys:

(1) The relatively high level of employment among East Belfast Protestants;

(2) The relatively high level of enrolment in ‘other Government Schemes’ among West Belfast Protestants;

(3) The relatively high level of return to school among East Belfast Catholics;

(4) The relatively high level of unemployment among West Belfast Catholics.

(b) Examinations

It has often been argued that the pattern of Catholic disadvantage in employment can be explained, at least in part, by lower levels of educational attainment. The boys interviewed here were entered for GCE 'O' levels and/or Certificate of Secondary Education (CSE) examinations—if they were entered for examinations at all. There were quite considerable school-based differences in the proportions of boys in each school, *presented* for examinations, and in the subsequent levels of attainment in examinations. However, in terms of the above argument boys in the two Catholic schools generally performed at similar levels to boys from the better of the two Protestant schools. This evidence fits with the findings from a previous study of levels of educational attainment in the two communities (see chapter 7 and Osborne and Murray, 1978). The evidence so far gathered suggests that, at least for the contemporary period, levels of educational attainment in GCE 'O' levels and CSEs in the two communities has ceased to be significantly different, and hence to offer a possible basis to account for different employment profiles in the two communities.

(c) Boys in Employment

The clearest indication of the source of Protestant advantage is to be found in table 8:3.

Table 8:3

SOURCES OF HELP IN FINDING EMPLOYMENT

	Family and Friends	*Careers Service*	*School & Work Experience Programme*	*Advertisement and Direct Approach to Employer*	*Other*	*Total*	*N*
Protestant	55.7	13.9	6.3	19.0	5.1	100	79
Catholic	50.0	32.5	2.5	7.5	7.5	100	40
All Schools	53.8	20.2	5.0	15.1	5.9	100	119

Source: *Present survey*

For all the boys who had found employment, personal and family friends, together with family members themselves, had been the most instrumental in helping them find employment. Thereafter, Catholic boys relied more on the Careers Service (32.5 per cent), while Protestant boys found advertisements and approaching employers directly (19.0 per cent) a useful source of finding work. However, in interpreting this finding it should be remembered that 60.8 per cent of Protestant boys were in employment compared to only 37.2 per cent of Catholic boys. Boys in both communities relied heavily on friends and family to help them find work. As we saw above in the Social Context section, Protestants in the schools' catchment areas were more likely to be in employment and, moreover, their employment profiles displayed a greater diversity of types of employment than the equivalent profiles for Catholics. Hence, Protestant boys were more likely to have friends and family members who had jobs and were in a position to 'put in a good word' for them if and when a position became available at their place of work. The advantages of Protestant fathers and mothers appeared to be passed on to their sons through the informal channels by which employers tended to recruit labour. Personal recommendations, rather than extensive interviewing and/or the use of formal examinations, appeared to be the criterion most frequently used by employers.

The lack of currency of formal qualifications was a source of frustration and disillusionment for many of the boys: more than half the Protestant boys in employment took no formal examinations before leaving school, but less than a quarter of the Catholic boys. Catholic boys, in particular, were disillusioned about the usefulness of examinations in finding work. Moreover, despite the somewhat higher levels of educational attainment, Catholic boys in employment appeared to have found jobs which had less good prospects, at least in terms of skill levels and training. An indicator of this is the number of boys in employment offering 'day release'—usually one day off work per week to attend a local college for further education and training: 45.5 per cent of Protestant boys were in employment offering day release compared to 26.8 per cent of Catholic boys.

The engineering sector was found to be a pre-eminent source of employment for Protestant boys as it was for their fathers: for the boys, this sector accounted for close to one in three of jobs found. Thereafter, perhaps the most notable feature of the jobs profile of Protestant boys was its diversity: services, construction and manufacturing all being well represented. In contrast, Catholic boys were found to be much more concentrated in a few significant employment sectors. The engineering sector was a major employer but not to the same extent as it was for Protestants: one in six Catholic boys were employed in engineering. The construction industry and services were the major sources of employment for Catholic boys.

Finally, worthy of note was the religious composition of the work forces where the boys had found work. Less than one in three Catholics work where the other workers were thought to be all or mostly Catholics; while more than two out of three Protestants work mainly with other Protestants. Clearly, therefore, for the boys in this survey, many more Catholics would appear to work in mixed workforces than Protestants.

(d) Boys Unemployed

The transition from school to work is best seen as a process. Boys may, for example, leave school to take the first job offered, only to leave it within a few weeks to move to a better job. Others may become unemployed for weeks or months before returning to school or entering one of the Government programmes for school leavers. The literature on the transition from school to work suggests a complex process involving the interaction of labour market opportunities and aspirations which are constantly changing in the light of those opportunities. Aspirations, moreover, which have taken shape, and continue to be modified and/or amplified in the context of family, school and peer group culture.

Table 8:2 gave the location of the boys at the point of the post-school interviews. However, to some extent, this disguises the flux of the situation. Only a minority of the boys went straight from school to work. For 68 per cent of the boys who left school their first labour market position was unemployment. When interviewed five to eight months after leaving school 21 per cent of these boys who left school (i.e. excluding the 17 per cent who returned to school or college) were unemployed.

Unemployment levels varied greatly by religion and by areas of the city. From table 8:2 it can be seen that 13.5 per cent of Protestant boys in East Belfast were unemployed, compared to 16.9 per cent of Catholic boys; a figure for Catholics most likely deflated by the much larger numbers returning to school. In the West of the city, 16.1 per cent of Protestant boys were unemployed compared to 27.1 per cent of Catholic boys. The Housing Executive Survey revealed an unemployment rate of 14 per cent for household heads in the Belfast District Council Area (Housing Executive, 1979). Working from the same data we calculated unemployment rates in the school catchment areas as follows: 10.2 per cent in Protestant East, 25.1 per cent in Protestant West, 23.1 per cent in Catholic East, and 26.7 per cent in Catholic West. Hence, the extent of unemployment differentials by religion and geographical area is well documented.

Without taking account of the subsequent economic downturn and the concomitant rise in unemployment, the situation of the boys interviewed must have deteriorated in terms of the numbers of those unemployed, unless one makes the dubious assumption that the third, who entered Government schemes or returned to school, are all now in employment.

Of the twenty-four Catholic boys unemployed, seven had three or more 'O' levels while ten had CSEs; three of the nineteen Protestant boys had one 'O' level, none had CSEs. Hence, it would seem that for Catholic boys the possession of three or four 'O' levels is no immediate guarantee of a job. CSEs would seem to have little currency in the job market. Not surprisingly when asked about public examinations these boys in particular were generally disillusioned about the usefulness of certificates, but especially CSEs.

Unemployment was most definitely an unattractive experience for these boys. The lack of money and the boredom of long days with nothing to do was frequently mentioned. While Government programmes are clearly one answer, the high rate of turnover noted below among the boys interviewed, together with the high numbers who remain unemployed, suggests that they are not yet perceived by many as offering something either interesting or worthwhile.

(e) Boys in Government Schemes

In 1978, 6,000 places were available throughout the Province in various YOP schemes. These schemes vary greatly in their aims and hence in their activities. However, two broad orientations can be discerned in the schemes available. On the one hand, there are those schemes designed to provide the first stage of a standard apprenticeship training. At the end of a course lasting up to a year the young people are expected to enter the employment of their sponsor, or to find an employer with whom to complete their apprenticeships. Government Training Centres (GTCs) are the major location of such training. On the other hand, there are schemes which involve a mixture of work training together with an attempt to develop social and personal skills deemed appropriate in enhancing 'their attractiveness to prospective employers' (Ulster Year Handbook, 1978–79). These are called 'Other Government Schemes' in this study.

The stated aim of the last Labour Government was to provide a place on one or other of these schemes for any young person who wanted it. Despite the quite radically different policies being pursued by the present Conservative Government, they too have made this commitment. The increasing percentage of school leavers entering YOPs, together with the level of Government investment and involvement in the schemes, is what prompts us to suggest we are here witnessing the beginnings of a major restructuring of the transition from school to work.

In table 8:2, 15.2 per cent of the boys were found in YOPs. However, when we look at the experience of the boys interviewed in terms of process, rather than at one point in time (the date of the interview), it is clear that many boys had experience of YOPs: nearly one-third of all the boys who had left school.

West Belfast Protestants recorded the highest level of participation in YOPs at 36 per cent of those interviewed, while the level for East Belfast Catholics was the lowest at 15 per cent. The low East Belfast Catholic levels of enrolment may be due to the large number of boys who return to full-time education. A second feature worthy of note is the movement of Protestant boys out of GTC craft courses. Nineteen Protestants (15 per cent of boys interviewed) and fourteen Catholics (12 per cent) were recruited to these courses; most of the Protestants left, while all the Catholics remained. There was no clear pattern of destination for the boys who moved out: seven took up other apprenticeships, three obtained semi- or unskilled work, and four were unemployed.

This movement of Protestants out of GTCs suggests the need for further research on perceptions of the utility of GTC craft courses in the two communities. Speculatively, we might suggest that for Catholics, GTCs provide very scarce opportunities for training in a craft; opportunities which for Protestants were perceived to be more readily available in their communities.

(f) Boys in Full-Time Education

Almost one boy in six returned to full-time education (17 per cent). This figure would have been closer to one in ten if it had not been for the very high rate of return to full-time education for East Belfast Catholics. Two-thirds of the boys who returned to full-time education returned to school. The other one-third took a range of courses in Belfast Further Education colleges. The boys returned to full-time education to take one of three options: a GCE 'A' level course, a GCE 'O' level course, or to train for a job. The last type of course was always taken in a Further Education College. The majority of boys in the two Catholic schools and in the Protestant East school returned to take an 'A' level course, while in Protestant West the majority returned to take 'O' levels, or went on to colleges for job training.

A number of the boys who returned to full-time education would appear to have done so for negative reasons, in particular, to avoid becoming unemployed. Many of them, based on previous examination performances, would not seem to be equipped with the necessary abilities to take advantage of the type of courses presently available in schools. But, having returned to educational institutions, their aspirations were raised: 79 per cent of them expected to get a better job as a result of further education.

Two observations are worth making here. First, there has yet to be undertaken the necessary rationalization of post-compulsory school leaving age educational and training provision. In this it would seem particularly wasteful not to incorporate the schools with all their facilities, resources and current over-capacity. Second, it seems grossly unjust that young people on YOPs receive a Government-provided allowance while those young people who return to school receive no such allowance.

Conclusions

At this level of entry to the labour market, that is, mainly into manual jobs, the major method of recruitment utilized by employers was informal recommendations from friends or family members of the potential recruit. Clearly, the use of such informal mechanisms will tend to reproduce the existing patterns of job distributions both in terms of religion and geographical area. We found a remarkable degree of openness in the areas in which boys suggested they would be willing to work. Hence, a major conclusion of the study is that those who exhort the unemployed, particularly in areas like Catholic West Belfast, to be more prepared to move to find work should perhaps spend an equivalent time persuading employers to institute recruiting procedures which take account of this potential mobility of labour.

While the study focused primarily on entry to manual work, it is worth suggesting, albeit somewhat speculatively, that recruitment to non-manual jobs may be different. Non-manual employers tend to be larger organizations, more directly amenable to pressure to institute formal procedures. In saying this we fully recognize the problems faced by small employers instituting such procedures, e.g. the expense, the time involved, the disadvantages in terms of employing a worker known to be 'safe' and vouched for by an employee, versus recruiting an 'unknown' through formal procedures. It is clearly difficult to convince small employers of the social utility that may result from such procedures. Moreover, there is no guarantee that formal procedures on their own result in greatly improved opportunities for disadvantaged groups.

Nevertheless, marked differences in the employment profiles of the two communities exist. Undoubtedly such differences contribute to the present 'troubles'. Governments, in the recent past, have committed themselves to fair employment legislation and greater equality of job opportunities. If such legislation is not to be seen as a mere palliative, then much more direct and forceful attempts to implement measures to achieve equality of opportunity will be required; measures involving not only employers and government, but also trades unions.

The most important aspect in the transition from school to work is the recent intervention of the government in the provision of various types of post-school pre-work education and training (YOPs). Ultimately, however, we must ask: training for what? The prospects of work for this generation of school leavers is a distant dream. Whether or not the prospects will be better for the next generation is an open question, to which a pessimistic answer currently seems the most appropriate response.

(ii) The Londonderry and Strabane Study: Out and Down in Derry and Strabane

D. Murray and J. Darby

The aim of this chapter is to describe the main findings of a research project carried out in 1978–79 into the vocational aspirations, expectations and experiences of male school leavers in Londonderry and Strabane.

Initially the research is placed in the context of the general employment situation in Northern Ireland. The demographic patterns of both areas are discussed, including the geographic and social milieux in which the schools are located. This section also includes a statement of general research aims and the methodological procedures adopted to accomplish them.

Second, an account is presented of the Phase I questionnaire which was answered by the boys shortly before they left school. This instrument provided information on such topics as expectations of employment, perceived influences on vocational choice and family employment history.

The third section, which deals with the post-school interviews, strives to demonstrate how successful, or otherwise, the school leavers had been in actually obtaining employment, as well as the processes and networks they used to obtain work—family, government agencies, career teachers. The role the Government's YOP schemes play in the early careers of school leavers is also considered. Comparison is made between the experiences of Roman Catholic and Protestant school leavers with regard to their experience in the job market in the four months subsequent to their leaving school.

The fourth theme is a consideration of the schools as preparation agents in placing students in employment. This function is considered in the light of pupils' perceptions of, and reactions to, the school system and also with regard to the academic qualifications of the school leavers.

Finally, three main conclusions of the research are discussed more fully—the economic climate and its effects, the differential experiences of the job market for Protestant and Roman Catholic boys, and the role of the school.

Methodology and Demographic Background

The main purpose of the research was to examine the influences upon sixteen-year-old male school leavers in the Londonderry and Strabane areas of Northern Ireland which shaped their attitudes towards jobs and their first experiences in the labour market. More specifically the study sought to:

(1) Discover the vocational aspirations and expectations of the school leavers;
(2) Compare the aspirations of Roman Catholic and Protestant school leavers;
(3) Examine the influences which determined their aspirations and expectations;
(4) Study the experiences of the young people after they have left school and attempted to enter the job market.

The research was carried out in five schools—three in Londonderry (one Controlled Secondary, one Maintained Secondary and one Technical College) and two in Strabane (one Controlled Secondary and one Maintained Secondary).[1]

In Londonderry the Maintained school was situated in the Creggan ward to the West of the city, the Controlled Secondary was located in the East of the city and the Technical College near the commercial centre.

Londonderry is Northern Ireland's second largest town, with a 1971 population of 52,205. Strabane with 9,413 inhabitants is similar in size and structure to the many market towns which are characteristic of the Province. They are both located in the north west of Northern Ireland, about 15 miles apart and both are close to the Donegal border of the Irish Republic (see frontispiece).

Historically they have both experienced economic and social disadvantages due in part to their remoteness from the industrial heart of the Province which lies to the East, and especially in the Greater Belfast area. At the time of the study, the official unemployment figure for Strabane was 23.1 per cent and 15.1 per cent in Londonderry. Male unemployment was particularly serious, with the official figures for Strabane standing at 28.9 per cent and Londonderry's (with Limavady) at 18.1 per cent. More recent evidence (Darby and Murray, 1980) suggests that male unemployment in both Londonderry City and Strabane is over 30 per cent.

Strabane's population is more than 80 per cent Roman Catholic although the country areas surrounding the town are predominantly Protestant. Some parts of Londonderry, which has an overall Catholic population of 67 per cent, have become highly segregated by religion; in 1971 Creggan ward in the West of the city was 96 per cent Roman Catholic, and wards to the north and east of the city were more than 66 per cent Protestant.

The largest employers in Londonderry (industrial and engineering complexes) are situated to the south and east of the city. Its commercial centre lies to the west of the River Foyle.

The teachers in each school who were responsible for career guidance were approached at the start of the project and lists obtained of all sixteen-year-old males who planned to leave school in the school year 1978/79. They also completed a questionnaire which helped to build up a profile of the schools and their catchment areas.

Two research instruments were used during the study. The first was a questionnaire which was distributed while the boys were still at school. The second was based on individual interviews which were carried out four months after the boys had left school.

Within the first instrument questions were constructed around a number of major themes: job aspirations; job expectations; perceptions of job market; career guidance; job description; family employment; history and job location. All of the pupils who expected to leave school in June 1979 completed the questionnaire in small groups in the presence of the researchers. A total of 223 pupils completed questionnaires of whom 62 were attending Technical College. During the second phase of the research, it was considered that useful and perhaps more meaningful information would derive from an ethnographic approach. An attempt was made therefore to interview all the original respondents individually in order to allow them to elucidate and elaborate upon the expectations and aspirations which they had articulated during the first questionnaire; 93.3 per cent of the boys from the original sample who had actually left school in June 1979 were personally interviewed.

Constant contact was maintained with the teachers throughout the research project. This contact was vital since it continually provided information which enabled more sense to be made of the complex matrix of perceptions, values and attitudes which are formed towards employers and employment within the areas under study.

The Phase I Questionnaire

The persistently high unemployment rate in the Londonderry/Strabane areas has clearly produced a degree of fatalism among the area's young people. This was reflected by the fact that overall 35.4 per cent of the school leavers did not expect to secure employment after leaving school. This fatalism was not engendered solely by a general perception of unemployment, but also by acute personal and familial experience. In one Maintained school in the Creggan area of Londonderry 41.4 per cent of the boys' fathers were unemployed; in this same school 47.1 per cent of the boys did not expect to have a job when they left school.

There was also an interesting disparity of response between Roman Catholic and Protestant pupils. In Londonderry 36.4 per cent of Roman Catholic boys did not expect to have a job when they left school while only 11.4 per cent of Protestant school leavers had this pessimistic expectation. The Roman Catholic school leavers did not appear to consider that they would be discriminated against because of their religion, since only 5.3 per cent of them gave this as a possible reason for their failure to get a job. The differences between the expectations of Protestant and Roman Catholic school leavers should be considered within the overall economic depression affecting both their employment prospects. There was, however, evidence of considerable differences in the distribution of unemployment between the two religious groups. When the total responses are analysed by religion, more than twice as many Catholic fathers (33.7 per cent) than Protestant fathers (14.0 per cent) were unemployed. Whatever the reasons for these differences it seems probable that they may be a key factor in explaining the generally pessimistic views of Catholic pupils about their vocational future.

Table 8:4

PATERNAL AND MATERNAL UNEMPLOYMENT OF LONDONDERRY AND STRABANE SCHOOL LEAVERS

	School A maintained (RC)	*School B controlled (Protestant)*	*College C*	*School D controlled (Protestant)*	*School E maintained (RC)*
Father unemployed	41.4	17.1	27.4	9.1	29.4
Mother not in employment	61.4	34.3	54.1	45.5	52.9

The depressed state of the job market clearly affected the expectations of the school leavers. In this context, the difference between the jobs they would most like to get and the jobs which they actually expected to get was revealing. The three most popular jobs were

Electrician (chosen by 17 per cent of the sample), Joiner/Carpenter (15.2 per cent) and Mechanic (7.6 per cent). However only 39 per cent of the boys who wanted to become electricians expected to attain their ambition and, for the prospective joiners and mechanics, figures were 50 per cent and 41 per cent respectively. With regard to the influences affecting the vocational choices of the school leavers, the family seemed to play a relatively minor role. Although 88.3 per cent of unemployed fathers had been out of work for more than six months, this did not seem to result in an acceptance of unemployment among their offspring. Some 88.7 per cent of respondents expressed unhappiness at the prospect of being in receipt of unemployment benefit. Neither was there a high correlation between the job expectation and aspirations of the school leavers with the jobs held by their fathers. Only 4.8 per cent of the boys wanted to do the same job as that held by their fathers and only 5.1 per cent expected to do so. In the majority of cases where there was a positive correlation, the school leavers expected to go into a family firm or farm.

While the boys were still attending school their attitudes towards it were very postive: 76.7 per cent declared that they would not have left school a year earlier had it been legally possible to do so. Their views on those aspects of schooling which were specifically geared towards their acquiring jobs were also sympathetic: 91.5 per cent of the pupils who had undergone work experience (temporary placement in employment while still attending school) considered that it would be helpful afterwards. Similarly with careers guidance in the schools: 75.8 per cent anticipated that this would be helpful later. The most interesting response, in the light of subsequent experience, was that 92.7 per cent of the boys considered that formal qualifications (mainly General Certificate of Education and Certificate of Secondary Education) would benefit them when they left school. This high regard for educational qualifications was often combined with a low regard for their own abilities.

In addition to the external influences of the family and the school, the qualities and appeals of different jobs which either attracted or deterred school leavers were examined. The boys were asked to rank a range of eight jobs with regard to salary, usefulness and pleasantness, and then to state their preference for one of them.

It is important to record that all of the respondents had been labelled as 'non-academic' at the age of eleven. This may to some extent explain that, while doctors and teachers occupy the higher

Table 8:5

PREFERENCES AND RATINGS OF EIGHT NOMINATED JOBS

	Job Preference (ranked) %	*Estimates of salary (rank order)*	*Estimates of importance to community (rank order)*	*Estimates of most pleasant conditions (rank order)*
1. Plumber	31.4	5	4	5 =
2. Bricklayer	26.5	2 =	3	7
3. Bank Clerk	9.9	4	8	1
4. Teacher	9.4	2 =	2	2
5. Doctor	7.6	1	1	3
6. Civil Servant	4.0	6	6	4
7. Factory worker	4.0	8	5	5 =
8. Labourer	3.1	7	7	8

rated estimates for salary, 'importance to the community' and 'most pleasant working conditions', neither occupation features at the top of the preference scale. It appears probable that although these jobs are highly regarded they are not seriously considered as possibilities by the boys. Instead, dominating the list of preferences are the craft jobs of plumber and bricklayer, which would seem to be perceived as both desirable and attainable. The less clearly defined jobs of factory worker and labourer which were seen as being both badly paid and having unpleasant working conditions were relegated to the bottom of the job preference hierarchy.

The Post School Interviews

Apart from the fact that almost one in five of the boys who decided to leave school in June 1979 had in fact returned in September, the most notable characteristic of the school leavers' post-school

Table 8:6

DESTINATION OF SCHOOL LEAVERS WHO COMPLETED PHASE 1 QUESTIONNAIRE

	Completed Phase 1 questionnaire	*Returned to school %*	*Employed %*	*Unemployed %*	*G.T.C. and other schemes %*	*Not located %*
School A	70	12.9	40.0	20.0	27.1	—
School B	35	31.4	42.9	11.4	5.7	8.6
School C	62	19.3	41.9	17.7	16.1	4.8
School D	22	18.2	36.4	13.6	9.1	22.7
School E	34	26.5	29.4	—	41.2	2.9
Total	223	20.2	39.0	14.3	21.1	5.4

experience was that only 39 per cent had succeeded in getting a job. The percentages were roughly similar for Roman Catholics (38.6 per cent) and Protestants (40.4 per cent). There was a marked difference, however, in the attendance by Catholic and Protestant boys at Government Training Centres, youth opportunities schemes and other community based projects: 28.1 per cent of Catholic boys were attending such establishments but only 7.4 per cent of Protestants.

It is revealing to consider the post school experience of the boys in more detail.

(a) The Employed

Of all the boys, 39.4 per cent had succeeded in securing employment by the October following their departure from school. They were asked how they had heard about these jobs in the first place.

Members of the immediate family, especially the father, were the informants in 34.4 per cent of the cases, and 20.6 per cent of the boys heard about their jobs from the careers teacher or someone else in the school. The much greater importance of the careers office and the labour exchange (a government department responsible for both placing individuals in work and paying them relief, or 'dole', until they do) for Roman Catholics is noteworthy. Not one Protestant had heard about a job through these sources, while 26.6 per cent of Roman Catholics named them. Protestants, on the other hand, more often heard about their job through their family.

The jobs which the boys obtained covered a broad spectrum of unskilled, semi-skilled and skilled occupations, but shared three disquieting characteristics. The first is that only 44.8 per cent of the employed boys were working in the job they had originally wanted. The second is the remarkably low level of wages. The overall gross weekly wage for the 87 boys who had managed to get jobs averaged £25.97. This ranged from one Strabane boy on £12 per week to a boy employed as an apprentice engineer at Du Ponts on £53 per week. Wages were particularly low in Stabane, where 61 per cent of the employed boys earned £23 per week or less. The third characteristic, which once again underlines the remarkably depressed state of the local economy and the boys' resignation to it, was that only 9.2 per cent expressed dissatisfaction with their jobs.

Data were also gathered about the type of employment obtained by the school leavers (table 8:7).

Table 8:7

PERCENTAGES OF ROMAN CATHOLIC AND PROTESTANT SCHOOL LEAVERS IN SKILLED AND UNSKILLED EMPLOYMENT

Type of Employment	*Roman Catholic school leavers %*	*Protestant school leavers %*
Skilled	45.3	73.9
Unskilled	54.7	21.8
Unclassified	—	4.3
Total	100.0	100.0

Boys deemed to be in skilled occupations were those who had gained entry to apprenticeships to trades (electricians, carpenters, mechanics, plumbers and so on). There was a disproportionate representation of Protestant school leavers in this 'skilled' section of the job market. In keeping with the pattern demonstrated by respondents with regard to the acquisition of jobs in general, the boys' own views of the important factors for obtaining an apprenticeship were 'good information' and 'having someone to speak for you'. In this respect it is of note that 75 per cent of the Protestant apprentices stated that they had got their job through the efforts and advice of relatives compared to the 38.8 per cent of Roman Catholic boys in apprenticeships.

Table 8:8

MAIN SOURCES OF INFORMATION ABOUT THE JOB (Per cent)

	Family Relations	*Labour Exchange/ careers office*	*School/ careers teacher*	*Friend*	*Myself*	*Local newspaper*
School A	28.6	32.2	10.7	14.3	17.9	3.6
School B	47.8	—	20.0	20.0	—	6.7
College C	30.7	16.5	38.5	3.8	11-5	11.5
School D	50.0	—	13.6	37.5	—	—
School E	20.0	40.0	—	40.0	—	—
Overall	34.4	20.6	20.6	17.2	9.1	6.8

Note: As two answers were sometimes offered, the total percentages for each school may exceed 100.

(b) The Unemployed

Overall 14.5 per cent of the original sample were unemployed at the time of the second interviews. There is no evidence to suggest that they were in this situation by choice, since 87.3 per cent of the boys had applied unsuccessfully for two or more jobs since leaving school and 31 per cent had actually obtained a job only to lose it again.

Of these unemployed boys, 15.6 per cent had attended a full-time short course at a Government Training Centre, thus postponing the almost inevitable unemployment experience, (it is to be recalled that only 39.4 per cent of the school leavers had actually succeeded in obtaining full-time employment).

Another facet of the relationship between Government Training Centres and the unemployment situation was that 37.5 per cent of the unemployed boys had actually applied for positions in such establishments but had been unsuccessful. What is also notable is that this figure of 37.5 per cent totally comprised Roman Catholic boys. This would seem to provide further evidence that the Protestant boys, even those who had been unemployed for several months, did not consider Government Training Centres or schemes as either alternatives to employment or aids in the attainment of further employment.

Unemployment relief benefits were certainly not considered as an acceptable alternative to employment by many of the school leavers: 84.4 per cent of those unemployed stated that they were unhappy at being on the dole, and 40.6 per cent considered that they would still take a job even if it only paid the same as unemployment relief.

(c) Boys at Government Training Establishments

There were three Government centres in the areas covered by this report. In Londonderry there was a centre on either side of the river (at Maydown and Springtown). There was also a centre in Strabane.

The single most impressive aspects of Government Training Centres in Londonderry and Strabane is the major part they seem to play in alleviating, and perhaps masking, the unemployment situation in those areas.

The overall percentages relating to those boys who actually left school in 1979 demonstrates this point graphically, with 19.7 per cent in Londonderry and 33.5 per cent in Strabane finding positions in Government sponsored institutions.

These overall figures tend to obscure the fact that these institutions are attended more often by Roman Catholic school leavers than by Protestants. Three times as many Catholic boys in Londonderry and five times as many in Strabane were attending such centres.

It does not seem to be the case that school leavers end up in government-sponsored institutions as a result of having poor academic qualifications. Indeed these boys seem to be marginally better qualified academicallly than those who succeeded in getting a job, although 74.4 per cent of them had no GCE passes and 40.4 per cent lacked any CSE passes.

There is, in fact, evidence to support the view that the boys considered Government Training Centres as being normal employment: 76.6 per cent of the boys from both Strabane and Londonderry stated that it was what they had wanted to do and 97.9 per cent of respondents stated they were either 'happy' or 'very happy' with their situation.

This response must be viewed in the context of how many other jobs they had applied for. From both towns, 25 per cent of Protestant boys and 62.8 per cent of Roman Catholic boys attending Government Training Centres had applied for at least one other job, and 28.0 per cent of Catholic school leavers had applied unsuccessfully for three or more jobs.

Consistent with other findings in the study, family and personal efforts seem to be of paramount importance in placing boys after they leave school. What is also of interest is the low perception of the boys of the benefit of schools and careers guidance in this respect. When asked how they had heard of the Government Training Centre, 67.0 per cent cited 'through their own efforts', 15.1 per cent mentioned their family and 17.1 per cent named either the school or careers guidance.

Education and Schools

The responses of the boys with regard to their perceptions of the usefulness of schools, in influencing their suitability for employment and jobs choice, were sought before they left school and afterwards, when they had been in the job market for four months. Their perceptions changed dramatically in this intervening period.

In the Phase I questionnaire the impression was given of general supportiveness for school structures and courses. This applied particularly to specific aspects of schooling directly geared to preparing them for employment: 91.5 per cent considered that the work experience they had had while at school could be helpful or very helpful in getting them a job afterwards. There was a similar high regard for career guidance and careers teachers. Examinations taken in school were also perceived to be a considerable influence on getting a job. These included the more practically based CSE examinations and the more academic GCE: 92.7 per cent of the school leavers considered that such qualifications would help in getting them a job.

When the boys were asked why they thought they would not get the job they wanted, more of them pointed to their lack of educational qualifications than to any other reason. This was frequently expressed as 'not good enough' or 'not smart enough' or some other self-perception of inadequacy. Indeed this tendency of school leavers to regard themselves as failures was one of the most consistent themes in the study.

This sense of failure was reinforced when the boys left school. It is perhaps not surprising that, since only 39 per cent of them actually got jobs, they would as a result become less impressed with the preparation and training they had received in school. However, even the responses of the school leavers who had subsequently obtained employment seem to support such an hypothesis. Of the 92.7 per cent who had predicted that the securing of qualifications would be helpful to them getting a job, only 37.9 per cent felt the same way four months later. In fact their reaction seems well founded. Of the 87 employed boys 81.6 per cent had no GCE passes and 49.9 per cent had no CSE passes. This appears to suggest that lack of qualifications was not a major disadvantage in securing jobs, as these figures by no means distinguish the employed boys from those who were unemployed, where 81.2 per cent had no GCEs and 62.5 per cent no CSEs, or indeed those attending Government Training Centres where 74.5 per cent had no GCEs and 40.4 per cent no CSEs.

A similar retrospective disillusion with other aspects of schooling was also evident. While 75.8 per cent had anticipated that their school's careers guidance would be helpful or very helpful, only 57.5 per cent still held this view afterwards. Even work experience was rated less highly. Here the percentages declined from 91.5 per cent of boys who considered it helpful while at school to 29.9 per cent who still held this view after they had left. Only in the Technical College, where 46.2 per cent of the employed boys still maintained their original view, was the decrease less marked.

Conclusions

In this section it is intended to emphasise features of the study which have particular relevance for social, economic and eduational policy.

The Economic Climate and its Effects

Throughout the study the economically depressed state of both the Londonderry and Strabane areas, and its effects on the boys' perceptions of their own futures, were repeatedly underlined. Some

28.7 per cent of their fathers were unemployed, and almost 90 per cent of them had been out of work for more than six months. The picture was similar for their mothers, with 53.4 per cent of them unemployed. It is clear, however, that the school leavers themselves expected to occupy the bottom ranks in the area's economic hierarchies and that these expectations were realised when they left school. Only 64.6 per cent of the boys who completed the Phase I questionnaire while still at school in April and May 1979 expected to have a job when they left. In fact, when the same boys were interviewed during the following October, only 39.4 per cent of the original total were employed. Even more significant, given that the Phase I questionnaire was carefully limited to those boys who had determined to leave school in June 1979, was the fact that 19.3 per cent of them had in fact returned to school in September. Many of these returns were the consequence of a disillusioning summer when the number of job applications was simply greater than the number of vacancies.

The school leavers were entering an environment dominated by high unemployment and many either went back to school or deferred their entry into the unemployment statistics by entering a Government Training Centre or Community work scheme. This is only part of the picture. Most of the boys who secured jobs remained part of the same deprived community as those who did not. Their average salary was £25.97 which, at the time of writing, was just £3.00 per week higher than the income of those attending Government Training Centres. In such a buyer's market for employers there is some evidence, both from salary levels and from interviews with careers teachers and careers officers, that the situation is being exploited by some employers, especially in Strabane. While it is not easy to suggest what might be done to remedy this situation, short of a general economic recovery, it is important to emphasise that employed and unemployed are located close together in an economic continuum, and that their material conditions are often similar. Londonderry and Strabane's depression therefore should not be measured simply by their high unemployment figures.

Catholics and Protestants

One of the major themes in the study was a comparison of the vocational expectations and experiences of Protestant and Roman Catholic school leavers. It is notable that only 6.3 per cent of the boys anticipated that they might be discriminated against on religious grounds, and that a slight majority of these were Protestants. The percentage is obviously too small for even tentative conclusions.

The major difference between the two religious groups seemed to reflect their relative shares of the job market. The key factor here was that 33.7 per cent of the Catholic fathers were unemployed, against 14.0 per cent of the Protestants. It was not surprising therefore that more of the Protestant-employed boys than the Catholics (44.0 per cent compared to 29.0 per cent) had first heard about their job from a member of their family, most often their father. Catholics, with fewer influential contacts in the job market, were much more inclined to seek their jobs through the employment exchange or the Careers Officer. In fact 26.6 per cent of the Catholic boys had heard about their job in this way, and no Protestants. Whatever the historical reasons, there is an important endemic residual imbalance in the employment prospects of the two religious groups. The realization of this situation has obviously affected their approaches to employment. If, as the figures suggest, the majority of Protestant boys learn of available jobs through parents or relatives, and if Protestants presently hold a disproportionate share of the job market, then there seems little chance in the near future of rectifying the imbalance in employment, which seems to exist between the two main religious groups. This general situation is reflected in the different Catholic and Protestant attitudes to Government Training Centres and community projects. While only 7.4 per cent of the Protestant boys were working in these Centres, 28.1 per cent of the Catholic boys were. It is clear, both from the earlier questionnaire returns and from these data, that such government-financed schemes perform a significant role in keeping Roman Catholic unemployment figures down, and the interviews support the view that some school leavers regard these Centres as job equivalents. Indeed 42.6 per cent of the boys attending government Training Centres had opted for the schemes without applying for any jobs. Almost inevitably, given Northern Ireland's sectarian sensitivities, the preponderance of Catholics in Government Training Centres has led to their being perceived as Catholic institutions by some Protestants. One Protestant floor tiler from Strabane remarked during his interview that he was 'scared to go to the Government Training Centres because they are Catholic', and other Protestants declared an unwillingness to attend them without specifying the reason. Davies and McGurnaghan (1975) have demonstrated Northern Ireland's growing dependence on public rather than private investment and employment. The violence of the last decade, among other factors has had the effect of deterring industrial investment, expecially from outside the United Kingdom. This effect has been disguised to some extent by considerable increases in public investment, through bodies like the Local Enterprise Development Unit and the Northern Ireland Development Corporation, and by means of industrial subsidies. Davies and McGurnaghan estimated that more than 20,000 jobs were created by 1975 by government action as a result of the troubles. It is not surprising then, that dependency on Government Training Centres is particularly marked in depressed areas like Strabane, where 28.6 per cent of the boys were working in them. The social and economic implications of the growing importance of these institutions are clearly important, but have not yet been the subject of serious study. Equally important is the evidence in this report that the increased dependency of young people on the Centres is significantly greater for the more depressed Catholic community. There is an urgent need for an investigation of the policy implications of these trends. All of them should be viewed in the context of the depressed economic position of Northern Ireland in general and of Londonderry and Strabane in particular. Nevertheless the fact that Roman Catholic and Protestant school leavers seem to be differentially affected within this milieu of Northern Ireland is disturbing and demands further attention. While no evidence of discrimination against Catholics was observed, it is clear that the networks used to obtain jobs operates most favourably for Protestants. Such a system will inevitably result in the perpetuation of an employment imbalance between the two religious groups.

The Role of the School

While the school leavers were still at school they had a conspicuously high regard for education and its supposed importance in helping them to get jobs. Some 69.5 per cent reckoned that they would return to education in some way after leaving school, and 46.2 per cent thought that their lack of educational qualifications would be the major obstacle to their securing the job they wanted. It was anticipated by the boys that the schools' career-oriented activities, careers guidance, work experience and the gaining of educational qualifications would all play important roles in helping them to become employed after they left school.

This view of the school changed dramatically after the boys' first experience on the job market. The high esteem in which the schools' career-oriented activities were held collapsed, most markedly in their views of work experience (91.5 per cent thought it helpful while at school; 29.9 per cent after they had left) and educational qualifications (from 92.7 per cent to 37.9 per cent). It seems likely that part of the reason for this disillusionment may be found in the fact that educational qualifications appear to offer no real advantages when the young men were seeking jobs. The number of GCE and CSE passes held respectively by those boys who were employed, those who were unemployed, and those attending Government Training Centres, were surprisingly similar; indeed the boys attending Government Training Centres were actually better qualified than those with jobs.

All this points to a serious need for a reconsideration of the schools' effectiveness in preparing school leavers for employment. How relevant are academic qualifications to 16-year-old school-leavers when employers appear largely to disregard them? How can the liaison between careers teachers and the careers office be improved? Do those schools which do not offer work experience seriously disadvantage their pupils? Perhaps of most concern is the extent to which the curricula of the schools are irrelevant to the job market and how much the academic bias in such schools (which were originally conceived specifically to avoid such bias) is responsible for the disturbingly low self-esteem of many school-leavers. When boys give as the most likely reason for their failure to get a job the fact that they are 'not smart enough' or are 'not qualified', it is reasonable to ask if the schools should not reconsider what responsibility they have had in encouraging so many school-leavers to regard themselves as failures.

Note

1. In general 'Controlled' can be treated as synonymous with Protestant and 'Maintained' as being Roman Catholic. Although Technical schools have both Roman Catholic and Protestant students, all the 16-year-old school leavers who were present when the questionnaires were presented were Roman Catholic.

9. Political Arithmetic, Higher Education and Religion in Northern Ireland

R. D. Osborne, R. J. Cormack, N. G. Reid and A. P. Williamson

This chapter is concerned with applying a 'political arithmetic' approach to participation in higher education with particular reference to religion in Northern Ireland. Traditionally, political arithmetic studies have focussed on social class (usually defined in occupational terms) and latterly sex as key variables in the analysis of the education system and, in particular, access to higher education. In Northern Ireland, religion is of equivalent and special importance and interest in any assessment of higher education. Religion, both as a label denoting communal affiliation and attitudes, and in terms of demarcating different beliefs and doctrines, lies near the core of the Northern Ireland conflict. The various religious denominations have played a major and controversial role in the organisation and control of Northern Ireland's schools, resulting in the virtual segregation of schools at both primary and secondary levels between Protestants and Catholics. The segregation of education in this fashion has been regarded as both a cause and a symptom of the social and political conflicts in Northern Ireland consequently attracting the interest of both politicians and researchers. Religion, therefore, is a critical theme in any analysis of higher education in Northern Ireland.

The political arithmetic tradition of analysing the education system in terms of either class or religion is not well developed in Northern Ireland, as demonstrated by the paucity of both academic studies and official statistics. A primary function of this chapter, therefore, is to chart some of the basic characteristics of Protestant and Catholic participation in higher education. Data for this investigation are largely drawn from a research project designed to provide information for this and related analyses. While the main focus is on religion, class and sex as important variables interacting with religion, are also discussed.

The structure of the chapter is as follows: first we briefly examine the major developments in higher education particularly in terms of access, in the light of 'political arithmetic' studies of the education system; second, we outline the major elements of the structure of higher education in Northern Ireland and how it has changed over time. These two sections provide the basis for the empirical assessment of religion and higher education participation. Finally, these findings are reviewed and the implications for the labour market are briefly considered.

Until recently, a degree virtually guaranteed access to the more attractive and well-paid jobs in society. Despite the job prospects of current graduates being much less good, the expansion of higher education places in the UK during the past 20 years has meant increasing numbers gaining access to 'good' job opportunities. The expansion of places during the 1960s suggested to some that a stage of mass *higher* education was starting in the same manner, as mass *secondary* education had emerged in an earlier period (Trow, 1966). Certainly, the evolving pattern of enrolments in higher education in the United States in the post-war period indicated such a trend in that country. In Britain, the Robbins Report's (1963) guiding principle, that 'courses of higher education should be available for all who are qualified by ability and attainment to pursue them and wish to do so', inaugurated, or more accurately accelerated, the growth of higher education provision.

Although the primary concern of Robbins was with the economic benefits thought to result from increasing the stock of human capital there was also a social concern with the 'wastage of ability': bright, intelligent students who, for a variety of reasons, did not apply or were not admitted to institutions of higher education. In particular, Robbins identified a need to increase participation in higher education by women and individuals from working class backgrounds. This wastage in terms of social class is elegantly expressed, in the following passage from one of the classics of the 'political arithmetic' tradition, J. W. B. Douglas' *The Home and the School* (1967:168):

> In recent discussions there has been a tendency to assume that there is only a limited number of persons who can benefit from higher education and that there is a clearly defined 'pool of talent' on which to draw for university places. It has been said, however, that what is extracted from the pool depends much less on its content than on the effectiveness of the pump; it is clear from the present study that the pump is leaking badly at the points of secondary selection and early

> leaving. The pool of talent found at the end of the secondary school period is likely to be only a portion of that which would be found if it were possible to draw fully on potential rather than realised ability. Over a period of three years in the primary schools, there is a substantial loss of ability in the manual working-class children which could be prevented.

This study was first published in 1964 and Halsey et al (1980:204) quote this passage appreciatively and, on the basis of their study of men born between 1913 and 1952, suggest:

> . . . class differentials widen at each rung up the educational ladder . . . A service-class boy in our sample was four times as likely as his working-class peer to be found at school at the age of 16, eight times as likely at the age of 18, and eleven times as likely to enter a university.

The pump, to continue Douglas' metaphor, is clearly malfunctioning. Douglas found the worst leaks at the points of secondary selection and early leaving, while Halsey et al suggest that considerable losses occur at the point of entry to the sixth form. Farrant (1981:48) argues:

> . . . the number and proportion of school children who elect to stay in education after the school year in which they reached the age 16 is at present a, perhaps the, major determinant in the number of entrants to higher education.

These studies and investigations have augmented and confirmed the statistical evidence of a continuing under-representation of students from working-class backgrounds despite the expansion of places in the post-Robbins era. On the other hand the representation of women has increased quite markedly during the period of expansion although this still does not approximate the female proportion of the population. Hutchinson and McPherson (1976) argue that in Scotland women have displaced working-class males, although Farrant (1981), on the basis of changing subject choices of working-class males in England and Wales, suggests that this may be temporary. There is still strong evidence, however, that the subject distribution of women students reflects and thereby helps reproduce traditional female labour market roles (Reid and Goldie, 1981).

Almost twenty years after Robbins, the extent to which a variety of groups are under-represented in higher education has been much more fully documented (see the essays edited by Warren Piper (1981)). Thus, in Britain, the virtual absence of black ethnic minority groups in higher education has led Little and Robbins (1981) to call for US style quotas as a priority. The predominance of 18 to 20-year-olds experiencing higher education means that older students are denied parity of access (Woodley, 1981), while the problems of handicapped students receive scant attention (Sturt, 1981). Finally, the marked disparities in the participation rates of different geographical regions imparts a notion of spatial deprivation in access (Richardson, 1981). Burgess (1981), however, has sounded a note of caution arguing that a preoccupation with such issues may preclude a proper discussion of the appropriate content and purpose of higher education.

Higher Education: Structure and Change 1845–1980

In this short section we seek to give a brief outline of the development of the higher education system in Northern Ireland. In 1845 three Queen's Colleges were set up in Ireland, at Belfast, Cork and Galway under an Act which prohibited any preference for any religious denomination. Barritt and Carter (1962) state that the Belfast college was mainly attended by Presbyterians with Trinity College, Dublin, attracting Anglicans, and Cork and Galway recording some Catholic students. Under the 1908 Irish Universities Act the Queen's College of Belfast was established as a separate university—the Queen's University of Belfast—and the principle of non-discrimination was preserved, although less than 10 per cent of students in 1908 were Catholic. Several subsequent innovations including the establishment of a department of Scholastic Philosophy and the appointment of a lecturer in Celtic languages and literature may be regarded as friendly gestures towards Catholics and it has been suggested that the acceptance by Cardinal Macrory of an honorary degree in 1929 was '... a kind of public expression of approval' (Moody and Beckett, 1959:542). From 1875, Catholics, North and South, had been prohibited by the Catholic hierarchy from attending Trinity College, Dublin, a ban which was not finally lifted until 1970 (FitzGibbon, 1981). A further institution, established by the Presbyterian Church, was Magee University College in Londonderry which provided the other non-teacher training higher education institution in Northern Ireland, and which taught the first two years of certain courses at Trinity College, Dublin, and some first year courses for Queen's University, Belfast. Barritt and Carter (1962) state that few Catholics attended Magee.

The provision of teacher training in Northern Ireland has been an area of controversy since shortly after the state was founded.

Debates between the Protestant churches and the Northern Ireland government, and between the Catholic church and the government in relation to teacher training provision, have been well analysed by Akenson (1973). The resolution of these conflicts resulted in the foundation of Stranmillis College in 1922 attended mainly by Protestants. Female Catholic students continued to attend St Mary's College, founded in 1900, while male Catholic student teachers briefly attended Stranmillis College before arrangements were made for them to study at 'Strawberry Hill' (St Mary's) in Middlesex. This latter arrangement survived until after the War when Trench House was opened as the men's department of St Mary's and before it attained independent status as St Joseph's in 1961. Post-graduate teacher training without regard to religion was provided by Queen's University.

The basic structure of higher and advanced further education was radically altered following the recommendations of the Lockwood Report (1965). The Lockwood Committee was set up by the Northern Ireland government following the Report of the Robbins' Committee in Britain. Two important recommendations were made. The first was that there should be a second university in Northern Ireland, located at Coleraine in the north of the Province. The second concerned the establishment of a regional technical college, located in the Greater Belfast area to provide for advanced further education at sub-degree level.

The recommendation to set up a second university was accepted by the government although the decision to locate the institution in Coleraine aroused considerable controversy (Osborne, 1982c). In accepting this recommendation, the government did not close Magee College as suggested by Lockwood but linked it with the new university. The New University of Ulster, as it was titled, admitted its first students in 1968. The proposal for a regional technical college, while accepted by government, was not implemented in the recommended form. Rather the new institution, located on the northern outskirts of Belfast was designated a polytechnic and, in keeping with polytechnics in Britain, offered degree programmes as well as advanced further education.

Northern Ireland had a new framework for higher education provision. There were three degree awarding institutions (with the Ulster Polytechnic awarding CNAA degrees). Both the New University at Coleraine and the Polytechnic also offered undergraduate teacher education programmes. This meant that professional teacher training was provided at no less than six major institutions in Northern Ireland by the mid 1970s, (seven if the small teacher training section in Londonderry Further Education College is included).

However, by the late 1970s, just as the system was settling down, a number of important patterns were emerging which were to have a major influence on higher education provision in Northern Ireland. The economic recession with its limitations on social spending, together with a drop in the numbers of children entering the education system as a whole, coincided with the approaching end of the Lockwood forecasting period. In 1978, a major review of higher education was set in motion by the Labour Government (administering Northern Ireland under Direct Rule arrangements) with an independent review committee chaired by Sir Henry Chilver.[1] The Interim Report of the Committee (DENI, 1980) concerned with teacher training provision caused a storm of opposition to its central proposal to relocate the Catholic St Mary's and St Joseph's Colleges on the Stranmillis site. Concerted and powerful opposition was mounted by the college's trustees nominated by the Catholic Church (Trustees of the Catholic Colleges, n.d.).

A further important trend having major implications for the development of higher education in Northern Ireland was the doubling, to over 30 per cent or more, of the average proportion of students leaving Northern Ireland for study compared to the 1960s. At the same time, the number of undergraduate students entering Northern Ireland from elsewhere dropped dramatically. This upset one of the planning assumptions of Lockwood, that the in-flow and out-flow of students would broadly balance each other. The full impact of this net loss of students on the Northern Ireland institutions during the 1970s has been partially masked by the general rise in the numbers entering higher education. However, the New University of Ulster, in particular, has not grown as anticipated. At the end of the 1970s the three major institutions had the following number of undergraduates: Queen's University, 5354 (full-time) and 245 (part-time): the New University of Ulster 1543 (full-time) and 15 (part-time); and the Ulster Polytechnic 3768 (full-time) and 2111 (part-time).

Religion, Class, Sex and Mobility in Higher Education

Data

Most of the data utilized in this chapter have been generated from an SSRC supported study on participation in higher education of

Northern Ireland undergraduates.[2] The study has produced three data sets:[3]

(i) Data from each of the grant awarding authorities in Northern Ireland on all students receiving a grant for the first time in 1973 and 1979 for study leading to a primary degree.

(ii) Each of the students in these two cohorts were sent questionnaires to obtain additional social, educational and attitudinal information. The response rate for the 1973 entrants was 51.4 per cent with 1,273 respondents, and for 1979 it was 73.9 per cent with 2,658 respondents. (The 1973 response rate, while low, was achieved using addresses which were in most cases 4/5 years old).

(iii) Students studying for a BEd (Education) degree are funded by the Department of Education for Northern Ireland (DENI). Each member of this 1979 cohort also received a postal questionnaire.

Response to the questionnaires demonstrated remarkably little bias when compared with the sex, class and other breakdowns of the overall cohorts derived from the Boards. We are satisfied, therefore, that the questionnaire data are valid and highly reliable representations of the two entry years of 1973 and 1979.

Central to this particular analysis of the Board and two main sets of questionnaire data (we are excluding the BEd data in this analysis) is that of religious affiliation. In the absence of official statistics researchers wishing to undertake analyses including religion in Northern Ireland have two basic choices. The first is to ask a direct question seeking religious affiliation—as used in the Department of Manpower Services cohort survey (see chapter 5) or in the 1971 census—a strategy which, based on these examples, might be expected to produce a 90 per cent response. The alternative strategy is to use schools attended to infer a religious affiliation. The basis on which this can be done is extensively discussed in chapter 7 and it is therefore not necessary to repeat that discussion here. The strategy of using schools gives a high reliability to our findings.[4]

Participation

In 1908–9, the last year for which denominational statistics were officially published, 8.5 per cent of students at Queen's College were Catholic. Moody and Beckett (1959) suggest that in the ensuing six years the number of Catholics rapidly increased to represent approximately 25 per cent of the student body in 1915, while in the population at large Catholic representation was about 35 per cent. This proportion, they suggest, dropped over the next decade as Catholics failed to keep pace with the expansion of student numbers. Before World War II, therefore, the evidence suggests that Catholics were underrepresented in higher education when judged against their proportion in the population. For the post-war period, some information on participation is available from the published reports of the Catholic chaplaincy at Queen's. These data are shown in table 9:1.

Table 9:1

CATHOLICS AT QUEEN'S UNIVERSITY, BELFAST, 1953–1969

Catholics as percentage of each Faculty

Year of Entry	*Catholic as % Total*	*Arts*	*Agriculture*	*Law*	*Social Economic Studies*	*Science*	*Med./ Dentist.*
1953–54	19.1	33.5	3.9	31.8	18.1	6.7	18.7
1955–56	19.6	32.6	—	30.0	25.2	8.0	18.8
1956–57	20.2	31.1	3.3	26.5	21.0	11.2	19.7
1957–58	21.6	35.4	4.8	32.9	22.6	11.9	19.8
1958–59	21.9	35.4	6.2	29.7	20.4	14.2	19.0
1959–60	22.2	36.3	7.3	31.9	22.4	13.5	19.2
1961–62	23.8	38.3	7.9	27.3	25.6	15.1	17.9
1962–63	23.6	35.8	9.1	25.9	28.4	16.9	18.2
1964–65	25.9	36.9	11.0	30.0	30.6	19.2	16.5
1965–66	25.9	36.1	13.4	31.3	31.4	18.3	16.6
1966–67	27.2	39.9	10.3	30.4	28.5	19.2	16.9
1967–68	26.0	37.8	8.5	24.9	26.6	20.2	18.9
1968–69	27.4	38.9	9.6	35.9	29.3	21.0	21.3

Source: Calculated from annual reports of the Catholic chaplaincy, Queen's University, Belfast.

During the 1950s approximately 10 per cent of all students went to the Republic of Ireland and a further 5 per cent to Britain, and during the 1960s the proportion leaving the Province steadily increased. In using these figures for evidence on participation it should be remembered that data for Queen's University alone represent a declining proportion of the total cohort. From these figures, however, it can be inferred that during the twenty years or so following 1945 there was a steady growth in the numbers of Catholics entering higher education in general, and Queen's in particular. The increase at Queen's generally outpaced the overall increase in students at that institution. Notwithstanding this apparent growth it is unlikely, however, that Age Participation

Rates (APR) for Catholics and Protestants could have been equal even by the end of the 1960s. This can be asserted with some confidence because of the evidence from the estimated APRs for 1973 and 1979 as shown in table 9:2.

Table 9:2

AGE PARTICIPATION RATES BY RELIGION, 1973 AND 1979

	Protestant			*Catholic*		
	Male	*Female*	*Total*	*Male*	*Female*	*Total*
1973	13	9	11	9	7	8
1979	14	11	13	13	11	12

Note: Age Participation Rates are defined as $\frac{\text{Young initial entrants}}{\text{Single relevant age group (18)}}$.

Sources: Figures for entrants derived from Higher Education Project (omitting B.Ed. entrants). Figures for age cohorts derived from extrapolated 1971 census data (omitting those who did not state a religious affiliation).

In 1973 a Catholic APR of 8 is markedly lower than that for Protestants and particularly for males. The position in 1979, however, indicates virtual parity between Catholics and Protestants, reflected in the increase in the proportion of Catholics in the cohort from 35 per cent in 1973 to 40 per cent in 1979. The APRs for the 1970s suggest, therefore, a quite marked increase in Catholic participation during that decade as compared with the gradual rates of increase in the previous two decades. Between 1973 and 1979 overall student numbers increased by approximately 45 per cent; Protestant numbers increased by about 39 per cent and Catholic numbers by 71 per cent.

Richardson (1981) has recently redirected attention to the nature and importance of geographical variations in participation in higher education as a further important feature in evaluating access to higher education. Similarly Neave (1979) has argued, in a European context, that such regional variations are often a function of the socioeconomic structures of the different regions acting to promote or depress participation. The following table presents evidence concerning variations in participation between Protestants and Catholics across the regions of Northern Ireland (table 9:3).

For Protestants, in 1973, a uniform pattern of APRs prevails across the regions and these are generally above the Catholic rates in each region. Catholic APRs in 1973 are lower in the West and Greater Belfast with the latter figure a product of a particularly low figure for females. In 1979, Protestant APRs are notably higher in the

Table 9:3

REGIONAL APRs FOR PROTESTANTS AND CATHOLICS

	Protestant		*Catholic*	
Region	*1973*	*1979*	*1973*	*1979*
West	10	10	8	10
North	11	14	11	12
South	11	11	9	11
Greater Belfast	11	13	8	14

Note: Regions defined by the following district council areas:
West—Londonderry, Strabane, Limavady, Fermanagh, Omagh, Cookstown, Dungannon, Magherafelt.
North—Coleraine, Moyle, Ballymoney, Ballymena, Antrim, Larne.
South—Down, Newry & Mourne, Banbridge, Armagh, Craigavon.
Greater Belfast—Belfast, North-Down, Newtownabbey, Castlereagh, Carrickfergus, Lisburn, Ards.
Sources: As in table 9:2.

North and Greater Belfast with the South and the West lagging. A similar pattern is shown for Catholics, with Greater Belfast now recording the highest rate. It is not perhaps surprising to find the West recording the lowest APRs for both groups in view of its more rural character and its greater distance, in time and accessibility, from the main Northern Ireland institutions of higher education.[5] The West is, however, an area of greater importance for Catholics in population terms accounting for 34 per cent of the Catholic 18-year-old cohort, compared to 16 per cent of the Protestant (based on the 1971 census). In 1973, however, only 29 per cent of Catholics and 13 per cent of Protestant entrants came from the West. This under-participation in the West is compensated for by 'over-participation' in Greater Belfast, demonstrated particularly well for Catholics in 1979. Thus, while 33 per cent of the Catholic 18-year-old cohort resided in Greater Belfast, the same region accounted for 40 per cent of Catholic entrants. For Protestants the parallel figures were 55 per cent and 58 per cent. For Catholics especially, therefore, the underparticipation in the numerically more important West requires a markedly higher level of participation in Greater Belfast to enable Catholic APRs to match those of Protestants for Northern Ireland as a whole.

Occupational class[6]

Studies of access to higher education have invariably focused on class background as a major source of disadvantage. As we saw earlier, recent English studies seem to suggest that substantial pupil losses occur immediately after the compulsory school leaving age (Farrant, 1981). In chapter seven it is suggested that a higher proportion of Northern Ireland school pupils from working-class backgrounds were gaining 'O' and 'A' level GCE passes in schools attended by Catholics. For the class assessment of participation in higher education the benchmarks are the occupational class profiles of the two groups produced by Aunger in chapter two. Aunger uses the Hall-Jones system of categorising *occupations* while the *occupational clas backgrounds* of students are classified using the Registrar General's system (*The Classification of Occupations*, 1970). (The problems of using two systems are reduced by the following discussion being based mainly on a manual/non-manual division and specific occupations and occupational groups). Aunger's class profiles revealed a strong over-representation of Catholics in manual occupations with Protestants over-represented in non-manual occupations. Unemployment is experienced at a higher rate by Catholics than by Protestants (chapter 5). The occupational class profile of higher education entrants reflect these differences as shown in table 9:4.

Table 9:4

OCCUPATIONAL CLASS PROFILES OF PROTESTANT AND CATHOLIC HIGHER EDUCATION ENTRANTS, 1973 AND 1979 (Per cent)

	1973		*1979*	
Occupational Class	*Protestant*	*Catholic*	*Protestant*	*Catholic*
I	20.3	8.5	20.0	11.8
II	40.6	38.8	41.6	36.6
III N–M	14.0	9.8	10.0	5.8
III M	12.6	18.9	15.4	18.5
IV	6.3	8.1	6.1	8.4
V	1.3	3.9	1.3	3.2
Unemployed, Sick, Retired	4.9	12.1	5.6	15.7
TOTAL	100	100	100	100
N	1209	645	1783	1187

Note: Missing observations for 1973, 622; and for 1979, 627. These class distributions from the Board data are confirmed by the questionnaire data for the two years.
Source: Higher Education Project, Board Data.

The table clearly indicates that Protestant entrants are more likely to come from non-manual backgrounds than Catholics: 72 per cent of Protestants compared to 54 per cent of Catholics in 1979. Conversely, Catholics are more likely to come from a manual background that Protestants: 46 per cent of Catholics and 28 per cent of Protestants. (Note that this table includes the unemployed, sick or retired as a separate category). Catholics formed a majority of those entering from occupational class V and of those from an unemployed background. Some of these differences can be further highlighted by examining the specific occupational categories of fathers of entrants at the time of entry into higher education. In 1973, for example, 12 per cent of Catholic male and 18 per cent of Catholic female entrants came from a farming background compared to Protestant figures of 10 per cent and 15 per cent respectively. In 1979, the proportions declined for both groups. In 1979, 5 per cent of Protestant males and 2 per cent of Catholic males came from engineering/technological backgrounds while 10 per cent of Catholic males and 3 per cent of Protestant males had fathers employed as construction workers or general labourers. Some 12 per cent of Protestants' fathers were employed as managers or senior administrators compared to 6 per cent of Catholics. Protestant entrants are more likely to come from a sales worker background: 14 per cent in 1979 compared to 9 per cent of Catholics. An interesting feature is the relative importance of publicans and clergymen. In 1973, for example, some 6 per cent of Catholic male entrants' fathers were publicans while 3 per cent of Protestant entrants' fathers were clergymen. In 1979, the figure was 3 per cent for both groups.

At first sight these occupational differences in the background of entrants seem to broadly mirror the general differences in the class and occupational structures of the two groups and, therefore, not to justify extended comment. The general under-representation of individuals from manual backgrounds is, however, one of the enduring characteristics of higher education participation (Williamson, 1981). The relatively higher representation of individuals from manual backgrounds in the Catholic profile is, therefore, worthy of comment. Taken together with the evidence of chapter 7 there seems to be an emerging picture of Catholic schools, at least in part, diverging from the usual correlation between class and educational attainment. This pattern is an area which would repay a thorough investigation of the factors behind the aggregate patterns. Two possible explanations in particular could be examined. The first suggests that the relative disadvantage of Catholics in employment has encouraged a view in the Catholic community of education as the ladder for social and geographical mobility. Only through success in the education system can potential change from an impoverished and restricted environment be achieved. Protestants, particularly working-class Protestants, through their historically and, generally, better access to job opportunities, may not have developed the same attitude. A second explanation would stress the role of the school system itself and particularly a supposed ethos, derived from particular religious values and disciplinary attitudes apparently present in Catholic schools. While some evidence exists that Catholic schools are more successful than state schools in the United States (Greely, 1981), clearly to support such a conclusion in Northern Ireland requires further research.

In advocating such research it should be remembered that, on the basis of the higher education data, what is being identified is a tendency for working-class students to form a higher proportion of Catholic entrants than of Protestant entrants. Clearly, however, class is an important factor determining Catholic and Protestant entrants in 1973 and 1979 suggest interesting evidence of change class—and we should stress that we are not suggesting that class is insignificant in the Catholic education system.[7]

Courses studied

The discussion of 'O' and 'A' level patterns in chapter seven indicated broad differences in subject areas between Protestants and Catholics; Catholics, for the years studied, showed a bias towards the arts and related subjects while Protestants inclined towards scientific subjects. These differences applied to both males and females. The extent to which this pattern has carried on into the higher education sector can be gauged initially by the data for the 1950s and 1960s for Queen's University (table 9:1). Using the proportion of Catholics in the student population as a yardstick, it is clear that Catholics are over-represented in the Faculties of Arts and Law, particularly the former, while they are under-represented in Science, Medicine/Dentistry and Agriculture. The data for all entrants in 1973 and 1979 suggest interesting evidence of change (table 9:5). Examining the profile section of the table it can be seen that one of the largest changes is in the proportion of Catholics who are enrolled in Language/Literature courses in 1979 at 11.2 per cent compared with 20.7 per cent in 1973. Language/ Literature together with Arts courses accounted for one third of Catholic entrants in 1973 and one quarter in 1979, a proportion similar to that for

Table 9:5

COURSE OF STUDY OF PROTESTANT/CATHOLIC ENTRANTS, 1973 AND 1979

				Profile					
1973	*Educ/ Arts*	*Med. Dent. Health*	*Eng. Tech.*	*Agric. Fo. Sci. Vet. Sc.*	*Science*	*Soc. Ad. Bus. St.*	*Arch. T. Prof. Voc. St.*	*Lang. Lit. Area. St.*	*Total %*
Prot.	12.0	11.8	10.1	1.8	18.6	27.0	3.1	15.6	100
Cath.	13.2	8.1	7.2	1.5	17.3	30.2	1.8	20.7	100
1979									
Prot.	12.2	11.6	11.0	2.6	17.0	27.6	4.4	13.6	100
Cath.	14.1	9.1	8.0	1.0	15.0	36.2	5.3	11.2	100
1973				*Representation*					*N*
Prot.	62.4	72.6	72.0	68.4	66.3	61.9	75.9	57.7	1421
Cath.	37.6	27.4	28.0	31.6	33.8	38.1	24.1	42.3	781
1979									
Prot.	56.4	65.4	67.2	80.3	62.9	53.3	55.6	64.6	2015
Cath.	43.6	34.6	32.8	19.7	37.1	46.7	44.4	35.4	1345

Source: Higher Education Project, Board Data.

Protestants. By far the largest single subject area for both religious groups is Social Science/Business Studies. By 1979 over one-third of Catholic entrants were in this area. The important areas of Science and Engineering/Technology show no major change for the two years accounting for 28 per cent of Protestant entrants and 23 per cent of Catholic entrants in 1979. Agriculture and related subjects continues as an area of Catholic under-representation, a surprising feature given the proportion of Catholic entrants from farming backgrounds. Disaggregating these data for sex shows that the major differences in subject areas lie between males and females but that there are also some religious differences. Thus while males are far more likely to be enrolled in Science courses than females, Protestant females are more likely (13.5 per cent) than Catholics (10.5 per cent) to be engaged in such courses. Catholic females are far more likely to be in Social Studies/Administration/Business courses (43.8 per cent) than Protestant females (33 per cent) and, indeed, Catholics, male and female, are more likely to be studying these subjects than Protestants. For males, over half of Protestants (53.5 per cent) are in Medicine, Agriculture, Science, Engineering or Technology, while the comparative figure for Catholics is 40.3 per cent.

Variations in subjects studied can be observed by religion and these differences can be traced for both males and females. The nature of these differences, particulary in the Protestant emphasis on science related subjects sustains and enlarges the evidence from 'O' and 'A' levels reported in chapter seven.

Geographical Mobility

In this section, a number of issues of attainment will be examined within the basic framework of the geographical distributions of Protestants and Catholics entering higher education and their subsequent mobility upon graduation. One of the main characteristics of Northern Ireland's higher education in the past decade has been the proportion of students leaving the Province for study (see figure

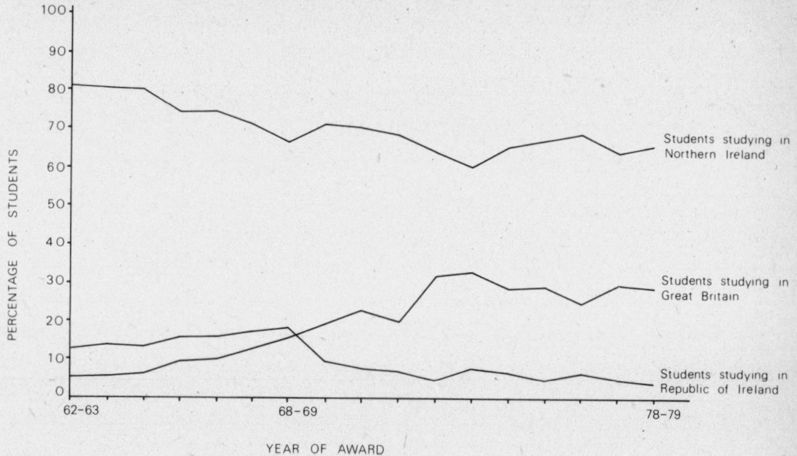

Figure 9:1 Study destinations for Northern Ireland undergraduates, 1962–79.

9:1). In the early 1960s just over 80 per cent of students remained in Northern Ireland while during the 1970s this gradually declined to around 65 per cent at the end of the decade. The main destination is Britain while most of the remainder go to the Republic of Ireland which, however, has taken a decreasing proportion.

The basic flows of Protestant and Catholic entrants are shown in table 9:6.

Table 9:6

DESTINATION OF ENTRANTS BY RELIGION (Per cent)

	Protestant		*Catholic*	
	1973	*1979*	*1973*	*1979*
Northern Ireland	57.8	62.0	62.9	75.4
Great Britain	39.6	35.3	22.5	17.6
Republic of Ireland	2.6	2.7	14.6	7.0

Source: Higher Education Project, Board Data.

Figure 9:2 Northern Ireland students: place of study (1973 entrants) and place of domicile (1980).

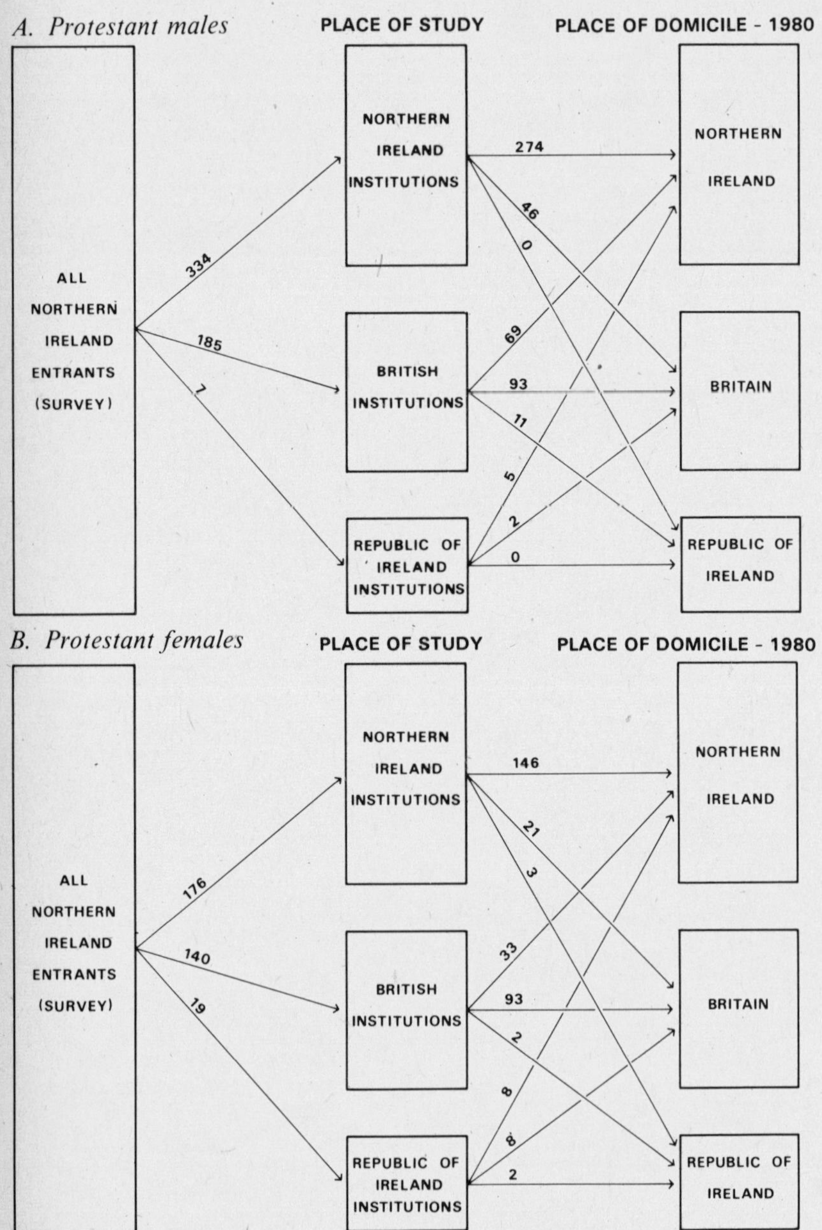

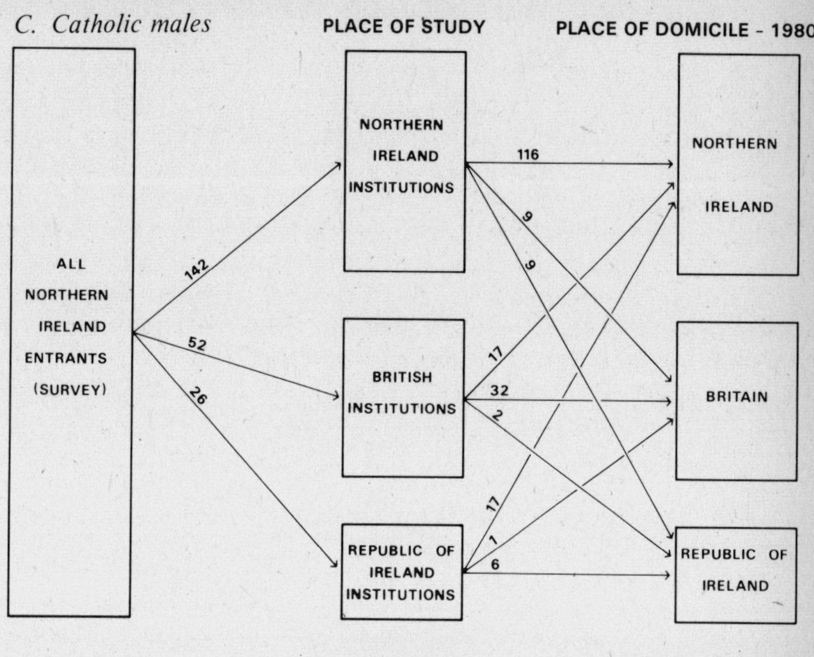
C. Catholic males
PLACE OF STUDY
PLACE OF DOMICILE - 1980
ALL NORTHERN IRELAND ENTRANTS (SURVEY)
NORTHERN IRELAND INSTITUTIONS
BRITISH INSTITUTIONS
REPUBLIC OF IRELAND INSTITUTIONS
NORTHERN IRELAND
BRITAIN
REPUBLIC OF IRELAND
142
52
26
116
9
9
17
32
2
17
7
6

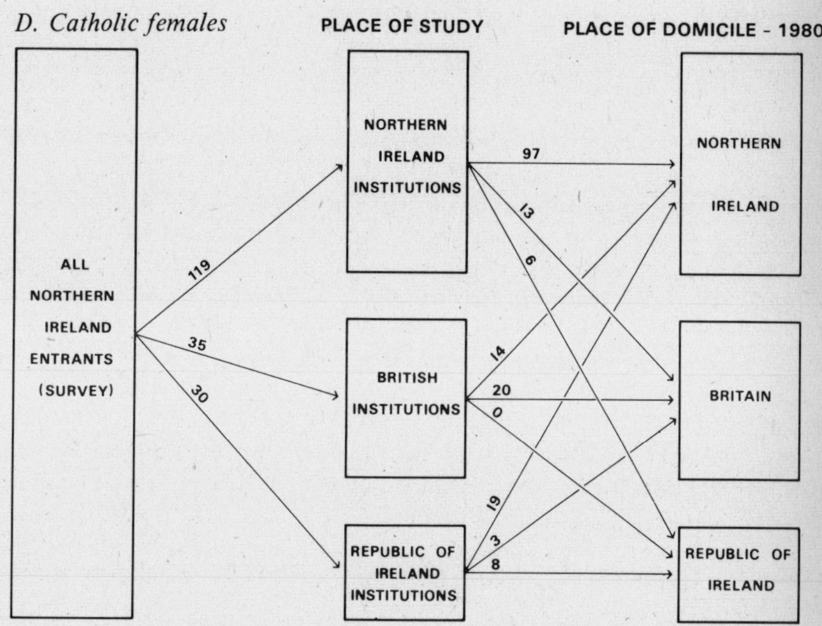
D. Catholic females
PLACE OF STUDY
PLACE OF DOMICILE - 1980
ALL NORTHERN IRELAND ENTRANTS (SURVEY)
NORTHERN IRELAND INSTITUTIONS
BRITISH INSTITUTIONS
REPUBLIC OF IRELAND INSTITUTIONS
NORTHERN IRELAND
BRITAIN
REPUBLIC OF IRELAND
119
35
30
97
13
9
14
20
0
19
3
8

These data, based on the information gained from the grant-awarding bodies, show differences between Protestants and Catholics and changes over time. Taking the proportions remaining in Northern Ireland for study first, in 1973 a slightly greater proportion of Catholics than Protestants attended the Northern Ireland institutions (62.9 per cent; compared to 57.8 per cent) but in 1979, while some 62 per cent of Protestants remained, no less than 75.5 per cent of Catholics did so. Moreover, the destinations of those leaving for study also changes. In 1973 while some 39.6 per cent of Protestant entrants went to Britain and 22.5 per cent of Catholics did likewise, in 1979 35.3 per cent of Protestants went to Britain compared to 17.6 per cent of Catholics. The Republic of Ireland's institutions attracted 2.7 per cent of Protestants and 14.6 per cent of Catholics in 1973 and 2.7 per cent of Protestants and 7 per cent of Catholics in 1979.

One of the strengths of our questionnaire data for 1973 lies in our ability to examine patterns of mobility of those entrants in terms of their place of domicile in 1980, seven years after entering higher education. The appropriate data are shown in figure 9:2 for Protestants and Catholics, broken down separately for males and females. Almost half of Protestant females, 47.4 per cent, left Northern Ireland for study compared with 36.8 per cent of Catholic females, while the proportions for males were 36.8 per cent of Protestants and 35.4 per cent of Catholics. Of those leaving Northern Ireland in 1973 some 63.2 per cent were recorded as domiciled outside the Province in 1980: 67.1 per cent of Protestants and 53.5 per cent of Catholics. Most of this difference is attributable to contrasting behaviour of females. Thus, 38.5 per cent of Protestant males had subsequently returned compared to 43.6 per cent of Catholic males, while 29.7 per cent of Protestant females had returned compared to 49.3 per cent of Catholic females. (Of those commencing study in the Province, 82.9 per cent are recorded as domiciled in Northern Ireland in 1980: 83.4 per cent of Protestants and 81.6 per cent of Catholics.)

The net result of these movements is that the 1973 entrants recorded as domiciled in Northern Ireland in 1980 comprise 65.7 per cent Protestant and 34.3 per cent Catholic; 70 per cent Protestant and 30 per cent Catholic for males and 58.9 per cent Protestant and 41.1 per cent Catholic for females. These quite marked differences, if sustained over a number of years, could have important implications for the graduate labour market in Northern Ireland. Unfortunately, there is no direct evidence of the representativeness of these patterns for other years. Speculatively, however, if these broad patterns of graduate mobility were applied to the greater proportions of Catholics commencing study in 1979 in Northern Ireland (75 per cent compared to 62 per cent of Protestants) then it is quite possible that the graduate labour market in Northern Ireland will be showing an increasing proportion of Catholics.

Of the 1973 entrants, in 1980, over 85 per cent of women, married or single, Protestant or Catholic, were either in full-time employment (80 per cent), part-time employment, or full-time post-graduate education. These high rates of female economic activity suggest that although the Catholic proportion of the Northern Ireland graduate labour market is biased towards females, it is nonetheless recording a high level of availability for employment.

Attainment

Within this framework of mobility, differences in the educational attainments of entrants can be examined. Those with 'A' level qualifications accounted for more than 95 per cent of entrants in 1973 and 1979.

In table 9:8 are shown the overall 'A' level distributions of Protestant and Catholic entrants in 1973 and 1979, broken down by sex.

Table 9:8

'A' LEVEL SCORES, BY RELIGION AND SEX, 1973 AND 1979 (Per cent)

	*Points Categories**									
	1973					*1979*				
	(N)	*1–4*	*5–8*	*9–14*	*15–20*	*(N)*	*1–4*	*5–8*	*9–14*	*15–20*
Protestant males	(487)	12.1	33.3	41.5	13.1	(817)	13.5	30.1	42.1	14.3
Catholic males	(208)	10.0	33.0	44.0	12.9	(514)	18.3	39.1	32.5	10.1
Protestant females	(327)	3.7	30.3	52.9	13.1	(680)	12.1	34.6	44.4	9.0
Catholic females	(181)	6.6	37.6	47.0	8.8	(462)	16.7	40.9	36.1	6.3
	X^2 significance n.s.					X^2 significance 0.001				

* Points allocated: Grade A = 5, B = 4, C = 3, D = 2, E = 1.

Source: Higher Education Project, Questionnaire Data.

The 1973 entrants' 'A' level distribution shows no statistically significant differences with reference to religion whereas the 1979 entrants' distribution is significant (p = .001). Examining the 1979 patterns it is clear that a larger proportion of Protestants, males and females, have 9 points or more (equivalent to 3 'C' grades or better) than Catholics. In average terms, Protestants record a score of 9.4 and Catholics 8.3 in 1979 whereas in 1973 the respective figures were 9.9 and 9.5.[8] It would seem, therefore, that the expansion of places in the 1970s has involved, particularly for Catholics, an increase in those entering higher education with lower grades. This analysis can be considered further by examining the mean 'A' level scores in terms of destination for study, as shown in table 9:9.

Table 9:9

MEAN 'A' LEVEL SCORES FOR PROTESTANTS AND CATHOLICS BY DESTINATION FOR STUDY

1973	*Northern Ireland*	*Great Britain*	*Republic of Ireland*
Protestant	9.1	11.3	10.9
Catholic	9.0	9.9	11.3
1979			
Protestant	8.8	10.3	10.9
Catholic	8.0	8.8	11.3

Source: Higher Education Project, Survey Data.

In 1973, Protestants and Catholics who left Northern Ireland for study had higher mean 'A' levels than those who remained in the Province. For Protestants, those going to Britain had the highest mean score while for Catholics those going to the Republic of Ireland recorded the highest score. In 1979, as in 1973, the lowest scores for Protestants and Catholics are recorded by those remaining in Northern Ireland. In 1979, more of those Protestants with an 'A' level score between 15–20 points left Northern Ireland (59.1 per cent) than similarly qualified Catholics (45.7 per cent).

It is clear, therefore, that during the 1970s those Catholics leaving Northern Ireland for study were, on average, better qualified amongst those going to the Republic, although the numbers involved are small, while Protestants are on average better qualified amongst the much larger numbers going to Britain.

The consideration of attainment can be extended further to the degrees obtained by the 1973 entrants (table 9:10). Only small differences are apparent in the degrees obtained, with Protestants slightly more likely to obtain an honours degree and a higher classified honours degree, while Catholics are more likely to have obtained a general degree.

Table 9:10

DEGREE QUALIFICATIONS OF PROTESTANT AND CATHOLIC 1973 ENTRANTS

	Protestants	*Catholics*
Honours degree, upper second or above	29.3	25.9
Honours degree, lower second or below	36.3	35.8
General degree	11.5	16.4
Pass, ordinary or other degree	16.4	15.1
Still studying	0.9	1.2
No degree	5.5	5.5
N	860	402

Source: Higher Education Project, Questionnaire Data.

Occupations of 1973 entrants

From our 1973 entrants we gained information on the jobs which they held in 1980. Since this information is gained at one point in time, a few years after graduation, these jobs and their status do not represent the ultimate career destinations of this cohort of graduates. However, differences evident at this stage may well become more marked as careers develop. The data are shown in table 9:11. For males, the most prominent difference lies in the

Table 9:11

OCCUPATIONS OF 1973 ENTRANTS AS RECORDED IN 1980 (Per cent)

	Male		*Female*	
*Occupations**	*Protestant*	*Catholic*	*Protestant*	*Catholic*
Routine Clerical	4.9	8.6	13.8	9.2
Teachers (including University)	11.6	14.2	24.6	35.0
Doctors/Dentists	9.2	8.6	9.6	4.3
Other health and related	2.3	1.9	3.3	2.2
Engineers (all)	12.9	5.5	0.3	—
Technologists/scientists	6.1	4.6	3.3	1.6
Lawyers	4.0	4.5	2.4	2.7
Social welfare and related	2.3	3.2	7.5	10.8
Laboratory asistants and technicians	5.5	4.1	4.5	4.4
Surveyors/Architects/Planners	3.4	2.3	0.9	0.5
Accountants	4.0	5.6	1.2	1.6
Managers/senior government officials	6.5	6.5	5.5	2.6
TOTAL	72.7	69.6	76.9	74.9

* Classified according to Registrar General's Classification of Occupations, 1970, HMSO, London.

Source: Higher Education Project, Questionnaire Data.

proportions employed as engineers, technologists or scientists. Some 19 per cent of Protestants are in these occupations while 10.1 per cent of Catholics are similarly employed. In contrast, 26 per cent of Catholic men are in teaching, routine clerical jobs or social welfare or related occupations compared with 18.8 per cent of Protestants.

For females, the largest contrasts are with the jobs obtained by males but some differences between Catholics and Protestants are observable. Teaching accounts for around one-quarter of Protestants while over one-third of Catholics are teachers. Teaching, routine clerical jobs and social welfare occupations account for 55 per cent of Catholics compared with 45.9 per cent of Protestants. Almost 10 per cent of Protestants are doctors and dentists compared with only 4.3 per cent of Catholics, and together doctors, engineers and technologists and scientists account for 13.2 per cent of Protestant females while only 5.9 per cent of Catholics are in these occupations.

In summary, there are certain differences in the occupations held which seem at least partially to continue the occupational differences noted in the analysis of the 1971 census by Aunger in chapter two. Engineering and technical occupations are more significant for Protestants—males and females—while teaching and social welfare-related occupations are more significant for Catholic males and females. In other areas, however, there are broad similarities in the proportions recorded in management/administration, for example, or as lawyers or accountants. No information on the location of these jobs in terms of public or private sector has been obtained and so we are not in a position to gauge whether employment in either of the two sectors is occurring at similar rates.

Summary and Discussion

Perhaps the most significant feature described in this chapter is the steady increase of Catholic participation in higher education both in terms of participation rates and absolute numbers. During the 1970s, Catholics formed an increasing proportion of a growing cohort entering tertiary level education. Protestant participation also increased although at a slower rate, so that APRs at the end of the 1970s were virtually equal. The expansion of Catholic participation, however, has apparently taken place at the lower end of the entry qualifications scale, so that significant differences existed in the mean entry qualifications of Protestants and Catholics in 1979. Occupational class differences were also apparent and these differences tended to reflect the variations in the wider class profiles between Protestants and Catholics in Northern Ireland. Broadly, Catholics were more likely to come from manual backgrounds and Protestants from non-manual backgrounds. This has been argued as noteworthy in view of the marked under-representation of entrants from manual backgrounds which is a widespread characteristic of participation in higher education.

The differences in geographical mobility of Protestants and Catholics, in terms of both entry into higher education and subsequently as graduates are also significant. Although similar proportions of Protestants and Catholics were likely to leave Northern Ireland for study in 1973, Protestants were significantly more likely to leave in 1979. Graduate patterns of geographical mobility suggest that over 80 per cent of those commencing study in Northern Ireland remain in the Province. Of those leaving Northern Ireland for study, two-thirds remained outside the Province and this was more the case for Protestants than Catholics. If these graduate mobility patterns are generally true for the seventies and early eighties, rather than unique to 1973 entrants, the graduate 'pool' in Northern Ireland could be recording an increasing proportion of Catholics. Linking this evidence with the labour market can only be speculative. However, the rapid growth of job opportunities in the public sector in Northern Ireland during the early 1970s occurred with a graduate pool available for recruitment which, at its least, was similar to the Protestant/Catholic balance in entrants and may have shown increasing Catholic representation. Differences by sex and subject areas qualify this general position.

With regard to access, it is important to note that Catholics in Northern Ireland are currently not underrepresented amongst entrants, although this is a position apparently reached only very recently. Class, and to a lesser extent sex, remain important areas of concern as does the significant underrepresentation of Protestant working class entrants. The evidence on subjects studied and the subsequent occupations of 1973 entrants suggests that Catholics, working-class students and women are likely to be particularly vulnerable to policy changes in curtailing places in the social sciences, arts and humanities and the retrenchment in public sector job opportunities in teaching and the social services, for example. Clearly the 1980s could witness the reverse of many of the advances made by these groups in the 1970s as higher education becomes less egalitarian and opportunities for upward social mobility are progressively reduced.

Notes

1. The Group ('The Chilver Committee') was set up in December 1978 'to consider the present provision of higher education in Northern Ireland, to review both the general and particular needs of the Northern Ireland community in the 1980s and 1990s for higher education (including advanced further education) and to make recommendations'.
2. The project funded by the Social Science Research Council is entitled: 'Participation in higher education: trends in the social and spatial mobility of Northern Ireland undergraduates' under the direction of R. Cormack, R. Osborne, N. Reid and A. Williamson. The Research Officer employed by the project was Ms R. Goldie and the Data Preparation Officer was Mrs E. Cole-Baker.
3. The two years 1973 and 1979 were chosen because 1973 was the first year for which raw data were available owing to a major reorganization of the Northern Ireland educational administration in that year. 1979 was the latest year for which information could be obtained at the time data were being collected.
4. In our attempts to assess the extent of Catholic attendance at non-Catholic schools we asked a panel of experts to attempt estimates of the actual proportions of each school's population in Protestant/Catholic terms. We were fortunate to have accurate figures for two schools commonly thought to have a high proportion of Catholics from the headmasters. In both these cases our experts considerably overestimated the headmasters' figures. Our religious affiliation figures therefore have been based on a binary division with each school designated as either 'Protestant' or 'Catholic'. We estimate that on this basis our data on religious affiliation are highly accurate for the Board data and probably even better for questionnaire derived data where we were able to make use of other information.
5. Assessing the institutional and geographical destinations of students entering higher education from the West in 1979 shows 30.8 per cent going to Queen's University, Belfast, 37.4 per cent to institutions outside Northern Ireland, 13.3 per cent to the New University of Ulster and 18.4 per cent to the Ulster Polytechnic.
6. In the literature 'occupational class' and 'social class' tend to be used synonymously even though in the latter case it is usually based on occupation. For the analysis of the higher education data, class classifications are based on occupations.
7. Related to this issue is the type of school previously attended by entrants. In 1973, 6.3 per cent of Protestants and 4.7 per cent of Catholics had attended secondary intermediate schools prior to entering higher education, while in 1979, the figures were 8.5 per cent of Protestants and 16.2 per cent of Catholics ($p=.001$).
8. Part of the difference in mean 'A' level scores in 1979 is accounted for by variations in the number of 'A' levels of Protestant and Catholic entrants. Some 74.0 per cent of Protestant males and 75.6 per cent of Protestant females enter higher education with three or more 'A' levels while the parallel figures for Catholics are 68.5 per cent and 66.8 per cent. The difference is more striking for those entering with four 'A' levels: 20.6 per cent of Protestant males and 10.6 per cent of Protestant females compared with 12.9 per cent of Catholic males and 6.8 per cent of Catholic females. For those entering higher education with four 'A' levels the mean scores are: Protestant males 14.9, Protestant females 15.3, Catholic males 14.8 and Catholic females 14.7.

10. The Experience of the Legal Enforcement of the Fair Employment (Northern Ireland) Act 1976

C. McCrudden

The Fair Employment (Northern Ireland) Act 1976 (FEA, 1976) confers two major duties on the Fair Employment Agency (FEA): the promotion of equality of opportunity in employment in Northern Ireland between people of different religious beliefs, and, secondly, the elimination of unlawful discrimination on the ground of religious belief or political opinion.

Part III of the Act makes unlawful, in relation to employment or occupations, discrimination on the grounds of religious belief or political opinion by those to whom the Act applies. In addition the Act makes unlawful any victimisation of persons concerned in proceedings under the Act, the publication of discriminatory advertisements, or aiding, inciting, procuring or inducing another person to commit an act of unlawful discrimination. The Agency is to receive discrimination complaints and investigate them. If it decides that there has been unlawful discrimination it is to attempt to conciliate, but if unsuccessful it is able to issue recommendations to the employer or other respondent. If these are not complied with the Agency may take action, on behalf of the complainant, in the County Court. This Court has power to award damages or issue an injunction, or both.

The ways in which equality of opportunity is to be promoted are set out in Part II of the Act. As required by the Act, a Guide to Manpower Policy and Practice has been issued by the Northern Ireland Department of Manpower Services. The FEA, also as required by the Act, has encouraged employers and other bodies to subscribe to a Declaration of commitment to the principle of equality of opportunity. Potentially much more important, however, are the powers of investigation given to the Agency. Where the Agency is of the opinion, following an investigation, that the person concerned has failed to afford equality of opportunity, either generally or in relation to any class of person, the Agency is required to use its best endeavours to ensure that he takes such action for promoting equality of opportunity as is in all the circumstances reasonable and appropriate and to secure a satisfactory written undertaking by him that such action will be Taken (s.13(1)). Where the Agency is unsuccessful in this 'conciliation state', because the undertaking is not given, the Agency may decide that further action is appropriate. If it does so, the Agency is required to serve on the person concerned a notice containing directions. If an undertaking has been given but not complied with, the Agency is required either to serve on him a notice containing directions which then supersedes the undertaking or to make an application to the County Court (s.13(2)). In such notices the Agency may 'in particular' direct the person found not to be affording equality of opportunity that he abandon or modify, in accordance with any instructions given in the directions, any practice which results or may result in failure to afford equality of opportunity. Directions may include a provision that new practices specified by the Agency be substituted or adopted. The Agency is also empowered to require whatever it considers necessary to ensure that the directions are duly carried out. The Agency, in addition, has a general power to issue such directions to the person investigated as it considers 'reasonable and appropriate for promoting equality of opportunity' (s.13(3)). Each notice served must inform the person concerned of a right of appeal to an Appeals Board against the directions (s.13(4)).

In this chapter I shall attempt to put some flesh on the rather dry, bare bones of these statutory provisions. I shall examine the experience between 1976 and the end of 1981 of attempts to identify and eradicate religious and political discrimination in employment, and to reduce inequality of employment opportunity between the two religious communities. A brief consideration of the origins of the Act should help to identify some themes which will be of importance in examining post-enactment enforcement.

The Van Straubenzee Working Party Report

The Fair Employment Act is one of the few surviving parts of the Northern Ireland constitutional settlement developed in the first period of 'direct rule' (1972–1974). A Working Party was established in 1972 by the Minister of State in the Northern Ireland Office.

> To consider what steps, whether in regard to law or practice, should be taken to counter religious discrimination where it may exist in the private sector of employment in Northern Ireland.

The Minister of State (at first Mr. Paul Channon, later Mr. William van Straubenzee) chaired the Working Party. Its members were appointed by the Minister and were members of the Northern Ireland Committee of the Irish Congress of Trade Unions (five members), and the Northern Ireland Chamber of Commerce and Industry (two members). The Working Party reported on the 23rd May, 1973 and recommended, *inter alia*, that antidiscrimination legislation be introduced. The Fair Employment Act is the result, although it goes further than the Working Party recommended in extending its protections to employment in the public sector as well. It received the Royal Assent on the 22nd of July 1976 and the Fair Employment Agency was established on the 1st September of the same year.

The Act implements four fundamental recommendations of the van Straubenzee Working Party. The first was that a voluntary approach to the eradication of discrimination must be supplemented and supported by legal machinery. This was based on the view that '[w]hilst it is reasonable to expect some response to exhortation, it would only be reasonable to foresee a substantial number of exceptions' and that '[i]t would be wrong to allow the progress which might be achieved through the tolerance and fair-mindedness of some to be vitiated by the intransigence of others'. Secondly, although discrimination should be made unlawful, the civil rather than the criminal process should be used. 'Of all the measures that could be adopted criminal penalties are amongst the most likely to provoke sectarian hostility in industry and thus be counter productive'. In addition the civil legal process could provide redress for the victim and embody 'positive means for reducing the incidence of discrimination'. Thirdly, an independent regulatory Agency should have the major responsibility for enforcing the law. Fourthly, this Agency should not only be given power to investigate and determine complaints of unlawful discrimination, it should also be given a much wider responsibility 'to take constructive action which will help to rectify such inequality of opportunity as may have arisen in the past' (Ministry of Health and Social Service, 1973).

The Effect of the Absence of an Anti-discrimination Law Tradition

Each of the four principles which underlie the approach adopted in the Act was heavily influenced by the lengthy American (and more recent British) experiences of attempting to eradicate racial discrimination by law (McCrudden, 1981a). There are, however, a number of contrasts which may be drawn, particularly with regard to the context in which anti-discrimination law in the United States operates, which may illuminate various aspects of the problem the Agency faces in carrying out its functions in Northern Ireland.

Most obviously perhaps, unlike the United States, the tradition of using law for such purposes in a sustained way is of recent origin in Northern Ireland. Limited statutory protection against religious discrimination had been provided in the Government of Ireland Act 1920. Section 5 provided that any enactment of the Northern Ireland Parliament might be challenged in the High Court on these grounds. Section 8(6) prohibited certain discriminatory uses of executive powers. Despite these provisions however the legal system had little effect on the growth and virulence of discrimination.[1] Prior to the 1960's, most anti-unionists concentrated on parliamentary (or more often extra-parliamentary) opposition to the existence of Northern Ireland as a state. Discrimination was regarded as inherent in the nature of the state itself. Minority political leaders who might in other countries (and did in the United States) use legal means of redress often, in Northern Ireland, refused to recognise the legitimacy of the courts or ignored them altogether.

Even after the beginning of the civil rights campaign in the mid 1960's in which reforms within Northern Ireland were sought rather than a new constitutional settlement, the protections provided in the 1920 Act were not used. The limitations of section 5 and 8(6) were severe (Calvert, 1968; United Kingdom Government, 1975). Neither section prohibited discrimination on the basis of political opinion; neither section prohibited discrimination in other than the public sector. Even as regards the public sector there was uncertainty whether either section 5 or section 8(6) applied to the actions of local councils.[2] In addition the political climate in Northern Ireland was such that there continued to be a lack of confidence that the courts were a sufficiently impartial forum in which to try complaints against unionist officials, especially in view of the number of ex-unionist politicians sitting in the superior courts. Moreover, lawyers were often unwilling to become involved in an area as controversial as discrimination (Carrol, 1973). There was, finally, a lack of tradition among Northern Irish lawyers of using litigation to bring about such a change due in some part to the absence of other formal constitutional guarantees, in particular of individual rights. And the lack of such a tradition also influenced the judicial approach.

On the limited occasions during the 1960's when judicial review of allegedly discriminatory administrative action was sought on grounds other than those possible under the 1920 Act, the problems of using the institutional mechanism of courts in an attempt to bring about social change became apparent. Those cases, for example the Dungannon litigation, which sought redress for allegedly discriminatory actions of local authorities on administrative law grounds, often proceeded on the basis of very precise and apparently rather technical issues, rather than the broad discrimination issue which underlay the dispute (*Campbell and Casey* v. *Dungannon RDC,* unreported, 19 March 1971, N.I. High Court, Chancery Division; *McLoughlin et al.* v. *Dungannon UDC,* unreported, 19 April 1971, N.I. High Court, Chancery Division; Hadden and Hillyard, 1973). The complexities of administrative law review made the taking of an action procedurally uncertain. The difficulties concerned with proving bias increased the initial hesitation to take cases. The cost of litigation was an additional deterrent and when, in the early 1960s, there was a well-publicised refusal to grant legal aid for a case alleging discrimination in the allocation of local government housing, the attempt to develop a litigation strategy lost much of the little support it had (Campaign for Social Justice, no date).

Only since 1968 have measures other than those provided in the 1920 Act been introduced to enable the legal process to be used more effectively to reduce discrimination. In 1969, the Parliamentary Commissioner for Administration (popularly known as the Ombudsman) was appointed to investigate cases of maladministration (including religious discrimination) by Northern Ireland Government Departments (Parliamentary Commissioner Act (N.I.), 1968). Soon afterwards a similar Ombudsman (the Northern Ireland Commissioner for Complaints) was established for local councils and public authorities (Commissioner for Complaints Act (N.I.), 1969). An anti-discrimination clause was introduced in all Northern Ireland government contracts. In 1972 a permanent Local Government Staff Commission was established with advisory powers to assist local authorities in the selection of candidates for senior and designated appointments (Local Government Act (N.I.), 1972).

After the introduction of Direct Rule in 1972 the British Government provided additional sources of protection in the Northern Ireland Constitution Act 1972. Primary legislation by any new

Northern Ireland legislative body was void if discriminatory. Discriminatory secondary legislation applying to Northern Ireland was also void. Actions by public bodies discharging functions relating to Northern Ireland were unlawful if discriminatory. Only one case has so far been taken under these sections of the Act (*Purvis v. Magherafelt D.C.* [1978] N.I. 26).

The lack of tradition of using law to eradicate discrimination has had a number of effects. The perception, among those whom the law was passed to protect, of what can be achieved is likely to be uncertain. This will be discussed subsequently. Equally important however, is the lack of experience among those given the task of interpreting and enforcing the law. The Northern Ireland courts lack experience in dealing with the issues which legal enforcement of anti-discrimination and the legal promotion of equality of opportunity necessarily raises. The role which the courts have been given under the Fair Employment Act is, for them, largely novel.

Nor has a *modus vivendi* yet been reached between the relevant government departments and the Agency, nor between the Agency and the courts. The effect of the evolving relationship between the courts and the Agency will be discussed below. A similar, though politically more controversial, evolution is taking place between the Agency and the supervisory Department of Manpower Services. Allegations have received wide publicity in the press of attempts by the Department to block Agency investigations into the composition of the Northern Ireland Civil Service and the employment practices of Ford Autolite and Short Brothers (*Hibernia*, 1979).[3]

Whatever the truth of these allegations, it is clear that the Department is ultimately responsible for the Agency and that certain consequences flow from this. Politically, as can be seen from Commons debate on the Agency (Official Report, Northern Ireland Committee, 21 May, 11 June, 9 July 1980), problems associated with the Agency rub off on the Departmental Minister. Financially too, the Department may find itself responsible if the Agency loses particularly badly in the courts. Because of the Agency's future responsibilities with contract compliance (this will be discussed subsequently) the Department may well also find itself at loggerheads with other government departments. Where trust between the Agency and the Department is absent (and such trust is unlikely to have developed) it would be unsurprising if the Department had become more and more involved in Agency affairs.

Important as these are, the major adverse effect of the lack of tradition of anti-discrimination law enforcement has been on the FEA itself. The Agency has, in the Northern Irish context, only the work of the relatively recently appointed Ombudsmen as precedents. But there are substantial differences between the Ombudsmen and the Agency which render even these precedents of limited value as a guide. In particular, whereas the Ombudsman (in fact both offices are held by the same person) acts alone, the Agency is composed of 12 members (including the Chairman) appointed by the Department of Manpower Services, three on the nomination of the Northern Ireland Committee of the Irish Congress of Trade Unions, and three on the nomination of the Northern Ireland section of the Confederation of British Industry. Just as the relationships between the Department, the Agency and the courts is in flux, so too the relationships within the Agency, between the Chairman, the Agency members, and the staff are also still evolving.

In the formative years of equivalent British and American agencies, the uncertainties produced by all of these evolving relationships gave rise to criticisms that the quality of work produced was seriously affected. Often too there appears to have been a lack of clear definition of what the staff of such agencies were supposed to be doing, loose procedures, lack of adequate supervision of staff by superiors and lack of formalised staff training. Reminiscent of these are some recent criticisms of the FEA (Anon., 1980).

The small staff and low budget of the organisation (12 staff—in addition to a Chief Executive who is also Chairman of the Agency—with a budget, in 1980–81, of £208,000) is unlikely to have helped the Agency to meet its full potential. Its smallness is particularly remarkable when compared with the Northern Ireland Labour Relations Agency (with a budget in 1980–81 of £595,917), and with the Commission for Racial Equality (with a budget in 1980–81 of £7,036,000). When the amount provided the FEA and the CRE is divided by the minority population which each body was primarily established to protect, the contrast is equally clear: the CRE is provided with over twice as much per capita as the FEA. It is apparent too that the original proposers of the legislation imagined a considerably larger organisation. The explanatory memorandum to the Fair Employment Bill envisaged the Agency growing to have a maximum staff of 40 and a budget (in 1975 prices) of £280,000. And this was before the extra responsibilities given the Agency concerning contract compliance had been finalised.

The pattern of Agency staffing has had a number of other aspects which appear increasingly anachronistic. Most noticeable perhaps is the lack of specialisation of function within the Agency. The Chairman doubles as Chief Executive *and* is as involved in day-to-day administration as in policy formulation and liaison with outside bodies. The conciliation officers are involved in the investigation of complaints *and* their conciliation. The employment liaison officer is engaged in formal investigations as well as monitoring and promotional work. Most importantly, perhaps, there is no internal source of continuing legal advice, despite its importance in policy formulation in this area, and despite too the regular litigation of Agency findings in the ordinary courts. At the time of writing the legal advice of two firms of Belfast solicitors is requested *ad hoc*.

The Experience of the Legal Enforcement of Non-Discrimination

Each of these characteristics of the Agency has adversely affected the effective implementation of the ideas and techniques proposed by the Working Party and adopted in the Act. In particular, the value of Part III of the Act has proved to be more symbolic than instrumental. A number of other reasons have contributed to this. Relatively few people have come forward and alleged unlawful discrimination to the Agency. In the first four years of the operation of the Act ony two hundred and sixteen such complaints were made.[4] By March 1981 new complaints were running at only two or three a month. One factor identified by the Agency to explain the paucity of allegations emphasises the 'considerable reluctance' among members of the public to make complaints:

> In certain districts people consider it would do them harm if it became known they had made a complaint. White collar employees, despite legislative provisions outlawing victimisation, worry in case making a complaint would be detrimental to their future employment and promotional prospects (FEA, 1979:19).

Schmitt (1981:13) has pointed, too, to the 'still substantial cynicism by the minority community regarding the equity of government remedies' as an even more basic reason (Schmitt, 1981, 9). This is at least partly reflected, he writes, in a:

> . . . pronounced lack of concern from minority leaders and groups in support of the Fair Employment Agency. The Provisional IRA, being committed to total political change, sees fair employment legislation as

> entirely irrelevant and indeed is pleased when administrative efforts fail to achieve significant reform, thus weakening the legitimacy of the existing political system. The leadership of the SDLP, on the other hand, is much more concerned with achieving a political voice in government and tends to stress also the importance of economic development.

Another factor that appears to discourage complainants is the belief that as discrimination is so difficult to prove, there is little point in making a complaint. The figures of successful complaints supports the Agency's comment that such a belief is quite understandable. Up to the end of March 1981 there had been only ten findings of discrimination by the Agency out of the two hundred and sixteen complaints made. Of the eight Agency findings of discrimination which have been promulgated at the time of writing, six have been appealed to the County Court as permitted by the Act. Of those which have come to judgment (four of the six) findings of unlawful discrimination have been overturned by the County Court in each (*Northern Ireland Civil Service v. FEA*, undated; *Borough Council of Craigavon* v. *FEA*, 13 September 1979; *Newry and Mourne District Council* v. *FEA*, 24 June 1981). In one case the adverse County Court judgment has itself been overturned on appeal by the Agency to the Northern Ireland Court of Appeal (*FEA v. Borough Council of Craigavon* [1980] IRLR 316). If one way of assessing the success of the Agency in carrying out its statutory functions under Part III of the Act is its ability to have findings of discrimination supported in the courts, it has clearly failed.

There are a number of reasons for this failure. The difficulty of proof of intentional discrimination[5] is clearly vital. The Northern Ireland Commissioner for Complaints (NICC, 1971a:13) had described this ten years earlier:

> It is not difficult for a body if it is so inclined to profess policies of impartial selection and to point to ostensibly proper procedures, whilst following discriminatory practices. It can, for example, find plausible reasons for placing at the top of the list a candidate whom it prefers for a quite different reason. Also it may not be possible to establish discrimination through the examination of official documents, files and minutes etc. The minutes of local and public bodies relative to appointments that I have seen are extremely brief and contain the minimum of information. They usually report a bare decision without any reference to the arguments put forward or the factors taken into account. Such records often give no help in an investigation beyond confirming that a certain decision was made on a certain date.

The NICC (1971a) developed two methods to overcome the difficulties which he encountered. First,

> in some cases . . . it is necessary to question motive and to interrogate the body concerned about its reasons for preferring a particular candidate so that I may be informed of the factors which influenced the taking of a discretionary decision.

The Agency too has used this method of attempting to overcome the problem. It would be true to say however that the questioning by the Agency of the motives of respondents has not been successful, largely because the County Courts have regarded it as their function to second-guess the Agency's inferences where the Agency has found discrimination. The substitution by the courts of their opinions for those of the Agency in this way has been encouraged by the decision of Lord Lowry, C.J. in *FEA v. Craigavon Borough Council* ([1980]IRLR 316) that when an appeal against an Agency decision is taken to the County Court, 'the right procedure is to rehear completely the aggrieved person's complaint' rather than, as was proposed by the Agency, by way of a review of the Agency's findings and the reasons for them.

A second method adopted by the NICC (1971a) to reduce the problems of proof was by considering:

> the significance of statistical information about the religious denominations of the existing employees of a particular body, when allegations based upon such information are made by complainants. Evidence of this sort must be regarded with circumspection, but it is a factor whose significance I must carefully consider.[6]

So too the Agency has increasingly sought statistical evidence. In view of the courts' approach to appeals, there should be increasing reliance on making inferences of discrimination on the basis of 'harder' evidence of this type, and a decreasing reliance on intuitive judgment based on the 'feel' of a case.

However, even if those who consider that they had been discriminated against on a particular occasion do formally complain to the Agency and even if they are successful, reliance solely upon such complaints would be inadequate. The pattern of applications for employment in many areas in Northern Ireland reveals, in the Agency's words, 'the characteristics of what is now in effect voluntary religious segregation in seeking employment opportunities, (FEA, 1980:24). Few complaints are likely to be received against those firms which are known to be the most exclusionary since those who would be in the minority in a particular firm are unlikely ever to apply, considering that rejection would be a foregone conclusion. 'The bulk of complaints . . . come not from the areas of employment where the grossest imbalances take place but from areas where both communities have access to employment and where therefore such imbalances do not arise (Cooper, 1981:11).

Reliance simply on a non discrimination strategy is inadequate for a second important reason. As the Agency's research has amply demonstrated the present effects of past discrimination and the use of criteria for selecting and promoting employees which have the *effect* of disproportionately excluding Catholics, though they are not used intentionally to achieve this effect are just as important in perpetuating inequality of opportunity as intentional discrimination. The Van Straubenzee Working Party decided therefore that the legislation should seek to secure not only the absence of discrimination but the presence of equality of employment opportunity as well. Indeed it was to be the pre-eminent goal. They decided that the fundamental aim must be to promote '*full equality in all aspects of employment opportunity*'.

The Experience of the Legal Enforcement of Equality of Opportunity

It was by no means certain however that the Agency itself would decide that law enforcement techniques were the most appropriate or effective methods of securing equality of employment opportunity and, despite the Van Straubenzee Report's scepticism of change being brought about voluntarily, the Agency might have found the alternative too unpalatable. And so it appears it did for a number of years. Initially the efforts of the Agency in furthering the goal of equality of opportunity were largely promotional and educational: persuading organisations to sign the Declaration,[7] working with the Department of Manpower Services in producing the Guide to Manpower Policy and Practice, holding seminars and giving lectures. By the end of March 1979 only one formal investigation into inequality of opportunity had been completed in a small area of public employment.

There were other, additional reasons, of course. It was felt desirable that the Guide to Manpower Policy and Practice should be available to employers and that the Agency should have completed its initial research work into patterns of employment, before formal investigations were begun on any substantial scale.

With publication of the Guide and completion of the research these two self-imposed barriers disappeared. It became clear too, that voluntary changes were not taking place sufficiently quickly to justify further restraint.[3] Since 1979 therefore the use of powers to hold formal investigations into equality of opportunity under Part II of the Act has been recognised by the Agency as the major weapon which it should and would use. Not only has the number of investigations increased but more importantly the potential impact of the investigations initiated has been expanded through choosing 'strategic' targets (McCrudden, 1979, 71). At the time of writing, for example, two major investigations were taking place, one into the religious composition of the Northern Ireland Civil Service, the other into the engineering industry.

Most investigations, however, have seldom been part of a coherent plan thought out in advance and followed consistently. They are usually *ad hoc*, reactive to particular complaints and launched with little or no assessment of the burdens which such an investigation would place on the Agency. The result has been that few would seem to be progressing smoothly to completion. Only one minor investigation initiated under Part II had been completed by the end of 1981. No findings of inequality of opportunity arising from such investigations have yet been made, though the draft findings in an investigation of Cookstown District Council sent to the Council for comment have been publicised in the press.

The unplanned nature of the enforcement by the Agency of Part II has been accentuated too by the increasing use of section 27 of the Act which provides that where, following an investigation of a *discrimination* complaint under Part III, the Agency is of the opinion that the respondent has failed to afford *equality of opportunity,* the Agency is required to use its best endeavours to see that equality of opportunity is provided by the respondent in future (e.g. FEA, 1981, case No. 137). The Agency's view appears to be that, if information is obtained which gives rise to very serious concern about practices in an organisation, it is very difficult, and probably undesirable, to walk away from that situation and say that, since such an investigation was not part of the Agency's forward planning, one should not be initiated. The difficulty with this view is, however, that it diverts resources from effectively pursuing those priorities which have been ranked higher by the Agency in its strategic planning. Nor is it necessarily so that the problems exposed will be walked away from. Rather they could be tackled in a more effective, planned and efficient way by, for example, storing such information for future use as part of a larger, strategic investigation.

One of the few tangible benefits which increasing use of these provisions has brought is that a clearer meaning of 'equality of opportunity' has been formulated. The Van Straubenzee Working Party had been clear on the general approach which should be taken but not on the specifics of what exactly should constitute inequality of opportunity (Ministry of Health and Social Services, 1973). In the first Part II investigation to give a considered view of what constituted inequality of opportunity, the Agency adopted the position that religious imbalance in a workforce establishes a *prima facie* case of inequality of opportunity as defined in the Act. At each stage of the selection process one religious group may be favoured more than another group whether intentionally or not. Such factors as the level and type of education, success in aptitude tests, specific work experience, strength, place of residence, specific skills, performance at interviews, may be relevant for selecting from among applicants for a particular job. However where any factor is such that one religious group is placed at a disadvantage by its use, or where the manner of selection itself results in a disproportionate exclusion of a particular group, then it is necessary for a criterion having such an adverse effect on the religious group to be shown to be necessary. If it is not shown to be necessary then it must not be used, although a less exclusionary alternative may be substituted in some circumstances. The onus of demonstrating this business necessity lies on whoever wishes to use the criterion having the exclusionary effect (Northern Ireland Ministry of Health and Social Services, 1973; Northern Ireland Department of Manpower Services, 1978).

Because few Part II investigations have been carried out, and even fewer completed, examples of what are thought by the Agency to be the major factors perpetuating inequality of opportunity as thus defined are to be found mainly in opinions, using section 27, following Part III discrimination complaints. In one such case the Agency decided that the practice of recruiting by word of mouth and casual enquiry amounted to a failure to afford equality of opportunity to Catholics who might wish to work with the company (FEA, 1981, case no. 137). In its annual reports the Agency has given further examples of practices which it also regards, based on its own research, as perpetuating inequality of opportunity, including the filling of vacancies by the personal recommendations of existing employees, or contacts with one particular school in an area (FEA, 1979, 1981).[9]

While social science research has shown the importance of these factors in general, it is clearly a different operation for the Agency to establish that inequality of opportunity is not being provided in a *particular* case and in a way which is calculated to satisfy the Fair Employment Appeals Board (to which appeals against such findings may be made) or the superior courts (should a respondent seek judicial review of the Agency's decision). There has been little consideration of how best to produce information directly usable in the administrative and legal settings with which the Agency is concerned.

To a limited extent precedents established in the United States (and Britain) assist in setting out what needs to be demonstrated in order to establish a case of inequality of opportunity since the concept is basically similar to the expanded idea of indirect discrimination adopted there. Where they are of less assistance is in showing, in the Northern Irish context, *how* to establish these elements. Proving these elements is an onerous proposition in Northern Ireland, for a number of reasons (McCrudden, 1981b).

The method by which rules are established in Northern Irish industrial relations contributes to the difficulties. The informal system of industrial relations current in the United Kingdom during the 1950s and 1960s tended to increase the importance of work place bargaining. This was largely autonomous, fragmented, unwritten and work group (rather than trade union) influenced (see Report of the Royal Commission on Trade Unions and Employers' Associations, 1965–1968; Brown, 1972). Where discrimination was practised it tended therefore not to be formalised in collective agreements. Rather it tended to be informally agreed upon or carried out through custom and practice, localised to a particular work group or section, and unwritten. The informal system increases the burden of those seeking to establish discrimination and inequality of opportunity. The Agency is, too, often faced with the use of subjective factors which have an exclusionary effect and these are notoriously difficult to prove, being in many ways similar to intentional discrimination.

Secondly, though the approach which has been taken at the initial stage of establishing a prima facie case of inequality of opportunity is largely statistical (it is nearly always necessary to have reasonably accurate data on numbers of majority and minority in the relevant work group, factory, pool of applicants, or whatever), *how* to collect that information in Northern Ireland is a substantial problem.

Employers are not required to collect such statistics. For these reasons, the substantial benefits of Part II (in particular its scope and the ability of the Agency to initiate investigations without the need for a complaint) may well be lost, unless a strategy is devised to circumvent the difficulties and take advantage of these benefits.

The potential for using Part II investigations as a means of increasing equality of opportunity has been considerably increased by developments at the end of 1981 relating to the enforcement of anti-discrimination provisions in Northern Ireland government contracts.

The van Straubenzee Working Party had recommended that the FEA should take over the function of the Parliamentary Commissioner in enforcing the Northern Ireland Government contract provisions (Northern Ireland Ministry of Health and Social Services, 1973) and this was accepted by the Government. An additional scheme was, however, recommended and incorporated in the legislation. The Act provides as we have seen that the Agency is to invite such organisations as appear to it to be representative of employers, of organisations of workers and of persons engaged in occupations in Northern Ireland to subscribe to a declaration of commitment to the principle of equality of opportunity (to be known as the Declaration of Principle and Intent) and to encourage their members to subscribe to it. The Agency is also to use its best endeavours to encourage all employers and all vocational organisations to subscribe to the Declaration. The Agency is to keep a register of those who subscribe to the Declaration and each employer or organisation whose name is on this register is entitled to receive from the Agency and to hold a certificate describing him or it as an equal opportunity employer or organisation (FEA, 1976).

The published list of those who have signed the Declaration is distributed to all public authorities (FEA, 1976). The Minister in the debates noted that he assumed that government departments 'will take into account those who are and those who are not registered' (Official Report, Standing Committee on the Fair Employment Bill, col. 222). Mr. Powell stated, rather more directly, that there was 'a clear implication in the body of the clause that the public service in deciding between two contractors or two persons who may offer their services or sell their goods or services to a public authority should prefer the persons who were on the list of declarants to those who were not' (Official Report, Standing Committee on the Fair Employment Bill, cols. 219–220). This appears to have been assented to by those on the Government front bench.

The Agency is empowered to require a declarant, as a condition of remaining on the register, to re-affirm at such intervals and in such manner as the Agency may determine, his intention to adhere to the Declaration. More importantly, the Agency is empowered to remove from the register the name of any person who, among other things, is found by the Agency in consequence of an investigation under either Part II or Part III to have acted in a manner inconsistent with adhering to the Declaration (FEA, 1976, s.7). When an employer's name is removed from the register the Agency is required as soon as reasonably practicable to notify the removal to all the relevant public authorities. In addition, where a public authority forms the opinion that a contractor has acted in the course of performing a contract entered into with the authority in a manner inconsistent with the terms of the Declaration and his name has not already been removed from the register, the authority is required to inform the Agency of this opinion stating the reasons for it (section 9(4)). A person aggrieved by the removal of his name from the register may appeal to the Appeals Board against the removal.

These provisions had little effect. At the end of 1981, however, the British Government announced a considerable strengthening of their potential effect. Tenders for government contracts, from April 1982, will not 'normally' be accepted from firms within the scope of the Act unless they hold an equal opportunity certificate issued by the Agency (Official Report, House of Commons, Issue No. 1225, 10 December 1981, col. 473).

The Experience of Securing Remedies for Unlawful Discrimination and Inequality of Opportunity

Neither a finding of inequality of opportunity nor of unlawful discrimination is an end in itself. Assuming that the Act was intended to be more than symbolic in its effects (and it is an assumption with a considerable degree of support in the van Straubenzee Report) such findings are, in effect, preliminaries to the process of remedying the mischief found. There are two major issues which give rise to concern in the approach adopted by the Agency to the remedial process: one arising from the *method* adopted, the other from the *end* apparently chosen.

There are a number of important elements in the method adopted by Parliament for securing remedies in Part III of the Act. The Agency must initially attempt to settle the issue through conciliation. So too at each subsequent stage some degree of effort to reach agreement is contemplated before moving up to the next sanction. Thus it is only after conciliation by the Agency fails, that it is empowered to issue injunctive type orders. These orders are in turn backed up by mandatory injunctions available from the county courts enforcing them. In the event of subsequent non-compliance, monetary relief may be awarded by the county court to enforce the specific recommendations of the Agency. Somewhat similarly, negotiation and conciliation are contemplated as primary initial methods for remedying inequality of opportunity under Part II where it has been found.

Despite this, little attempt appears to have been made to consider the implications of this approach. The investigation and conciliation staff, as was pointed out above, are one and the same, thus giving rise to the likelihood of a counterproductive effect among respondents. So too planning for conciliation in order to further particular strategic ends has been virtually non-existent.

The second issue arises more particularly in the enforcement of Part II: what are the remedies appropriate when (or rather if) the absence of equality of opportunity has been established? I have described elsewhere the extent to which the van Straubenzee Working Party Report reflects the debate between 'affirmative action' and 'quotas' and how a compromise was reached of rejecting the concept of 'quotas' (narrowly defined) but accepting the intentionally broadly defined concept of 'affirmative action' (McCrudden, 1981c). The latter, it was said,

> involves deliberate programmes under which equality of employment opportunity may be achieved. It sets out explicitly and systematically to create this equality. It acknowledges that, in this way, employment proportions by and large will automatically reflect the denominational ratios in the community as a whole (Northern Ireland Ministry of Health and Social Services, 1973, para. 69).

The Agency too carefully distinguishes affirmative action from quotas:

> Final selection [in affirmative action] must be on merit. An employer who rejects a candidate in favour of one less suitable because he wants to improve the balance of his labour force would find himself in just as much difficulty with the Agency as an employer who adopts more traditional forms of discrimination . . . The work of the Agency will be complete not when there is an exact mathematical proportion of the two major sections of the community in every job or occupation in industry,

> but when it is clear that all artifical barriers of prejudice, custom and traditional practice have been removed (FEA, 1980: 24).

In one case, indeed, the Agency found against a respondent District Council on the grounds that they had practised 'benign discrimination' in order to rectify a religious imbalance in their workforce (FEA 1980, case No. 87).

While the Agency has been careful, therefore, to reject quotas it has not as yet fully utilised the possibilities provided by 'affirmative action'. Remedies which have been recommended in specific cases illustrate the comparatively limited range of techniques which the Agency has thus far regarded as appropriate. In one case a company was recommended to introduce means to enable the company to monitor applications as to the religion of applicants, incorporate a question on religion in the application form, and set a target for each recruitment to attract applicants in numbers which reflected the religious profile of the catchment area. In another case a company was recommended to place responsibility for the development and implementation of an equal opportunity policy with a member of senior management who should regularly monitor and report on its effectiveness, take steps to make all employees and job applicants aware of the company's commitment to equal opportunities, and fill all vacancies after advertisements in the press or through the Employment Service. The company should not recruit new employees on the recommendations of existing employees. In a third case the Agency recommended that, for each senior appointment which the organisation intended to make, it should appoint an independent assessor. The assessor's duties should be to assist those making the appointment in various ways. The use of consultants approved by the Agency was recommended. And the assessor was to report back to the Agency.

It is, of course, too early to say whether this limited approach will be successful in opening up opportunities for Catholics. Current indications are that it is unlikely, yet the Agency is, as yet, reticent in adopting the full-blooded affirmative action envisaged by the van Straubenzee Working Party, a reticence which appears largely to be due to the disastrous decline in Northern Ireland's economic prospects. The current assumption of the Agency appears to be that there are severe limitations to what can be done to increase equality of opportunity in a situation of economic decline (Cooper, 1981: Osborne, 1980).

It would have been preferable of course if attempts at providing greater equality of opportunity had taken place when the Northern Ireland economy was in better shape than it is now. No one is likely to disagree about the desirability of disguising the fact that redistribution from those who have to those who have not is taking place by increasing the total amount of goods which is to be distributed. Then everyone may get more or at least the same. An example may serve to illustrate the point. A parent has £1,000 to distribute each year to two children. In previous years she has been unfair, giving child A £750 and child B £250. This distribution has become such a regular occurrence that A has come to expect it and has made arrangements based on the expectation of his receiving that amount. This year however the parent wants to be fair to B. She now realises there is no justifiable reason why A should get more. But she is worried. A's expectations are that she will give him £750. If, however, she can increase the total amount which is to be distributed to, say, £1,500 then she can give £750 to each. A should be content because his expectation of receiving that amount is satisfied. B should be equally content because the unjustified distributional system has been rectified, at least for the future. In this way the tensions likely to be generated by bringing about changes in the proportion which each child gets have been lessened. (A may still complain of the change in differential between himself and B but this is much less worthy of sympathy in light of the unjust basis for that differential.)

Such a welcome solution is highly unlikely in Northern Ireland, at least in the short term, however much it might have been possible in 1973 when the van Straubenzee Working Party reported. The position in which some employers now find themselves is more similar to that which would face the parent if she were required to *decrease* the total amount for distribution. Where this issue arises at the remedial stage the Agency will have to decide whether to allow the presently unjust method of distribution to continue in order to satisfy the expectations of the Protestant community, or require the available resources to be distributed more justly at the cost of disappointing those expectations.[10]

Fortunately, however, some employers are not in this position. In some industries in certain areas it is likely that employment opportunities are being expanded in particular firms. In other industries it is likely that though employment opportunities have not increased there is still turnover of employees. The implications of these differences in the effects of a recessionary economy have not adequately been assessed by the Agency, in particular with regard to the direction formal investigations should take, and the way in which remedies should be formulated.

Conclusion

The experience of the legal enforcement of the Fair Employment Act is, therefore, a depressing picture of a massive task, of the possibility of change, but of an Agency which has failed to meet that challenge. A complete overhauling of the FEA is necessary. Agency procedures, structures, and policy must all be rethought before the type of forceful role for the legal process in the eradication of inequality of employment opportunity, envisaged by the van Straubenzee Working Party, is even remotely possible. Recently there have been some grounds for optimism that necessary reforms may take place. The Agency has, since the middle of 1981, been engaged in a review of these issues. It is by no means certain that the Act will prove successful even if the, I hope constructive, criticisms of the Agency made in this paper are accepted and changes adopted and implemented. What *is* clear, however, is that without such changes the ideals which the Act was meant to achieve stand little chance of success.

Notes

1. On only one occasion does either section appear to have been subject to judicial scrutiny in the context of alleged religious discrimination (see *Londonderry C.C. v. McGlade* [1925] NI 47).
2. Counsel's Opinion to the Campaign for Social Justice (October 1965) advised that it did not.
3. The Agency did not abandon any proposed investigation as a result of any suggestions from the Department (according to a letter from R. G. Cooper, chairman of the Agency, 1 February 1982).
4. 6 in 1976–77, 130 in 1977–78, 37 in 1978–79, 43 in 1979–80 (see FEA 1977–1981).
5. 'Discrimination' was defined by the Northern Ireland Commissioner for Complaints (1971(b)) as 'the taking of a decision in favour of, or against, a person which is motivated by considerations of the person's religious belief or political opinions.'
6. In coming to his conclusion that discrimination had occurred, the Commissioner in one case 'Looked at the overall picture presented, including the employment pattern itself and particularly the department in which the Complainant failed to get an appointment.' NICC, Case No. 175/74. For other cases in which discrimination was not found but in which the NICC looked at statistical patterns, see NICC Case Nos. 13/71; 600/70; 43/69; 356/70 (see also NICC 1972). A similar approach was taken by the Northern Ireland Parliamentary Commissioner, cf. Case No. 2212/100/E.

7. During the first two years of the operation of the Act adherence to the Declaration was only open to employers with 25 or more employees. By March 1972, 1,100 had signed, representing approx. 90 per cent of those firms with more than 25 employees. This number also included all the major trade unions and all but a small number of significant employers in both the public and private sectors. The only major area not represented was local government where only 7 of the 26 district councils had signed. On 1 September 1978 the exception was reduced to an employer with 10 or more employees. By the end of March 1979 a further 1,562 organisations had been invited to sign, and 646 of them chose to do so. By 31 March 1980 the total number having signed was 2414 (FEA Annual Reports 1977–1981).
8. Osborne (1980a) quotes an unpublished survey by Mapstone and Young which found that of 155 firms questioned, although 70 per cent had signed the Declaration, only 17 per cent had considered appraising employment practices.
9. The inequality of opportunity provisions thus, in the Agency's view, go considerably further than one author had earlier supposed, in providing a method of attacking the present effect of past discrimination (see Lowry, 1979).
10. It is not proposed to detail the various methods which might be adopted by the Agency. Fortunately the Agency has the considerable experience of the American courts and agencies in developing 'affirmative action' available to it, should it wish to embark on an effective remedial policy (see Schlei and Grossman, 1976).

11. Conclusions

R. D. Osborne and R. J. Cormack

Religion, education and employment are topics, the exploration of which take us to central issues of the Northern Ireland 'problem'. In this book these topics have been approached from a position we have identified as 'political arithmetic': argument, disciplined by facts and figures, addressed to issues of government. Aunger's (chapter 2) detailed analysis of the 1971 population census provided much of the impetus for the research reported and discussed. As Aunger notes, previous survey-based research had suggested relatively small differences in the employment profiles of Protestants and Catholics. Thanks to the careful work undertaken by Aunger, the nature of occupational, employment and unemployment differences between the two communities are now much more widely acknowledged and understood. Aunger's analysis of 1971 data has been extended by Hepburn's (chapter 3) cross-sectional comparison of employment profiles between 1901 and 1951 for Belfast. He convincingly demonstrates that occupational and industrial advantages for Protestants span the first half of the twentieth century and that there is little evidence of convergence during this time. He also observes that when comparing patterns of social mobility, upward mobility for working-class Catholics appears particularly limited. Miller's (chapter 4) careful analysis of social mobility, based on a sample of adult males drawn in the early 1970s, suggests that, although broad patterns of mobility between Protestants and Catholics are similar, the differences in the occupational bases from which these patterns develop are such that these occupational differences seem most unlikely to narrow in the future. Miller concludes it would be '. . . foolish to assume that present-day inequities are only legacies from the past that will somehow gradually fade into oblivion of their own volition'. Together these three chapters document the extent of Protestant advantage and Catholic disadvantage, and demonstrate the longevity of these differences.

Typically the focus has been on male employment. The position of women in the Northern Ireland labour market, especially in terms of religion, has not been researched to anything like the same extend as for men. Aunger (chapter 2), while being primarily concerned with the occupational characteristics of all Protestants and Catholics, offered a brief analysis of some sex differences in employment. Importantly he suggests, from 1971 census evidence, that occupational differences between Protestants and Catholics are more marked for males than for males and females taken together. He notes that the *non-manual* occupations with the highest proportion of Catholics tend to be 'feminine' occupations while those with the highest proportion of Protestants tend to be 'masculine' occupations. For non-manual occupations as a whole the majority of Protestant non-manual workers are men while the majority of Catholic non-manual workers are women. In absolute terms the number of Catholic women employed in non-manual occupations is 25 per cent greater than the number of Catholic men in the same occupations. Generally, Aunger notes that Catholic men seem in a more disadvantageous position than Catholic women in terms of employment opportunities.

Trewsdale (chapter 6) emphasises that being a woman is *the* major source of disadvantage women face in the Northern Ireland labour market. Analysing 1971 census data she suggests '(the) female unemployment rate in an area will naturally reflect the lack of job opportunities in that area.' Whatever differences exist between Protestant and Catholic women, she argues, can be explained by reference to the same geographical variable: the unequal balance between the spatial distribution of employment, and the distribution of the two communities throughout the Province. A secondary explanation suggests that 'social practice' produces some of the observed differences, e.g. Catholic teachers for Catholic schools.

Trewsdale is undoubtedly correct in the emphasis she gives to women's disadvantaged position in the labour market. However, we would suggest that governments' regional and industrial policies greatly affect local labour market conditions to the advantage and disadvantage of *both* women and men in different areas. Some commentators have seen such policies as a deliberate strategy to ensure the availability of employment opportunities to Protestants and the denial of opportunities to Catholics (Farrell, 1976; O'Dowd et al, 1980). Others have portrayed governments as unwilling or unable to grapple with powerful economic forces and positively encourage industrial development in often geographically peripheral Catholic areas (Hoare, 1981). While an adequate explanation will ultimately have to take account of these and other forces and circumstances, the location of new industries over the years has tended to be to the advantage of Protestants and disadvantage of Catholics, regardless of sex. Moreover, explaining the disadvantaged labour market position of Catholic women in terms of sex and geographical location fails to take account of significant areas where they share the same underrepresentation as males, e.g. only 18 per cent of female employees in 'Insurance, banking, etc' were Catholic (see table 6:2). Ultimately these disagreements on the interpretation of the data available reflect the under-researched state of women in the labour market in Northern Ireland and point in the direction of what future research requires to be done.

Unemployment in Northern Ireland by the early 1980s had reached 20 per cent with one in four males without a job. The absence of official figures precludes a detailed assessment of the extent to which patterns revealed by the 1971 census—with a Catholic male unemployment rate over twice that of Protestant males—has changed. Miller and Osborne's analysis (chapter 5) of a large government cohort survey of the unemployed conducted during 1976–77 is, therefore, particularly useful. It shows that at a time of increasing unemployment, Catholics were over-represented in the survey (compared with their representation in the economically active population), were more likely to have been unemployed in the previous 3 years, for that unemployment to have lasted longer, to experience a longer period before securing a job (for those obtaining a job), to receive from Employment Offices fewer job submissions, and to be disproportionately represented in those remaining unemployed throughout the year. Moreover, the analysis demonstrated that these differences could not be accounted for by variations in education, skill level (as measured by social class), geographical mobility or general motivation. Finally, geographical location was shown not to be the dominant explanatory variable with unemployment rates for Catholics higher than Protestant rates in *all* areas, and for Catholics to receive fewer job submissions irrespective of the area in which the Employment Office was located.

While the state is directly involved in the organization and control of employment opportunities through its 'Job Markets',

'Employment Offices' and its other employment agencies not all job vacancies are filled through such *formal* mechanisms. The two studies of young male school leavers (chapter 8) reported a high degree of reliance on informal mechanisms of recruitment by employers seeking recruits at this stage and level in the labour market. In both studies, of the minority of boys who actually found employment, many if not most had found work primarily through the auspices of family and friends. As Murray and Darby point out:

> . . . the majority of Protestant boys learn of available jobs through parents and relatives, and if Protestants presently hold a disproportionate share of the job market, then there seems little chance in the near future of rectifying the imbalance in employment which seems to exist between the two main religious groups.

In Britain the Institute of Personnel Management (1978) has recognised the importance of these practices in disadvantaging young blacks and urged all personnel officers to reject them. In Northern Ireland where employment patterns and practices have been laid down over many years it requires special efforts to ensure the provision of full equality of opportunity. Formal procedures—notifying 'Job Markets' of vacancies, advertising in the local press, holding proper interviews and so on—will not ensure equality of opportunity, but they do constitute a significant advance on current practices. They would, for example, allow much more direct scrutiny of recruiting procedures; while for employers, for very little extra cost, they can expand the quantity and quality of potential recruits.

Chapters 7 and 9, dealing with educational attainment, provide important evidence of the broad equivalence of Protestants and Catholics in gaining formal qualifications in terms of GCE 'O' and 'A' levels, and in entering higher education. This demonstration of parity marks out Northern Ireland as manifestly different from the situation of ethnic minorities in either Britain or the United States. Massive underachievement of, for example, blacks and Hispanics in the United States and children of West Indian origin in Britain exercises minority community leaders and educational policy makers. It could be argued that in the United States the particular development of anti-discrimination policies towards 'goals' and 'quotas', particularly within higher education as well as in the labour market, have been required as a result of the failure of these groups to attain proportionate representation in the various levels of the education system. Recently Little and Robbins (1981) have called for a 'quotas' policy to ensure adequate black representation in higher education in Britain. Such a policy in favour of Catholics within the education system in Northern Ireland is clearly irrelevant. Proportionate representation has been achieved without these or similar policies. It follows, however, that parity in the education system should be followed by a similar pattern of representation in the labour market, especially in terms of recent recruitment patterns, *if* employment decisions bear a close relationship to educational qualifications.

Murray and Osborne (chapter 7) argue that, in the past, educational attainment differences are inadequate as a complete explanation of the underrepresentation of Catholics in non-manual occupations. Educational qualifications were shown to have little currency in the predominantly manual sector of the labour market in which the young male school leavers studied in Chapter 8 were seeking work. However, given the formal procedures most usually utilised in recruiting staff to non-manual employment, and the greater currency of formal qualifications in this sector, we would expect there to be significant differences beginning to occur in the occupational profiles of Protestants and Catholics. The relative parity of educational achievement in the two communities occurred at a time of quite rapid recruitment to public sector employment. Hence, if there have not been substantial gains by Catholics in the numbers and quality of such jobs attained in the recent past, then a major piece of evidence to back the arguments made by those who assert that Direct Rule administrations in Northern Ireland since 1972 have failed to change pre-existing employment patterns, will have been found (O'Dowd et al, 1980).

Existing anti-discrimination policy in Northern Ireland, as McCrudden (chapter 10) makes clear, seeks to provide measures for the redress of individual grievances and the achievement of equality of opportunity in employment. There is no doubt that the Fair Employment Agency created under the 1976 legislation has had to work in an inhospitable political climate. Its existence and activities have been vigorously opposed by the major Protestant political representatives (Osborne, 1982a), although this has not prevented individual cases being brought to the Fair Employment Agency by them. It has also, perhaps, suffered from the organisational difficulties often encountered with the bureaucratisation of social reform. More specifically, however, in Northern Ireland the polarizing effect of continuing violence on social and political attitudes, most recently with the H-Block crisis and related events in 1981, together with massive recession in the Northern Ireland economy have combined to produce a widespread suspicion of the Agency's role and remit. In these circumstances an over-active policy all too easily becomes seen in 'zero-sum' terms; if 'they' are gaining, 'we' must be losing. This has been reflected in general attitude surveys by increasing proportions of Protestants feeling discriminated against (in general terms rather than specifically in employment) over the past decade. Nevertheless, a too cautious policy provides grounds for those who query the capacity for reform to effect real social change in Northern Ireland (O'Dowd et al, 1980) and provides a bleak message for those already disadvantaged in the labour market. There are major dangers in doing too little as well as too much.

No doubt, to many people in Northern Ireland much of the analysis and discussion in the preceding chapters has been couched in terms which have avoided the central issue: *discrimination*. The term itself is highly emotive and invites sharply contrary opinions; cool evaluations are few and far between. We have tended to prefer to use the term 'disadvantage' to refer to circumstances where one community compared to the other is markedly underrepresented, given their proportion in the population at large, especially in certain significant areas, e.g. in the distribution of occupations, and representation in institutions of higher education. 'Discrimination', on the other hand, is perhaps best reserved for those instances where individuals have *directly* experienced rejection for a job on the basis of the known or assumed community/religious identity of the individual.

Whyte's (1982) recent review of the social, economic and political situation in Northern Ireland, up to the end of the 1960s, is a convincing demonstration of the importance of discriminatory behaviour and practices in *some* areas while indicating its relative unimportance in others. We might also note here a former senior Civil Servant's retrospective view that anti-discrimination legislation should have been introduced in Northern Ireland in the early 1960s (Oliver, 1982). We do not propose to review Whyte's thorough discussion here, but it is appropriate to comment on the current importance of discrimination in employment, since much has been made by opponents of the fair employment legislation and the Fair Employment Agency of the fairly small numbers of cases found by the agency. There are clearly two related aspects to this discussion:

the actual incidence of discrimination and the number of cases investigated and the subsequent findings of the agency.

Most of the current evidence seems to suggest that the amount of religious discrimination, in terms of individually motivated behaviour, in employment, is relatively small. However, such a conclusion on discrimination could be deceptive in significant ways. Many of the patterns of disadvantage and segregation in employment, as contributions to this volume have demonstrated, have been laid down over a considerable number of years. The development of these long-standing and widely accepted practices and customs in employment has led to the acceptance of patterns of advantage, exclusion and segregation as part of every-day life in Northern Ireland, e.g. 'we' have never been employed in that factory and so 'we' look elsewhere for work. Given also the importance of informal networks for gaining job information and filling vacancies it does not necessarily require discriminatory behaviour to maintain such a situation. Current patterns of exclusion and disadvantage can be the result of past discrimination sustained by contemporary practices and behaviour which are not overtly discriminatory. Equally significant in this regard, is that individuals are rarely in a position to know or even suspect when a decision has been made on discriminatory grounds. There is no guarantee either that an individual will even know of mechanisms for redress which may be open to them if they suspect discrimination. In Northern Ireland, there are the additional problems of violence and intimidation to deter a potential complainant. The general inadequacy of an individual complaints-based system has for these and other reasons been well demonstrated in both the United States and Britain (Lester and Bindman, 1972; McKay, 1977).

'Discrimination', in the individual and direct sense defined above, is notoriously difficult to genuinely identify and to then provide conclusive evidence in often unsympathetic and untutored courts. Relatively few cases of discrimination have been brought to the Fair Employment Agency, and even fewer have been pursued to the point where a 'finding' of discrimination has been established and issued. However, it is clear that in making such a 'finding' much depends on the evidence that is deemed adequate. Under the fair employment legislation, Agency findings are subject to *judicial* review on appeal. But the Fair Employment Agency's brief is much wider than narrow legal criteria; it rightly encompasses, in addition, industrial and personnel practices of employers, just as do industrial tribunals in sex discrimination cases. A number of the early Agency findings were overturned in the County Courts and this undoubtedly had the effect of *raising* the threshold of 'acceptable proof' of discrimination before the Agency would make a 'finding'. The recent Appeal Court decision relating to the case of Fair Employment Agency v. Craigavon Borough Council (chapter 10; Osborne, 1982a) has now, however, defined much more clearly where the 'burden of proof' sits in discrimination cases when they reach the courts.

However, when long-standing patterns of *disadvantage* such as those discussed in the chapters of this book are admitted as evidence of improper practices, then *legal* remedies to structural inequalities in opportunities have some chance of success. The recent case of Cookstown Council provides a useful example of the importance of aggregate patterns rather than individual cases. The employment patterns and practices of Cookstown Council were subjected to a full investigation by the Fair Employment Agency upon representations by several individuals, but not as a result of a formal individual complaint of discrimination. The Agency, in the course of a detailed investigation, found evidence of 'inequality of opporunity' and that the Council's explanations were demonstrated empirically to be wholly inadequate (Osborne, 1982b). In such circumstances anti-discrimination legislation built solely around an individual complaints system would have been powerless to investigate the Council's record, far less lay down the basis for changing practices.

While we are sceptical of the relevance and efficacy of a United States-style 'quotas' policy to the problems of discrimination and disadvantage in Northern Ireland it is, nevertheless, surprising that such a policy option has never figured in the various 'solutions' and 'scenarios' to which the population has been subjected over recent years. Such policies have been developed in other parts of the world to resolve broadly similar conflicts. However, in Northern Ireland different national identities have been more consistently powerful sources of inspiration and mobilisation than civil rights and claims for fair shares of housing, jobs etc. Moreover, as we pointed out in the introduction, Catholic political parties have been more concerned with the question of the legitimacy of the Northern Ireland state than with the types of social democratic policies usually favoured by parties representing disadvantaged groups.

Nevertheless, the repeated attempts of British governments to resolve the conflict *within* Northern Ireland as presently constituted have centred on trying to ensure Catholic access to political power through power-sharing at Executive/Cabinet level. One of the reasons for seeking to deliver political power to Catholics in this way was clearly to encourage Catholic commitment to Northern Ireland and to reduce support for those seeking through violence to end the existence of the Northern Ireland political entity. A further reason, however, has been to try to ensure that Catholics gain a share of government benefits through public expenditure on employment, social services and so on, and to have *Catholic* politicians made partly accountable for such distributions. All attempts to achieve power-sharing, however, have failed. In this context a 'quotas' policy, strongly based on 'merit' to retain credibility (as in the case with national representation in the EEC Commission), in the public sector, could ensure many more opportunities than half a dozen cabinet posts. Such a policy of itself would not resolve the current demands of the Catholic political leadership. It might, however, be more attractive to many ordinary Catholics than the apparently less tangible benefits likely to accrue from power-sharing or even more distantly in a 'United Ireland.' To Protestants, such a policy is likely to be acceptable only if it greatly reduced, if not removed, the attacks, political and military, upon the legitimacy of the Northern Ireland political entity. Such possibilities can, perhaps, be dismissed as unrealistically speculative; based on an erroneous belief that both the desire for political power and national identity can be traded for socio-economic advantages. With the continuing political stalemate, however, and the sense of apathy and boredom amongst the electorate with traditional demands from party leaderships, the potential for such options may be greater than appears to be the case at first sight. On the other hand a 'United Ireland' would most decidedly require strong anti-discrimination provisions and a highly visible mechanism for ensuring equality of opportunity. While Garret Fitzgerald's (1982) recent claims for the strength with which the Irish Constitution protects individuals' rights has much force, much more precise legislation and institutions would be required to secure such rights, particularly in a period of 'integration'.

All this might, of course, be quite academic if the numbers and quality of jobs both in the North and South of Ireland continue to decline as they have in recent years. Redistribution policies work best in expanding economies where the new jobs can be directed towards disadvantaged groups (Goldthorpe et al, 1980). In a declining economy, however, there is little a government can do to significantly restructure past disadvantages. While the present Conservative government's policies have clearly exacerbated the problems we suspect that no government in the foreseeable future will be in a position to create, either directly or indirectly, substantial numbers of new jobs.

Whatever policies are pursued in the future they should be policies based on sound empirical evidence on the circumstances they are designed to tackle. In the past, all too often this has not been the case. The chapters in this book strongly suggest the importance of monitoring opportunities disaggregrated by religion. The producers of statistical information on Northern Ireland should be encouraged to disaggregate their data by religion wherever this is possible and appropriate. With this in mind it seems relevant to end this discussion with an agenda for future research.

Research Agenda

1. The most important research will undoubtedly result from analyses of the 1981 population census data. This will enable direct comparisons with the 1971 census to be made and an estimate of the total effects of the social, economic and political changes in the last decade to be ascertained.
2. A high priority should be given to comparing and contrasting the labour market position of Protestant and Catholic women. In particular Aunger's suggestion that employment differentials between men are greater than for women should be further investigated.
3. It is quite clear that monitoring the major role of the state in locating new industry, in the event of an economic recovery, would become a priority. If new jobs, by and large, go to those areas which gained most in the past then there is little potential for increasing equality of opportunity for future generations.
4. A greater geographical sensitivity to the situation in terms of employment patterns outside greater Belfast, in towns such as Newry, Ballymena, Omagh, Armagh, Craigavon, Enniskillen, Dungannon and Downpatrick should be developed. Just as Poole (1982) has drawn attention to the contrasting patterns of residential segregation outside Belfast, so too may employment patterns vary geographically.
5. A continuing monitoring of the education system at both secondary and higher levels to assess the impact the massive

increase in unemployment has on aspirations and attainment. Any restrictions on higher education places may well have different implications for Protestants and Catholics depending on whether particular subject areas are cut-back.

6. One factor not considered in this collection of essays is the potential significance for employment patterns of the demographic differences between Protestants and Catholics. The assertion that the higher birth rate and larger family size of Catholics is the *key* factor for understanding employment/unemployment experiences is not accepted by the editors. Indeed, the singlemindedness with which the importance of these demographic factors has been argued (Compton, 1981) is mirrored only by those who seek to attribute all differences and disadvantages to discrimination (Farrell, 1976). The significance of larger family size in prolonging unemployment (through maximising dependent related benefits) has been substantially questioned by Miller and Osborne in chapter 5. Nevertheless, a comprehensive analysis being undertaken by Dr D. Eversley with the Policy Studies Institute should enable the precise significance of the demographic differential for employment opportunity to be assessed.

7. A major part of any further research in the 1980s must examine the effectiveness of the fair employment legislation and the Fair Employment Agency. This could involve a monitoring of the recent linking of government contracts to signing the Agency's 'declaration of principle and intent', an evaluation of the investigations undertaken by their effectiveness in securing change, and the extent to which employers' organisations and trades unions go beyond verbal commitments to the legislation.

8. Finally, a debate over the adequacy of official statistics should be started. As many commentators have pointed out, official statistics are a by-product of administrative activities, rather than specially developed indicators. The inadequacies of the monthly unemployment figures are particularly well known in this respect. Nevertheless, as Bulmer (1980) has pointed out, such data are often used for policy development and figure in public debate hence their potential should be exploited fully, whilst acknowledging their limitations. In Northern Ireland, no major statistical series are broken down by religion. The forthcoming 1981 census reports, if valid, will enable an assessment of the broad occupational and employment situation, but it is inadequate and unwise not to have, for example, an up-to-date measure of the changing pattern of

unemployment between the two communities. If there is a commitment by government to the achievement of equality of opportunity then there should be a similar commitment to produce the statistics to enable a measure of the extent to which that goal is being achieved.

Afterwords

Research on many aspects of life in Northern Ireland is often controversial. In order to reflect this and to stimulate debate on the issues in this book, we invited Dr. F. W. Boal, a prominent social scientist in Northern Ireland, to offer his critical comments, to which we offer our response.

A Word of Dissent: F. W. Boal

The preceding chapters offer a meticulous and painstaking gathering and analysis of data directed towards a number of related objectives, with a focus on the relative position of Roman Catholics and Protestants in the occupational structure of Northern Ireland. The extent to which one group is relatively disadvantaged and the other relatively advantaged within this structure raises two sets of questions. The first set asks what has caused the situation and the second asks what should be done about it. In the former context it may be useful to briefly indicate the possible wide range of causal factors that have contributed to ethnic stratification in many parts of the world; in the latter context some very specific political and social aspects of Northern Ireland need to be pinpointed.

Raymond Breton (1979), in a recent article has suggested that there are three different but complementary approaches to the study of ethnic stratification—the individual competition approach, the class approach and the social closure approach. Each approach, from its own perspective, highlights factors that may contribute to ethnic stratification. The three approaches can be briefly reviewed. Firstly, when one adopts *the individual competition approach* to ethnic stratification, and if occupation differences are observed between people of different ethnic origins, then the causes of these differences will be thought to derive from the distribution of relevant personal attributes across the ethnic groups concerned, attributes which affect the processes of allocation in the occupational structure and which also affect performance on the job (Breton, 1979: 273). The attributes will be related to personal resources, for instance access to networks that may lead to information about or entry to jobs, and to inter-ethnic attitudes and discrimination. The sources of these attributes will lie in features such as child rearing practices, religious values, achievement and present/future orientations and education. The central point of the individual competition approach is that disadvantage derives from individual attributes, which however, may in turn derive from ethnic group characteristics. These individual attributes, on the one hand, can reduce a person's level of qualification for a particular job while on the other they can be used as signals or justification for discriminatory behaviour.

The class approach to ethnic stratification emphasizes people *in groups* rather than as individuals. The critical social units in this approach are classes which are 'groupings whose interests are defined in relation to the basic social organization of production' (Breton, 1979: 277). The critical factor in this relationship is the relative power of the classes. There seems to me to be two possible sets of circumstances where class relations and ethnic stratification impinge. The first is where the members of a particular ethnic group are disproportionately concentrated at either the upper or lower ends of the class spectrum. This situation, via class relations, would build-in advantage to that group disproportionately found in the upper echelons of the class system and disadvantage to that group disproportionately found in the lower echelons. The second set of circumstances where class relations could impinge on ethnic stratification is where members of the bourgeoisie have an ethnic affinity with a section of the working class. In this instance the particular section of the working class can receive relatively favourable treatment in the job market, either because of ethnic affinity or because the bourgeoisie are using ethnic difference as a wedge to weaken the working class as an effective opponent.

The third perspective within which ethnic stratification can be viewed is that of *social closure*. This approach assumes the existence of certain sets or domains of jobs. Here advantage accrues to an ethnic group that holds a position of dominance in respect to desirable job domains, particularly in a situation of scarcity (Breton, 1979: 282, 283). What matters here is the effectiveness of an ethnic group's social organization for the control of domains and of access to them. In consequence, occupational differentials are thought to derive from a group's ability to organize so as to either take or retain control of particular work domains. The process of domain control is known as closure, defined by Weber as 'the process by which social collectivities seek to maximize rewards by restricting access to resources and opportunities to a limited set of eligibles' (Parkin, 1979: 44).

The three complementary approaches to the study of ethnic stratification indicate that a wide array of factors may contribute to stratification—disadvantage or advantage deriving both from characteristics inherent to the group concerned and from forces acting externally to the group. Both types of factor are identified in the preceding chapters, but, as I see it, much greater emphasis is given to the latter.

When one turns to consider solutions to the perceived problem of inequality of position of Protestants and Roman Catholics in the occupational structure of Northern Ireland, several issues need to be raised. The first issue relates to what I will call proportionality—that is an expectation that all occupational slots in Northern Ireland should be composed of Roman Catholics and Protestants *in proportion* to their share of the population of employable age. This proportionality expectation dominates the contributions to this book. However should not allowance be made for factors such as geographic distribution of the population (where for instance, one group is less urbanized than the other), for some degree of ethnic occupational specialization (due to cultural differences that should not be ignored, but recognized as enriching contributions to society), or for the fact that Northern Ireland is a partly segmented society (that is, there is some degree of institutionalized separation between the two ethnic groups, and therefore, some parallel occupational specialization)?

Beyond these considerations, and indeed more fundamental, is the issue of national difference. Parkin claims that 'ethnic or communal conflict often seems to call for explanation by reference to the concept of nationalism as much as by the conventional categories of stratification theory' (Parkin, 1979: 41), while Lieberson notes that 'political separation offers a solution to disadvantaged groups in an ethnic stratification system that is not possible for groups disadvantaged on the basis of age, sex or economic stratification' (Lieberson, 1972: 200). Thus there is a lack of consensus on the very existence of Northern Ireland—arguments are not just about 'fair shares' or 'equality of opportunity' within an agreed constitutional frame. Those opposed to the very existence of Northern Ireland as a constitutional entity wish to opt out— indeed they wish to drag everybody else along with them. At an intermediate phase of such opt-out there has been a series of withdrawals from participation in parliament, from participation in the police force and from participation in local government.

An interesting and instructive parallel to the Northern Ireland situation can be found in a comment by the former Deputy Mayor of Jerusalem, Meron Benvenisti. This comment was made at a conference of American and Israeli mayors called to discuss problems of government in 'multi-ethnic cities'. Benvenisti wrote:

> There is no comparison at all between Jerusalem's problems and those of American mixed cities. The minority leaders in America do not deny the legitimacy of the government and refuse to participate in its operations. To the contrary, they fight to integrate into the ruling apparatus... they seek a bigger slice of the American national cake... The communal tension in Jerusalem stems from the fact that the Arab minority does not recognize the legitimacy of the government that was imposed on it... While the minority in U.S. cities seeks 'good government', the Arab community seeks 'self-government' (*Kol HaIr*, April 25, 1980).

Thus the crunch question to be asked is whether occupational proportionality is a realistic objective when there is a lack of consensus regarding the very state within which proportionality has to exist?

The objective of occupational proportionality which underpins this volume, and which I wish to question, leads the editors to call for 'a quotas policy strongly based on merit'. Such a call seems to be self-contradictory because a quotas policy would almost certainly mean that some jobs would be allocated not on merit but despite it, unless 'merit' be taken to include membership of the group seen to be disadvantaged. The call for quotas would also appear to be counter to *The Guide to Manpower Policy and Practice* (1978) which supplements the Fair Employment (Northern Ireland) Act 1976, where it is stated:

> It should be noted that quota systems, by which is meant systems which reserve specific proportions of places for persons of a given religious belief, are unlawful. Such systems are inherently discriminatory and contrary to the concept of equality of opportunity.

Occupational proportionality as an objective, particularly one to be achieved, in part at least, by a quota system, raises another fundamental but neglected issue. It is noted by several contributors to this volume that the economy of Northern Ireland is at present in a very depressed state, a state where any increase in job availability to one ethnic group must mean a decrease in availability to the other—the so-called zero-sum situation. This is undoubtedly true and greatly exacerbates matters. However there is a further dimension to this where the two ethnic groups display differential rates of numerical growth, or rather where one group is continuing to grow in size while the other is almost numerically stable (Compton 1981). In the instance of Northern Ireland, Catholics are a numerically expanding group, Protestants numerically stable. If proportionality applies, then an increasing proportion of jobs will go to Catholics. This seems very equitable until one considers that thereby Protestants are penalized for having small families, Catholics rewarded for having larger ones. Again, my point is not to suggest that the Catholic disadvantage displayed in the political arithmetic is not real, or that nothing should be done about it. My point is, however, that the political arithmetic presented in this book derives from a very complex set of causes and that any attempt to change that arithmetic should be based on a wide range of considerations rather than the unicausality of past or present discrimination. Raymond Breton's three approaches to the analysis of ethnic stratification outlined earlier will help to emphasize the need for a very broadly based approach involving change in individual characteristics, in social class characteristics and in the segmentary characteristics of ethnicity. However, over and beyond this, the fact that Northern Ireland is politically a profoundly divided society must remain the most central consideration of all. At the same time, a major improvement in the economic condition of the Province could fundamentally ease the environment for social and political change, whatever direction such change may take.

The Last Word: R. J. Cormack and R. D. Osborne

Boal's major and legitimate argument centres on the degree to which *proportionality* in the distribution of jobs, between Protestants and Catholics, can be expected to pertain in Northern Ireland. Proportionality, however, has been the traditional benchmark in political arithmetic studies (Karabel and Halsey, 1978), albeit with a clear recognition that there are reasons why proportionality may not pertain, e.g. lower levels of educational attainment amongst occupationally disadvantaged groups, discrimination against identified groups etc. This book has been centrally concerned with assessing such factors and the degree to which they may have affected proportionality.

As a geographer Boal gives pride of place to the argument that the spatial concentration of the Catholic population is in areas where there is a dearth of jobs. But what he chooses to ignore is that several chapters specifically sought to assess the role of such spatial factors. For example, in chapter eight, on young school leavers and the labour market, the research designs of both the Belfast and the Londonderry/Strabane studies explicitly focused on the potential role of geographical factors—not least in the locations selected in the two studies. In the Belfast study, the matching of schools in the East and West of the city was deliberately undertaken to coincide with the acknowledged uneven spatial distribution of jobs, together with an assessment of potential and actual journey-to-work patterns. Similarly, chapter five explicitly focused on geographical variations in the analysis of unemployment patterns. We could go on from chapter to chapter, but the important point is that for males, even when geographical area is controlled for, Catholic disadvantage is still manifest.

Boal suggests that occupational differences are to be explained in terms of a 'partly segmented society'. This may well be so, but he glosses over the central point by suggesting this leads to 'parallel occupational specialisation' resulting from cultural differences, which he disarmingly suggests make an 'enriching contribution to society'. The chapters in this book make it abundantly clear that there are *not* parallel occupational hierarchies in the two communities. Rather, Catholics are disproportionately represented in low status, low-paid jobs and in unemployment, compared to their Protestant counterparts. Moreover, the high numbers of Catholic 'publicans and innkeepers' (65 per cent in the Census of Population in 1971) may make an 'enriching contribution to society', but this hardly compensates for the dearth in other middle class professions e.g. in 1971, 6 per cent of 'mechanical engineers', 7 per cent of 'company secretaries and registrars' and 'personnel managers', 8 per cent of 'university teachers', 9 per cent of 'local authority senior officers', 19 per cent of 'medical practitioners' and 23 per cent of 'judges, barristers, advocates and solicitors' were Catholic. There is not so much a parallelism in the two communities but more a 'superimposition', to use Dahrendorf's term. In fact, the example of superimposition Dahrendorf (1959: 214) gives is apropos to the circumstances of Northern Ireland:

> We might suggest that in a given country there are three dominant types of social conflict: conflict of the class type, conflict between town and country, and conflict between Protestants and Catholics. It is of course conceivable that these line of conflict cut across each other in a random fashion, so that, e.g., there are as many Protestants among the ruling

> groups of the state as there are Catholics and as many townspeople in either denomination as there are country-people. However, here, too, we might suspect that dissociation and pluralism are empirically rather unlikely to occur. One would not be surprised to find that most Protestants live in towns and most Catholics in the country, or that only one of the denominations commands the instruments of political control. If this is so, we are again faced with a phenomenon of superimposition in the sense of the same people meeting in different contexts but in identical relations of conflict.

The policy goal of proportionality can be, in part, exacerbated or ameliorated by a number of factors, not least among them the differential rates of population increase in the two communities. On this point we would agree with Boal. However, where we part company is the *degree* to which we are willing to accept the interpretation placed on such demographic data offered by Compton, the author of the most widely quoted demographic work on Northern Ireland. Compton (1981: 141, 142) has argued:

> ...while some unfairness in job allocation may exist, it is structural imbalances generated by factors specific to the Roman Catholic community, such as a higher rate of population growth, lower social status, larger families, and a divergence between geographical distribution and the location of jobs, that account for a considerable part of the disparity between the respective denominational rates of unemployment, and hence contribute to inequality of job opportunity... the *only* (our emphasis) effective way to guarantee improvement in the relative position of Roman Catholics in Northern Ireland is through the encouragement of fundamental change in certain of the innate features of that community. Acceptance of the desirability to bring Roman Catholic family size and rate of growth closer to the national and European average would be an important step along the road to greater equality.

While the higher rate of population growth in the Catholic community may have contributed to that community's dire employment profile, these patterns of advantage and disadvantage were apparently established *before* contraceptive techniques were widely available especially to the working class (Hepburn and Collins, 1981). The 'only effective way to guarantee improvement in the relative position of Roman Catholics' will *not* come through requiring Catholics to break with the teachings of their Church and limiting their family size. The mechanisms reproducing disadvantage over the years are not solely, even significantly, to be found by 'blaming the victim' for having large families. Regardless of these arguments one wonders how in *policy* terms the issue is to be tackled.

Editorially, we made the decision to focus on the recent past and on issues of policy; nevertheless, we are well aware that policy-makers all too often fashion policies inadequately informed by a sense of history and of social structure. But, does the use of Breton's model mystify or clarify our understanding of social structure? All three approaches seem, at the end of the day, to operate, in large part, on the basis of discrimination. *Individuals* are either identified and discriminated against on the basis of a 'personal attribute', in the Northern Ireland case, on the basis of religion; or the Protestant *bourgeoisie* discriminate in favour of their working class co-religionists; or Protestants, as an *ethnic group*, organise themselves in such a way as to control access to the best, most powerful, most high status jobs.

Two comments seem appropriate at this point: one to do with the definition of discrimination, and the other the models employed to further our understanding. Discrimination and disadvantage are not synonymous as we pointed out in chapter 11. Disadvantage can be perpetuated without necessarily involving active discrimination.

Secondly, patterns of advantage and disadvantage have been looked at, in this book, in terms of the *distribution* of jobs between the two communities: the distribution of Protestant and Catholic men and women, school leavers, graduates etc. to jobs (Crompton and Gubbay, 1977). However, a legitimate and prior question concerns the organisation of *production*. Who, or which community, historically accumulated sufficient capital to enter into the phase of 19th century industrialisation? Who now owns/controls the principal units? Where were these units located? What are the relationships between the owners/managers and local, national and international capital? (Beckett and Glasscock, 1967; Beckett et al, 1982). Once the pattern has been set, powerful forces operate to reproduce the distribution of advantage, with or without discrimination, generation by generation. We willingly acknowledge that we have presented a cross-section of Northern Ireland society at one time and that other prior questions require resolution.

Within the range of policies designed to tackle long-standing patterns of disadvantage, quotas have become the focus of intense debate. Boal bases his rejection of a quotas policy on arguments developed in the United States by Glazer (1975). However, Glazer, in recent writings (Glazer, 1978), has indicated that quotas *can* be contemplated, even on his reluctant terms, in societies where the ethnic division seems unlikely to be breached (i.e. where assimilation or integration is not the dominant social process), and where the scale of disadvantage between ethnic groups is large and not apparently moving towards parity. Even Glazer, therefore, is not a whole-hearted opponent of quotas.

Boal does our discussion of quotas scant justice. We were concerned to evaluate where a quotas policy might fit into resolving aspects of the Northern Ireland problem; we did not issue a 'general call' for a quotas policy. We suggested a quotas policy might be contemplated in the public sector, albeit firmly based on meritocratic criteria. The recent evidence on patterns of employment in the Northern Ireland Electricity Service and in the Northern Ireland Civil Service (FEA, 1982; Pollack, 1982) suggests that strong policies to promote equality of opportunity are needed.

'It's fine in principle, but . . .'. That sentiment seems to run through debates on the politics of opportunity. The principle is one to be dusted-off and resurrected on grand occasions. It is what Price (1969) has reported has been called BOMFOG rhetoric ('Brotherhood of Man, Fatherhood of God'). It is time, however, to ask those who feel comfortable with the label 'liberal' just how liberal they are. It is not an emblem about which they need feel particularly modest; as we argued in chapter one it has a long history of social amelioration.

While the national question, as Boal suggests, is, and is likely to remain, centre stage we would repeat what we said in chapter one. Any likely political solution will have to be sensitive to the problem of minorities, whether a Catholic minority in Northern Ireland as presently constituted, or a Protestant minority in a united Ireland. In either case the claims of the minority community will inevitably be assessed in the light of the principle of equality of opportunity and the policies formulated to advance it.

Bibliography

Abrams, P. (ed.),
1968 The Origins of British Sociology 1834–1914. London: University of Chicago Press.

Akenson, D. H.
1973 Education and Enmity: The Control of Schooling in Northern Ireland 1920–1950. David and Charles: Newton Abbot.

Anderson, P.
1969 "Components of the National Culture", in A. Cockburn and R. Blackburn (eds.), Student Power. Harmondsworth: Penguin.

Anon.
1980 "The Fair Employment Agency: Northern Ireland's Damp Squib". Rights, 5, 6.

Aunger, E. A.
1975 "Religion and Occupational Class in Northern Ireland". Economic and Social Review, 7, 1–23.

Banks, O.
1982 "The Sociology of Education, 1952–1982". British Journal of Educational Studies, XXX, 18–31.

Barnes, J. H. and Lucas, H.
1975 "Positive Discrimination in Education: Individuals, Groups and Institutions" in J. Barnes (ed.), Educational Priority Vol. 31, Curriculum Innovation in London EPAs. London: HMSO.

Barritt, D. P. and Carter, C. F.
1962 The Northern Ireland Problem: A Study in Group Relations. London: Oxford University Pres.

Beckett, J. C. and Glasscock, R. E.
1967 Belfast: The Origin and Growth of an Industrial City. London: BBC Publications.

Beckett, J. C. et al
1983 Belfast, The Making of the City: 1800–1914. Belfast: Appletree Press.

Benn, T.
1979 Arguments for Socialism. Edited by C. Mullin. London: Jonathan Cape.

Bernbaum, G.
1977 Knowledge and Ideology in the Sociology of Education. London: Macmillan.

Beveridge, W. H.
1942 "Social Insurance and Allied Services" ('The Beveridge Report'). London: HMSO (Cmnd. 6404).

Bew, P., Gibbon, P. and Patterson, H.
1979 The State in Northern Ireland: 1921–1972. Manchester: Manchester University Press.

Black, B., Ditch, J., Morrisey, M. and Steele, R.
1980 Low Pay in Northern Ireland. Low Pay Unit: London.
Blackburn, R. and Mann, M.
1980 The Working Class in the Labour Market. London: Macmillan.
Blau, P. M. and Duncan, O. D.
1967 The American Occupational Structure. New York: Wiley and Sons.
Bland, R.
1980 "Structural and Exchange Mobility in Northern Ireland". Scottish Journal of Sociology, 4, 310–308
Boal, F. W.
1969 "Territorality on the Shankill–Falls Divide, Belfast". Irish Geography, 6, 30–50.
Boal, F. W.
1972 "Close Together and Far Apart". Community Forum, 2, 3–11.
Boal, F. W.
1978 Letter to the Editor. Belfast Telegraph, 17 April.
Boal, F., Doherty, P. and Pringle, D.
1974 The Spatial Distribution of Some Social Problems in the Belfast Urban Area. Belfast: Northern Ireland Community Relations Commission.
Boal, F. W. and Douglas, J. N. H. (eds.),
1982 Integration and Division, Geographical Aspects of the Northern Ireland Problem. London: Academic Press.
Boehringer, K.
1971 "Discrimination: Jobs". Fortnight Magazine, 14 May.
Booth, C.
1882–97 Life and Labour of the People of London. London: Macmillan.
Bowles, S. and Gintis, H.
1976 Schooling in Capitalist America. London: Routledge and Kegan Paul.
Boyle, J. F.
1977 "Educational Attainment, Occupational Achievement and Religion in Northern Ireland". Economic and Social Review, 8, 79–100.
Bramsted, E. K. and Melhuish, K. J. (eds.),
1978 Western Liberalism. London: Longman.
Breton, R.
1979 "Ethnic Stratification Viewed From Three Theoretical Perspectives" in J. Curtis and W. Scott (eds), Social Stratification: Canada (2nd edition). Ontario: Prentice-Hall.
Brown, W.
1972 "A Consideration of Custom and Practice". British Journal of Industrial Relations, 10, 42–61.
Budge, I. and O'Leary, C.
1973 Belfast: Approach to Crisis: A Study of Belfast Politics 1613–1970. London: Macmillan.

Bulmer, M.
1980 "Why Don't Sociologists Make More Use of Official Statistics?" Sociology, 14, 505–523.
Bulmer, M.
1982 The Uses of Social Research. London: Allen and Unwin.
Burgess, T.
1981 "Bias is of the Essence", in D. Warren Piper (ed.), Is Higher Education Fair? Papers presented at the 17th SRHE Annual Conference. Guildford: SRHE.
Burton, F.
1978 The Politics of Legitimacy. London: Routledge and Kegan Paul.
Byrne, D.
1980 "The Deindustrialisation of Northern Ireland". Antipode, 12, 87–96.
Calvert, H.
1968 Constitutional Law in Northern Ireland. Belfast and London: NILQ and Stevens.
Campaign for Social Justice in Northern Ireland.
1969 The Plain Truth. Dungannon: Campaign for Social Justice.
Campaign for Social Justice.
n.d. Legal Aid to Oppose Discrimination—Not likely. Dungannon: Campaign for Social Justice.
Central Advisory Council for Education.
1967 Children and their Primary Schools (2 vols.). London: HMSO.
Chilver Report
1980 "The Future Structure of Teacher Education in Northern Ireland, An Interim Report of the Higher Education Review Group". Belfast: HMSO.
Coleman, J. et al.
1981 "Draft Summary of Major Findings for Public and Private Schools". Chicago: Report to the National Center for Educational Statistics by the National Opinion Research Centre.
Collini, S.
1979 Liberalism and Sociology. Cambridge: Cambridge University Press.
Compton, P. A.
1976 "Religious Affiliation and Demographic Behaviour in Northern Ireland". Transactions (New Series). Institute of British Geographers, 1, 433–452.
Compton, P. A.
1978 Northern Ireland: A Census Atlas. Dublin: Gill and Macmillan.
Compton, P. A.
1981a "Demographic and Geographical Aspects of the Unemployment Differential Between Protestants and Roman Catholics in Northern Ireland", in P. A. Compton (ed.), The Contemporary Population of Northern Ireland and Population-Related Issues. Belfast: Institute of Irish Studies, Queen's University.

Compton, P. A.
1981b "Review of Population Trends in Northern Ireland 1971–78", in P. A. Compton (ed.), The Contemporary Population of Northern Ireland and Population-Related Issues. Belfast: Institute of Irish Studies, Queen's University.

Compton, P. A.
1982 "The Demographic Dimension of Integration and Division in Northern Ireland", in F. W. Boal and J. M. Douglas (eds.), Integration and Division: Geographical Aspects of the Northern Ireland Problem. London: Academic Press.

Cooper, R. G.
1982 "The Work of the Fair Employment Agency", in A. C. Hepburn (ed.), Employment in Divided Societies. Coleraine: New University of Ulster.

Cormack, R. J., Osborne, R. D. and Thompson, W. T.
1980 Into Work? Young School Leavers and the Structure of Opportunity in Belfast. Belfast: Fair Employment Agency for Northern Ireland.

Crompton, R. and Gubbay, J.
1977 Economy and Class Structure. London: Macmillan.

Daniel, W. W.
1974 A National Survey of the Unemployed. Report No. 546. London: Political and Economic Planning.

Darby, J.
1976 Conflict in Northern Ireland: The Development of a Polarised Society. Dublin: Gill and Macmillan.

Darby, J. et al.
1977 Education and Community in Northern Ireland. Research Paper. Coleraine: Department of Social Administration, New University of Ulster.

Dahrendorf, R.
1959 Class and Class Conflict in Industrial Society. Stanford: Stanford University Press.

Davies, R. and McGurnaghan, M. A.
1975 "The Economics of Adversity". National Westminster Bank Review, May 1975, 56–68.

Davis, K.
1949 Human Society. New York: Macmillan.

Davis, K. and Moore, W. E.
1945 "Some Principles of Stratification". The American Sociological Review, 10, 242–249.

Deacon, A.
1981 "Unemployment and Politics in Britain Since 1945", in B. Showler and A. Sinfield (eds), The Workless State. London: Martin Robertson.

Department of Environment.
1978 "Poleglass Area". Statement by Department of the Environment for Northern Ireland. Belfast: HMSO.
Devlin, B.
1969 The Price of My Soul. London: Pan.
Ditch, J. and Osborne, R. D.
1980 Women and Work in Northern Ireland: A Survey of Data. Occasional Paper in Social Policy. Belfast: School of Sociology and Social Policy, Ulster Polytechnic.
Doherty. P.
1980 "Patterns of Unemployment in Belfast". Irish Geography, 13, 65–76.
Donnison, D.
1973 "The Northern Ireland Civil Service". New Society, 5–7–73, 8–10.
Douglas, J. W. B.
1967 The Home and the School. London: Panther Books.
Eccleshall, R.
1980 "Ideology or Commonsense: The Case of British Conservatism". Radical Philosophy, 25, 2–8.
Edwards, O. D.
1970 The Sins of Our Fathers: Roots of Conflict in Northern Ireland. Dublin: Gill and Macmillan.
Edwards, J. and Batley, R.
1978 The Politics of Positive Discrimination: An Evaluation of the Urban Programme 1967–1977. London: Tavistock.
Eldridge, J.
1980 Recent British Socilogy. London: Macmillan.
Eurostat.
1978 "Labour Force Sample Survey, 1977". Luxembourg.
Fair Employment Agency for Northern Ireland.
1977 First Report of the Fair Employment Agency for Northern Ireland. Belfast: HMSO.
Fair Employment Agency for Northern Ireland
1978 An Industrial and Occupational Profile of the Two Sections of the Population in Northern Ireland: An Analysis of the 1971 Census. Belfast: Fair Employment Agency for Northern Ireland.
Fair Employment Agency for Northern Ireland,
1979 Second Report of the Fair Employment Agency for Northern Ireland. Belfast: HMSO.
Fair Employment Agency for Northern Ireland
1980 Third Report of the Fair Employment Agency for Northern Ireland. Belfast: HMSO.
Fair Employment Agency for Northern Ireland.
1981 Fourth Report of the Fair Employment Agency for Northern Ireland. Belfast: HMSO.

Fair Employment Agency for Northern Ireland.
1982 A Final Report by the Fair Employment Agency for Northern Ireland on Its Investigation Into the Employment Practices of the Northern Ireland Electricity Service. Belfast: Fair Employment Agency.

Farrant, J. H.
1981 "Trends and Admissions", in O. Fulton (ed.), Access to Higher Education. Monograph 44. Guildford: SRHE.

Farrell, M.
1976 Northern Ireland: The Orange State. London: Pluto Press.

Featherman, D. L. and Hauser, R. M.
1978 Opportunity and Change. New York: Academic Press.

Fitzgerald, G.
1982 Irish Identities. The Dimbleby Lecture. London: BBC Publications.

FitzGibbon, A. M.
1981 "Entrants to Trinity College, Dublin 1960–1980: Religious Affiliation and Related Variables". Paper read at SRHE Conference, Biases in Higher Education, Manchester.

Floud, J. E., Halsey, A. H., Martin, F. M. (eds.).
1956 Social Class and Educational Opportunity. London: Heinemann.

Fraser, M.
1973 Children in Conflict. London: Secker and Warburg.

Friedman, M. and R.
1980 Free to Choose. London: Secker and Warburg.

Galbraith, J. K.
1977 The Age of Uncertainty. London: BBC/Deutsch.

Gallagher, F.
1957 The Indivisible Ireland: The History of the Partition of Ireland. London: Gollancz.

Gamble, A.
1981 An Introduction to Modern Social and Political Thought. London: Macmillan.

George, V. and Wilding, P.
1976 Ideology and Social Welfare. London: Routledge and Kegan Paul.

Giddens, A.
1971 Capitalism and Modern Social Theory. Cambridge: Cambridge University Press.

Glass, D. V. (ed.)
1954 Social Mobility in Britain. London: Routledge and Kegan Paul.

Glazer, N.
1975 Affirmative Discrimination: Ethnic Inequality and Public Policy. New York: Basic Books.

Glazer, N.
1978 "Individual Rights Against Group Rights", in E. Kamenka and A. Erk-Soon Tay (eds.), Human Rights. London: Arnold.

Goldthorpe, J. H. and Hope, K.
1974 The Social Grading of Occupations. A New Approach and Scale. Oxford: Clarendon Press.
Goldthorpe, J. H. and Llewellyn, C.
1977 "Class Mobility in Modern Britain". Sociology, 11, 257–287
Goldthorpe, J. H., Llewellyn, C. and Payne, C.
1980 Social Mobility and Class Structure in Modern Britain. Oxford: Clarendon Press.
Graham, J.
1962 Divergent Thinking. Unpublished Dissertation. Belfast: Department of Psychology, Queen's University, Belfast.
Gray, J. L. and Moshinsky, P.
1938 "Ability and Educational Opportunity in Relation to Parental Occupation", in L. Hogben (ed.), Political Arithmetic. London: Allen and Unwin.
Greely, A. M.
1981 "Schooling in the United States of America". The Tablet. 9 May.
Hadden, T. and Hillyard, P.
1973 Justice in Northern Ireland. London: Cobden Trust.
Hakim, C.
1979 "Occupational Segregation: A Comparative Study of the Degree and Pattern of the Differentiation Between Men and Women's Work in Britain, the United States and Other Countries". Research Paper No. 9. London: Department of Employment.
Hall, J. and Jones, D. C.
1950 "The Social Grading of Occupations". British Journal of Sociology, 1, 31–55.
Halsey, A. H. (ed.),
1977 Heredity and Environment. London: Methuen.
Halsey, A. H., Heath, A. F., Ridge, J. M.
1980 Origins and Destinations. Oxford: Clarendon Press.
Harris, R.
1972 Prejudice and Tolerance in Ulster: A Study of Neighbours and Strangers in a Border Community. Manchester: Manchester University Press.
Harris, R.
1955 Social Relations and Attitudes in a Northern Irish Rural Area. Unpublished Thesis: University of London.
Hauser, R. M.
1978 "A Structural Model of the Mobility Table". Social Forces, 56. 919–953.
Hawthorn, G.
1976 Enlightenment and Despair. Cambridge: Cambridge University Press.

Hepburn, A. C. and Collins, B.
1981 "Industrial Society: The Structure of Belfast 1901", in P. Roebuck (ed.), Plantation to Partition. Belfast: Blackstaff.
Heath, A.
1981 Social Mobility. Glasgow: Fontana.
Hibernia,
1979 "Dirty Tricks in the North's Fair Employment Agency". Dublin: Hibernia, 26–7–79.
Hill, M. J., Harrison, R. M., Sargeant, A. V. and Talbot, V.
1973 Men out of Work. Cambridge: Cambridge University Press.
Hoare, A. G.
1981 "Why They Go Where They Go: The Political Imagery of Industrial Location in Northern Ireland". Transactions (New Series). Institute of British Geographers, 6, 152–175.
Hobhouse, L. T.
1964 Liberalism. Oxford: Oxford University Press.
Hogben, L.
1938 Political Arithmetic. London: Allen and Unwin.
Homans, G.
1961 Social Behaviour: Its Elementary Forms. London: Routledge and Kegan Paul.
Housing Executive.
1979 "Belfast Household Survey, 1978". Belfast: Housing Executive.
Hunt, E. K.
1981 Property and Prophets. New York: Harper and Row.
Hutchinson, D. and McPherson, A.
1976 "Competing Inequalities: The Sex and Social Class Structure of the First Year Scottish University Student Population: 1962–1972". Sociology, 10, 111–116.
Institute of Personel Management.
1978 No Problems Here? London: I.P.M.
Isles, K. S. and Cuthbert, N.
1957 An Economic Survey of Northern Ireland. Belfast: HMSO.
Jackson, H.
1971 "The Two Islands: A Dual Study of Inter-Group Tensions". London: Minority Rights Group:
Jackson, J. A.
1979 "Determinants of Occupational Status and Mobility in Northern Ireland and the Irish Republic—Final Report to the S.S.R.C.". (Typescript). Dublin: Department of Sociology, Trinity College.
Jencks, C., Smith, M., Acland, M., Bane, M. J., Cohen, D., Gintis, H., Heyns, B., Michelson, S.
1972 Inequality: A Reassessment of the Effect of Family and Schooling in America. New York: Basic Books.

Jensen, A. R.
1969 "How Much Can We Boost IQ and Scholastic Achievement?" Harvard Educational Review, 39, 1–123.
Jones, C.
1977 Immigration and Social Policy. London: Tavistock.
Jones, G.
1980 Social Darwinism and English Thought. Sussex: Harvester Press.
Karabel, J and Halsey, A. H.
1978 Power and Ideology in Education. New York: Oxford University Press.
Kennedy, D.
1971 "Catholic Education in Northern Ireland, 1921–1970", Paper Read at a Conference Organized by the Guild of Catholic Teachers, Dioceses of Down and Connor, March 1970. Belfast: St. Joseph's College of Education.
Kent, R. A.
1981 A History of British Empirical Sociology. Aldershot: Gower.
Keynes, J. M.
1936 The General Theory of Employment, Interest and Money. London: Macmillan.
Kirp, D.
1979 Doing Good by Doing Little: Race and Schooling in Britain. Berkeley: University of California Press.
Kreckel, R.
1980 "Unequal Opportunity Structure and Labour Market Segmentation". Sociology, 14, 525–550.
Kuhn, T.
1962 The Structure of Scientific Revolutions. University of Chicago Press: Chicago.
Lester, A. and Bindman, G.
1973 Race and Law. Harmondsworth: Penguin.
Lichtman, R.
1969 "The Facade of Equality in Liberal Democratic Theory". Inquiry, 12, 170–208.
Lieberson, S.
1972 "Stratification and Ethnic Groups" in A. H. Richmond (ed.) Readings in Race and Ethnic Relations, Oxford: Pergamon Press.
Little, A.
1981 "Education and Race Relations in the United Kingdom". World Yearbook of Education, 1981. London: Kogan Page.
Little, A. and Robbins, D.
1981 "Race Bias", in D. Warren Piper (ed.), Is Higher Education Fair? Papers presented at the 17th SRHE Annual Conference. Guildford: SRHE.

Little, A. and Westergaard, J.
1964 "The Trends of Class Differentials in Educational Opportunity in England and Wales". British Journal of Sociology, 15, 301–316.

Livingstone, J. C.
1979 Fair Game? Inequality and Affirmative Action. San Francisco: Freeman and Company.

Lockwood Report
1965 "Higher Education in Northern Ireland". Report of the Committee Appointed by the Minister of Finance (Cmd. 480). Belfast: HMSO.

Lowry, D.
1979 "Legislation in a Social Vacuum: The Failure of the Fair Employment (Northern Ireland) Act, 1976 and Alternative Solutions". New York Journal of International Law and Politics, 9, 345–388.

Lukes, S.
1975 Emile Durkheim. Harmondsworth: Penguin.

Mackenzie, D. A.
1981 Statistics in Britain 1865–1930. Edinburgh: Edinburgh University Press.

McCann, E.
1974 War and an Irish Town. Harmondsworth: Penguin.

McCrudden, J. C.
1979 "Strategic Uses of the Law", in Runnymede Trust, A Review of the Race Relations Act, 1976. London: Runnymede Trust.

McCrudden, J. C.
1981a Discrimination Against Minority Groups in Employment: A Comparison of Legal Remedies in the United Kingdom and the United States. D.Phil Thesis. On deposit in the Bodleian Library, Oxford University: Oxford.

McCrudden, J. C.
1981b "Anti-Discrimination Legislation and the Role of the Social Sciences", in S. Lloyd-Boxtock (ed), Law and Psychology. Oxford: SSRC.

McCrudden, J. C.
1981c "Legal Remedies for Discrimination in Employment". Current Legal Problems, 9, 211–233.

McInerney, M.
1970 Trade Unions Bid for Peace in North. Dublin: Irish Times Ltd.

McIntyre Report
1980 Report of a Working Party on Social Priority Schools. Belfast: HMSO.

McKay, D.
1977 Housing and Race in Industrial Society. London: Croom Helm.

Manpower Services Commission.
1978 Young People and Work. London: HMSO.

Marshall, T. H.
1963 Sociology at the Crossroads. London: Heinemann.
Martindale, D.
1960 The Nature and Types of Sociological Theory. Boston: Houghton Mifflin Company.
Maus, H.
1962 A Short History of Sociology. London: Routledge and Kegan Paul.
Mayhew, H.
1968 London Labour and the London Poor. New York: Dover Publications.
Miller, R. L.
1978 Attitudes to Work in Northern Ireland. Belfast: Fair Employment Agency for Northern Ireland.
Miller, R. L.
1979 Occupational Mobility of Protestants and Roman Catholics in Northern Ireland. Belfast: Fair Employment Agency for Northern Ireland.
Miller, R. L.
1981 "A Model of Social Mobility in Northern Ireland", in P. A. Compton (ed.), The Contemporary Population of Northern Ireland and Population-Related Issues. Belfast: Institute of Irish Studies, Queen's University.
Mills, C. W.
1959 The Sociological Imagination. London: Oxford University Press.
Mishra, R.
1981 Society and Social Policy. London: Macmillan.
Mogey, J. M.
1955 "Ulster's Six Counties", in T. Wilson (ed.), Ulster Under Home Rule. London: Oxford University Press.
Moody, T. W. and Beckett, J. C.
1959 Queen's Belfast, 1845–1949 (2 vols.). London: Faber and Faber.
Moore, B.
1967 Social Origins of Dictatorship and Democracy. Boston: Beacon Press.
Moore, R.
1972 "Race Relations in the Six Counties: Colonialism, Industrialisation and Stratification in Ireland". Race, 14, 21–42.
Mortimore, J. and Blackstone, T.
1982 Disadvantage and Education. London: Heinemann.
Moser, C. A. and Hall, J. A.
1954 "The Social Grading of Occupations", in D. V. Glass (ed.), Social Mobility in Britain. London: Routledge and Kegan Paul.

Murray, D. and Darby, J.
1978 The Vocational Aspirations and Expectations of School Leavers in Londonderry and Strabane. Belfast: Fair Employment Agency of Northern Ireland.
Neave, G.
1979 "Education and Regional Development: An Overview of a Growing Controversy". European Journal of Education, 14, 207–231.
Northern Ireland Commission for Complaints.
1970 Second Report. NIHC 2048. Belfast: HMSO
Northern Ireland Commission for Complaints.
1971 Third Report. NIHC 2101. Belfast: HMSO.
Northern Ireland Commission for Complaints.
1972 Fourth Report. NIHC 2181. Belfast: HMSO.
Northern Ireland, Department of Manpower Services.
1978 Guide to Manpower Policy and Practicies. Belfast: HMSO.
Northern Ireland, Department of Manpower Services.
1979 Cohort Survey of the Unemployed. Belfast.
Northern Ireland, Ministry of Finance.
1973 Digest of Statistics, Northern Ireland, No. 40. Belfast: HMSO.
Northern Ireland, Ministry of Health and Social Services.
1973 Report and Recommendations of the Working Party on Discrimination in the Private Sector of Employment. Belfast: HMSO.
Northern Ireland, Registrar General.
1965 Fertility Report, 1961. Belfast: HMSO.
O'Brien, J.
1966 "Science and Catholic Education". Catholic Teacher's Journal, 9, 16–17.
O'Dowd, L., Rolston, B. and Tomlinson, M.
1980 Northern Ireland: Between Civil Rights and Civil War. London: CSE Books.
Office of Population Censuses and Surveys.
1970 Classification of Occupations. London: HMSO.
Oliver, J.
1982 in "The Evolution of Constitutional Policy in Northern Ireland Over the Last Fifteen Years", D. Rea (ed.), Political Cooperation in Divided Societies. Dublin: Gill and Macmillan.
Oppenheim, A. N.
1966 Questionnaire Design and Attitude Measurement. London: Heinemann.
Osborne, R. D.
1978 "Denomination and Unemployment in Northern Ireland". Area. 10, 280–283.
Osborne, R. D.
1980a "Fair Employment in Northern Ireland". New Community, VIII, 129–137.

Osborne, R. D.
1980b "Religious Discrimination and Disadvantage in the Northern Ireland Labour Market". International Journal of Social Economics. 7, 206–223.

Osborne, R. D.
1982a "Equality of Opportunity and Discrimination: the Case of Religion in Northern Ireland". Administration, 29, 331–355.

Osborne, R. D.
1982b "Fair Employment in Cookstown? A Note on Anti-Discrimination Policy in Northern Ireland". Journal of Social Policy, 11, 519–530.

Osborne, R. D.
1982c "The Lockwood Report and the Location of a Second University in Northern Ireland", in F. W. Boal and J. N. H. Douglas (eds.), Integration and Division: Geographical Aspects of the Northern Ireland Problem. London: Academic Press.

Osborne, R. D. and Murray, R. C.
1978 Educational Qualifications and Religious Affiliation in Northern Ireland. Belfast: Fair Employment Agency for Northern Ireland.

Parkin, F.
1979 Marxism and Class Theory. London: Tavistock.

Parker, J.
1975 Citizenship and Social Policy. London: Macmillan.

Payne, G., Dingwall, R., Payne, J., Carter, M.
1981 Sociology and Social Research. London: Routledge and Kegan Paul.

Payne, G. and Ford, G.
1977 "Religion, Class and Educational Policy". Scottish Educational Studies, 9, 83–99.

Payne, G., Ford, G. and Robertson, C.
1977 "A Reappraisal of Social Mobility in Britain". Sociology, 11, 289–310.

Payne, G., Ford, G. and Ulas, M.
1979 "Education and Occupational Mobility". Mimeo. Plymouth: School of Behavioural and Social Science, Plymouth Polytechnic.

Paor, L. De
1970 Divided Ulster. Harmondsworth: Penguin.

Pearson, L.
1914 "On Certain Errors with Regard to Multiple Correlation Occasionally Made by Those Who Have Not Adequately Studied This Subject". Biometrika, 3, 181–187.

Petty, W.
1899 "The Political Anatomy of Ireland" and "Political Arithmetick", in C. H. Hull (ed.), The Economic Writings of Sir William Petty. Cambridge: Cambridge University Press.

Pfautz, H. (ed.)
1967 Charles Booth on the City. Chicago: University of Chicago Press.
Project Team
1976 Belfast: Areas of Special Social Need. Belfast: HMSO.
Price, D. K.
1969 "Purists and Politicians". Science, 3 January, 163, 3862.
Pollack, A.
1982 "The Civil Service Investigation: the FEA's Last Chance". Fortnight, October, 188, 8–11.
Poole, M.
1982 "Religious Residential Segregation in Urban Northern Ireland", in F. W. Boal and J. N. H. Douglas, (eds.) Integration and Division: Geographical Perspectives on the Northern Ireland Problem. London: Academic Press.
Queen's University, Belfast.
1981 Appointments Board Annual Report. Belfast: Queen's University, Belfast.
Quigley Report.
1976 Economic and Industrial Strategy for Northern Ireland. Belfast: HMSO.
Rees, T. L. and Atkinson, P. (eds.)
1982 Youth Unemployment and State Intervention. London: Routledge and Kegan Paul.
Reid, N. and Goldie, R.
1981 "Northern Ireland Women in Higher Education". Belfast: Equal Opportunities Commission for Northern Ireland.
Report of the Royal Commission on Trade Unions and Employers's Associations, 1965–1968.
1969 Cmnd 3623. London: HMSO.
Rex, J.
1961 Key Problems of Sociological Theory. London: Routledge and Kegan Paul.
Reynolds, H. T.
1977 Analysis of Nominal Data. London: Sage Publications.
Richardson, J.
1981 "Geographical Bias", in D. Warren Piper (ed.), Is Higher Education Fair? Papers presented at the 17th SRHE Annual Conference. Guildford: SRHE.
Robbins, D.
1982 "Affirmative Action in the USA: A Lost Opportunity?" New Community, IX, 399–406.
Robbins Report.
1963 "Higher Education", Report of the Committee Under the Chairmanship of Lord Robbins (Cmnd 2154). London: HMSO.

Rose, R.
1971 Governing Without Consensus: An Irish Perspective. Boston: Beacon Press.
Rose, S.
1976 "Scientific Racism: The IQ Racket from Galton to Jensen", in H. Rose and S. Rose (eds.), The Political Economy of Science. London: Macmillan.
Rowthorn, B.
1981 "Northern Ireland: An Economy in Crisis". Cambridge Journal of Economics, 5, 1–31.
Scarman, Lord
1981 The Brixton Disorders 10–12 April 1981. Report of an Inquiry by the Rt. Hon. the Lord Scarman, (Cmnd. 8427). London: HMSO.
Schlei, B. L. and Grossman, P.
1976 Employment Discrimination Law. Washington, D.C.: Bureau of National Affairs.
Schmitt, D. E.
1981 "The Consequences of Administrative Employees in Equal Opportunity Strategies: Comparative Analysis of the United States and Northern Ireland". Annual Meeting of the American Political Science Association, September 3–6, 1981.
Schwendinger, H. and J. R.
1974 The Sociologists of the Chair. New York: Basic Books.
Scott, R. D.
1973 "University Under Stress—The Peculiar Problems of Teaching in Ulster". Vestes, 16, 127–133.
Showler, B.
1976 The Public Employment Service. London: Longmans.
Showler, B.
1980 "Racial Minority Group Unemployment: Trends and Characteristics". International Journal of Social Economics, 7, 194–205.
Silver, H. (ed.).
1973 Equal Opportunity in Education. London: Methuen.
Sinfield, A.
1981 What Unemployment Means. London: Martin Robertson.
Sindler, A.
1978 Bakke, De Funis and Minority Admissions. New York: Longman.
Smith, A.
1976 An Inquiry into the Nature and Causes of the Wealth of Nations. Campbell, R. H. and Skinner, A. S. (eds.). Oxford: Oxford University Press.
Smith, D. J.
1981 "Unemployment and Racial Minorities". Policy Studies Institute, Report No. 594: London.

Spencer, H.
1884 The Man versus the State. London: Williams and Norgate.

Spencer, H.
1954 Social Studies. New York: Robert Schalkenbach Foundation.

Sturt, R.
1981 "Disability", in D. Warren Piper (ed.), Is Higher Education Fair? Papers presented at the 17th SRHE Annual Conference. Guildford: SRHE.

Tawney, R. H.
1931 Equality. London: Unwin Books.

Townsend, P.
1975 Sociology and Social Policy. London: Allen Lane.

Trewsdale, J. M.
1980 Unemployment in Northern Ireland 1974–1979. Belfast: Northern Ireland Economic Council.

Trewsdale, J. M. and Trainor, M.
1979 Woman Power No. 1: A Statistical Survey of Women and Work. Belfast: Equal Opportunities Commission for Northern Ireland.

Trewsdale, J. M. and Trainor, M.
1982 Woman Power No. 2: Recent Changes in the Female Labour Market in Northern Ireland. Belfast: Equal Opportunities Commission for Northern Ireland.

Trow, M.
1966 "The Second Transformation of American Secondary Education", in R. Bendix and S. M. Lipset, (eds.), Class, Status and Power. New York: The Free Press.

Trustees of the Catholic Education Colleges.
No date "Catholic Education and the Chilver Proposals". Belfast.

Ulster Yearbook 1978–79
1979 Belfast: HMSO.

United Kingdom Government.
1975 The Future of Northern Ireland. London: HMSO.

D. Warren Piper (ed.)
1981 Is Higher Education Fair? Papers presented at the 17th SRHE Annual Conference. Guildford: SRHE.

Werskey, G.
1978 The Visible College. London: Allen Lane.

Whyte, J. H.
1978 "Interpretations of the Northern Ireland Problem: An Appraisal" Economic and Social Review, 9, 257–282.

Whyte, J. H.
1982 "How Much Discrimination Was There Under Unionism, 1921–1968?" Unpublished Paper. Belfast: Department of Political Science, The Queen's University.

Williamson, B.
1981 "Class Bias", in D. Warren Piper (ed.), Is Higher Education Fair? Papers presented at the 17th Annual SRHE Conference. Guildford: SRHE.

Wilson, J. J.
1978 The Declining Significance of Race. Chicago: University of Chicago Press.

Winch, D.
1978 Adam Smith's Politics. Cambridge: Cambridge University Press.

Wolfe, D. A.
1981 "Mercantilism, Liberalism and Keynesianism: Changing Forms of State Intervention in Capitalist Economics". Canadian Journal of Political and Social Theory, 5, 69–96.

Woodley, A.
1981 "Age Bias", in D. Warren Piper (ed.), Is Higher Education Fair? Papers presented at the 17th SRHE Annual Conference. Guildford: SRHE.

Wrong, D. H.
1959 "The Functional Theory of Stratification: Some Neglected Considerations". The American Sociological Review, 24, 772–82.

Young, M.
1958 The Rise of the Meritocracy. London: Thames and Hudson.

Young, M. F. D. (ed.),
1971 Knowledge and Control. London: Collier-Macmillan.

Index